"Drawing from a broad range of [...] Middleton argues in compelling fashion that Abraham's silence in Genesis 22 was a failure. In so doing, Middleton more broadly makes the case for lament as an integral practice of faith in a God who welcomes chutzpah rather than blind obedience. Whether you agree or not, you will not read the Aqedah story in the same way. Or Job and the Psalms."

—**William P. Brown**, Columbia Theological Seminary

"Ecclesiastes 3 famously says there is a time for everything, including 'a time to keep silence, and a time to speak' (3:7). In this book, Middleton invites us to ponder the silence of Abraham before God and the words of Job and other voices of protest and lament. From Middleton you can always expect penetrating exegetical insight, but the deeper value here is his case for bold and vigorous prayer in the face of suffering and pain. Middleton's rich blend of breadth and depth makes for engaging and transformative reading."

—**Nijay Gupta**, Northern Seminary

"Generations of theologians, commentators, philosophers, writers, and artists—both Jews and Christians—struggled and are still struggling with the most puzzling and horrifying stories: the binding of Isaac (the Akedah), who is meant to be offered as a burnt offering by his father, and the suffering of Job, the 'blameless and upright, one who feared God and turned away from evil.' *Abraham's Silence* is a stimulating and important contribution to the ongoing study of these incredible biblical texts where God 'tests' his most faithful servants. The author straightforwardly discusses various theological, exegetical, and rhetorical issues in these Scriptures and sheds a fresh light on them."

—**Isaac Kalimi**, member ordinarius, Academia Europaea: The Pan-European Academy of Sciences, Humanities & Letters

"What do you say to God when bad things happen? In this fascinating and insightful study of Abraham and Job, Middleton invites us to reconsider what God desires from those who are suffering. Beware! This book will change the way you think about God and transform your spiritual life. A must-read for every student of Scripture."

—**Amanda W. Benckhuysen**, director of Safe Church Ministry, Christian Reformed Church

"Middleton brings together penetrating analysis of biblical texts, keen theological insight, and remarkable clarity of presentation. Middleton is not afraid to ask difficult, painful questions—about God, about Abraham, and about what a life of faith should look like. Whether you agree with his arguments or not, you will undoubtedly learn and grow from this provocative book."

—**Shai Held**, author of *The Heart of Torah*

"Long ago 'The Preacher' concluded, 'There is a time to keep silence, and a time to speak' (Eccles. 3:7). Now Middleton, in the wake of 'the preacher,' wades boldly into the enigma of silence and speech. He ponders the demanding speech addressed to God by Moses, the prophets, and most especially by Job. But then he turns to Abraham's stunning silence before God concerning the near-sacrifice of Isaac, the son whom Abraham loves. Middleton judges that Abraham's silence means that Abraham has not fully probed God's mercy, but settles for a God less than fully merciful. Middleton's indictment of Abraham is a daring judgment that collides with the usual practice of the piety and prayer of the faithful, both Jews and Christians, and with the judgment of our foremost interpreters. This is interpretation at its most daring and at its best."

—**Walter Brueggemann**, Columbia Theological Seminary (emeritus)

ABRAHAM'S SILENCE

THE BINDING OF ISAAC, THE SUFFERING OF JOB, AND HOW TO TALK BACK TO GOD

J. RICHARD MIDDLETON

ß

Baker Academic

a division of Baker Publishing Group
Grand Rapids, Michigan

Published by Baker Academic
a division of Baker Publishing Group
PO Box 6287, Grand Rapids, MI 49516-6287
www.bakeracademic.com

Printed in the United States of America

Library of Congress Cataloging-in-Publication Data
Names: Middleton, J. Richard, 1955– author.
Title: Abraham's silence : the binding of Isaac, the suffering of Job, and how to talk back to God / J. Richard Middleton.
Description: Grand Rapids, MI : Baker Academic, a division of Baker Publishing Group, [2021] | Includes indexes.
Identifiers: LCCN 2021017455 | ISBN 9780801098017 (paperback) | ISBN 9781540964328 (casebound) | ISBN 9781493430888 (ebook)
Subjects: LCSH: Abraham (Biblical patriarch) | Isaac (Biblical patriarch)—Sacrifice. | Bible. Genesis, XXII—Criticism, interpretation, etc. | Conversation—Religious aspects—Christianity. | Prayer—Biblical teaching. | Job (Biblical figure)
Classification: LCC BS580.A3 M49 2021 | DDC 222/.110922—dc23
LC record available at https://lccn.loc.gov/2021017455

Chapter 1 has been expanded from an article originally published as J. Richard Middleton, "Voices from the Ragged Edge: How the Psalms Can Help Us Process Pain," *Canadian Theological Society Newsletter/Communiqué de la société théologique canadienne* 14, no. 1 (November 1994): 4–7. Used by permission.

Quotations from "These Plastic Halos" used by permission. Words and music by Mark Heard © 1988 Curb Word Music (ASCAP). All rights administered by WC Music Corp. WC Music Corp. 100% On behalf of Curb Word Music.

21   22   23   24   25   26   27   7   6   5   4   3   2   1

For David Biberstein
and Werner E. Lemke (1933–2010)

Contents

Acknowledgments

No book is an island, and every author is indebted to many others who helped shape their views and who paved the way for their writing.

I begin with thanks for those who first opened up the Scriptures for me when I was an undergraduate student at Jamaica Theological Seminary—David Biberstein, Roger Ringenberg, Neil McFarlane (1946–2019), and Zenas Gerig (1927–2011). I am profoundly grateful to each of these faithful teachers for whetting my appetite for lifelong, in-depth study of the Bible.

Werner E. Lemke (1933–2010) and Darryl Lance inducted me into graduate-level work in Old Testament at Colgate Rochester Divinity School. Their insight into the Scriptures was amazing, and I am grateful especially to Lemke for introducing me to the psalms of lament and their role in addressing human suffering.

There are other Old Testament scholars with whom I never studied, yet who have been significant teachers for me, either through their writings or through knowing them personally (or both). Those who have impacted me most are Walter Brueggemann, Terence Fretheim, J. Gerald Janzen, and William P. Brown.

I am honored also by the many people who invited me to present portions of this work in progress. The opportunity to share my developing thoughts, and receive intelligent feedback, has been one of the joys of working on the material for this book.

John Garner hosted my first-ever presentation on the lament psalms at Harbour Fellowship Church, St. Catharines, ON (1993). For his encouragement and for coming up with the creative title "Voices from the Ragged Edge," he deserves a special note of gratitude.

Lyle Eslinger heard me give an academic paper on Job at the Canadian Society of Biblical Studies and invited me to expand it for the Peter C. Craigie Memorial Lecture at the University of Calgary, Calgary, AB (2005). Jamie Smith then brought me to Calvin University to present a public lecture on Job (2006). And Job was the topic I chose for the V. James and Florence Mannoia Lecture at Greenville College, Greenville, IL (2014); my thanks to Christina Smerick for the invitation.

Matthew Anstey and David Neville brought me to Australia for four wonderful weeks as Theologian-in-Residence at Charles Sturt University (during a 2016 sabbatical). I am grateful for the opportunity to interact with many biblical scholars and other interested persons through the presentations I gave in Adelaide (hosted by Matthew) and in Canberra (hosted by David). In Adelaide, Matthew Anstey organized a symposium on lament in the Bible and life at St. Barnabas College, centered around my research on the Aqedah; he also helpfully responded to my Aqedah paper. In Canberra, David Neville had me give the keynote paper on Job for a seminar in biblical theology at St. Mark's National Theological Centre; my thanks to Jeanette Matthews for responding to my paper. I was also delighted to be able to present a public lecture on the lament psalms at St. Peter's Cathedral, Adelaide, and at St. Mark's National Theological Centre, Canberra.

My thanks to Gordon Matties for inviting me to give the J. J. Thiessen Lectures at Canadian Mennonite University, Winnipeg, MB (2016); these lectures, given shortly after my return from Australia, focused on lament, Job, and the Aqedah.

The following year (2017) I embarked on a two-week speaking tour in the UK, during which I gave presentations on various topics, some of them relating to research for this book. I spoke on the lament psalms in Scotland—at the Logos Institute for Exegetical and Analytic Theology, University of St. Andrews (hosted by Tom Wright), and then at the School of Divinity, History, and Philosophy, University of Aberdeen (hosted by Grant Macaskill). I also presented on the lament psalms for the Thinking Faith Network in Leeds (hosted by David Hanson).

While in the UK, I had the privilege of presenting on the Aqedah in a doctoral seminar for Old Testament students at Durham University (hosted by Walter Moberly), and I gave a public lecture on the Aqedah at the College of the Resurrection, Mirfield (hosted by Dorothea Bertschmann). I ended the UK tour by presenting on Job in a research seminar for faculty and postgraduate students at Trinity College, Bristol (hosted by Jamie Davis). I'm especially thankful to David Hanson for organizing these speaking engagements in Scotland and England.

The following year, James Whitman hosted me for four lectures, addressing lament, Job, and the Aqedah, for the thirty-fifth anniversary celebration of the Center for Judaic-Christian Studies, Dayton, OH (2018).

I am especially glad that I was able to present some of this material to various audiences in my hometown of Kingston, Jamaica. When I was on sabbatical in 2009 teaching a course at the Caribbean Graduate School of Theology (CGST), I gave a presentation on Job at the United Theological College of the University of the West Indies, hosted by Lesley Anderson and Garnett Roper (2009). While I was teaching another course at CGST, I gave a workshop on lament psalms at Swallowfield Chapel at the invitation of David Harvey (2010). And I had the privilege of giving a public lecture on the Aqedah as the first annual Zenas Gerig Memorial lecture at Jamaica Theological Seminary (2012); my thanks to Garnett Roper for the invitation.

Finally, during the COVID-19 pandemic (in 2021), I was able to give (virtual) papers on the Aqedah on two occasions. At the invitation of Cornelia van Deventer and Bat Maniyka, I gave a presentation on the Aqedah for a graduate-student symposium at the South African Theological Seminary; the Aqedah was also the topic for my keynote lecture at the third annual symposium of the Centre for the Study of Bible and Violence, hosted by Helen Paynter and Trevor Laurence.

I am profoundly grateful for these opportunities to give formal presentations on my research for this book, as well as for the many courses in which this material has come up, and the informal discussions about lament, Job, and the Aqedah I have had with students, church members, and academic colleagues over the years.

The book has been greatly enriched by these interactions.

Finally, I want to thank the folks at Baker Academic for their support and dedication in preparing this book for publication. Special thanks to Jim Kinney, who asked me, after my last book with Baker Academic, what I wanted to write next. Jim's friendship, along with his interest and support in this project, has been inspiring. Kudos also to Melisa Blok and her amazing editorial team for making this a much better book that it would have been otherwise. I am deeply grateful.

Abbreviations

General Abbreviations

BCE	before the common era
CE	common era
chap(s).	chapter(s)
e.g.	*exempli gratia* / for example
Eng.	English
esp.	especially
ET	English translation
etc.	*et cetera* / and so on
Heb.	Hebrew
i.e.	*id est* / that is
orig.	original
p(p).	page(s)

Scripture Versions

ASV	American Standard Version
CEB	Common English Bible
CEV	Contemporary English Version
ESV	English Standard Version
HCSB	Holman Christian Standard Bible
JPS Tanakh	Jewish Publication Society Tanakh
KJV	King James Version
LXX	Septuagint
MT	Masoretic Text
NAB	New American Bible
NASB	New American Standard Bible
NET	New English Translation
NIV	New International Version
NJB	New Jerusalem Bible
NJPS	New Jewish Publication Society of America Tanakh
NLT	New Living Translation
NRSV	New Revised Standard Version
REB	Revised English Bible
RSV	Revised Standard Version

Hebrew Bible / Old Testament

Gen.	Genesis
Exod.	Exodus
Lev.	Leviticus
Num.	Numbers
Deut.	Deuteronomy
Josh.	Joshua
Judg.	Judges
1 Sam.	1 Samuel
2 Sam.	2 Samuel
1 Chron.	1 Chronicles
2 Chron.	2 Chronicles
Neh.	Nehemiah

Ps(s).   Psalm(s)   Dan.   Daniel
Prov.   Proverbs   Hos.   Hosea
Isa.   Isaiah   Jon.   Jonah
Jer.   Jeremiah   Mic.   Micah
Lam.   Lamentations   Nah.   Nahum
Ezek.   Ezekiel   Zech.   Zechariah

New Testament

Matt.   Matthew   Heb.   Hebrews
Rom.   Romans   1 Pet. 1 Peter
2 Cor.   2 Corinthians   2 Pet. 2 Peter
Eph.   Ephesians   Rev.   Revelation
Phil.   Philippians

Secondary Sources

AB   Anchor Bible
ABRL   Anchor Bible Reference Library
ArBib   The Aramaic Bible
ASJP   Amsterdam Studies in Jewish Philosophy
ASJR   *Association for Jewish Studies Review*
BBR   *Bulletin for Biblical Research*
BCOTWP   Baker Commentary on the Old Testament Wisdom and Psalms
BETL   Bibliotheca Ephemeridium Theologicarum Lovaniensium
Bib   *Biblica*
BibInt   *Biblical Interpretation*
BibInt   Biblical Interpretation Series
BJS   Brown Judaic Studies
BZAW   Beihefte zur Zeitschrift für die alttestamentliche Wissenschaft
CBQ   *Catholic Biblical Quarterly*
CBQMS   Catholic Biblical Quarterly Monograph Series
CV   *Communio Viatorum*
DBSJ   *Detroit Baptist Seminary Journal*
FAT   Forschungen zum Alten Testament
HAR   *Hebrew Annual Review*
HBT   *Horizons in Biblical Theology*
HSM   Harvard Semitic Monographs
HTS   Harvard Theological Studies
Int   *Interpretation*
ISBL   Indiana Studies in Biblical Literature
JBHT   *Journal of the Bible and Human Transformation*
JBL   *Journal of Biblical Literature*
JES   *Journal of Ecumenical Studies*
JSOT   *Journal for the Study of the Old Testament*
JSOTSup   Journal for the Study of the Old Testament Supplement Series
JSQ   *Jewish Studies Quarterly*

JTR	*Journal of Textual Reasoning*
LHBOTS	Library of Hebrew Bible / Old Testament Studies
LJI	Library of Jewish Ideas
LNTS	Library of New Testament Studies
LTJ	*Lutheran Theological Journal*
NICOT	New International Commentary on the Old Testament
OBT	Overtures to Biblical Theology
OTG	Old Testament Guides
OTL	Old Testament Library
OTR	Old Testament Readings
RevExp	*Review and Expositor*
SBLRBS	SBL Resources for Biblical Study
SPOT	Studies on Personalities of the Old Testament
TBN	Themes in Biblical Narrative
Them	*Themelios*
ThTo	*Theology Today*
UCOP	University of Cambridge Oriental Publications
VT	*Vetus Testamentum*
WW	*Word and World*
YJS	Yale Judaica Series

Introduction

Does Abraham's Silence Matter?

In Genesis 22 God tells Abraham to offer up his son Isaac as a burnt offering on a mountain he will be shown in the land of Moriah. Surprisingly, Abraham doesn't question the instruction—either to see if it is really from God or to ask why God would want such a thing. Nor does he intercede on behalf of his son. Instead, Abraham rises early the next morning and—in silence—sets about preparing for the journey and the sacrifice.

When he arrives (three days later) at the place God had indicated, Abraham builds an altar, spreads out the wood (which Isaac has been carrying), and binds (*'āqad*) his son in preparation for the sacrifice. It is the presence of the Hebrew verb *'āqad* that leads Jews to call this story the *Aqedah*, the "binding" of Isaac.[1] In Christian tradition the story is known as the sacrifice (or near sacrifice) of Isaac. By whatever name, this is a disturbing text.[2]

For many years I have been troubled by Abraham's silent obedience in Genesis 22. If, I reasoned, I ever heard a voice asking me to sacrifice my son, I would *not* instantly comply, certainly not without some resistance and questioning. So I have found Abraham's response to God puzzling.

---

1. The word *Aqedah* has many spellings in the secondary literature, including Akedah, Akeda, and Akeidah.

2. Leon R. Kass puts it well: "No story in Genesis is as terrible, as powerful, as mysterious, as elusive as this one. It defies easy and confident interpretations, and despite all that I shall have to say about it, it continues to baffle me." Kass, *The Beginning of Wisdom: Reading Genesis* (New York: Free Press, 2003), 333.

1

The Value of Vigorous Prayer

Abraham's response is especially puzzling in light of the prominence of prayers of lament or complaint in the book of Psalms. I came to value such vigorous prayers after a time of darkness and silence, when I had lost my way. Having experienced a season of questioning regarding my vocation, and even my purpose, combined with doubt about God's goodness, I simply stopped praying. After all, what is there to say to One who has disappointed you, to the Source of all goodness and love, if you feel that this goodness has dried up and this love is gone.

But, thankfully, I did not remain in the darkness. Or in the silence. By the grace of the very God to whom I had stopped praying, I discovered the psalms of lament in the Bible. And these psalms led to a vigorous renewal of faith.

Lament psalms, composing perhaps as much as one-third of the Psalter, are the dominant form of prayer in the book of Psalms, indeed, the dominant genre of psalm.[3] In these prayers, ancient Israelites grappled with God, complaining about their intolerable situations (often blaming God for abandoning them or even targeting them) and pleading for deliverance.

It was the darkest of such psalms, the eighty-eighth, that precipitated a reawakening of my faith.[4]

The Darkness and Desperation of Psalm 88

Psalm 88 is a prayer *in extremis*, where the psalmist has experienced life as so compromised by suffering it is as if he has already gone down (alive) to Sheol, the place of the dead (88:3–5 [4–6 MT]).[5] In his desperation, the psalmist accuses God of being the source of his troubles.

---

3. See the classification of psalms in Bernhard W. Anderson, with Stephen Bishop, *Out of the Depths: The Psalms Speak to Us Today*, 3rd ed. (1983; repr., Philadelphia: Westminster, 2000), 219–24 (Appendix B: "Index of Psalms according to Type").

4. My introduction to the lament psalms came through a course on the Psalms taught by Prof. Werner E. Lemke at Colgate Rochester Divinity School in 1986. I did a class project on lament, using Ps. 88 as the core of a memorial service to help the community grieve the recent death of the young dean of students at the divinity school. Planning, participating in, and preaching at this service changed my life. My thanks to Werner Lemke (who passed away in 2010) for his incisive teaching and supportive mentoring when I was his student, and also for his friendship when I became his faculty colleague in 1996.

5. In Old Testament passages the verse numbering of the Hebrew Masoretic Text (MT) is sometimes different from the English verse numbers in Christian Bibles. This is often the case in the Psalms, since the MT counts the superscription or heading of a psalm as verse 1 (as do

> *You* have put me in the depths of the Pit,
> in the regions dark and deep.
> *Your* wrath lies heavy upon me,
> and *you* overwhelm me with all *your* waves. *Selah*
> *You* have caused my companions to shun me;
> *you* have made me a thing of horror to them. (88:6–8)[6]

Beyond having consigned the psalmist to the realm of the dead, it seems that God has abandoned his would-be worshiper, refusing to answer his prayer for help. This leads to poignant questioning: "O LORD, why do you cast me off? / Why do you hide your face from me?" (88:14). And the psalm ends on a note of sorrow, even despair, in the darkness:

> Wretched and close to death from my youth up,
> I suffer your terrors; I am desperate.
> Your wrath has swept over me;
> your dread assaults destroy me.
> They surround me like a flood all day long;
> from all sides they close in on me.
> You have caused friend and neighbor to shun me;
> my companions are in darkness. (88:15–18)

Most individual laments (of which Ps. 88 is an example) are composed of subgenres such as *complaint* (an honest description of what has gone wrong), *confession of trust* (an affirmation of the prior goodness of God), *petition* (the psalmist's request, even demand, that God intervene), and *vow of praise* (a commitment to respond appropriately after the intervention).[7] However,

---

the Greek Septuagint [LXX] and the Latin Vulgate), whereas superscriptions are not usually included in the verse numbering of Protestant or ecumenical English Bibles. Translations that count the superscriptions as verse 1 include Jewish translations, like the JPS Tanakh, which follows the MT numbering, Orthodox translations, which follow the LXX, and most Catholic Bibles, which follow the Vulgate (the LXX and Vulgate also number some psalms differently, so that Ps. 88 is counted as Ps. 87). After the first citation of Ps. 88 (which includes the MT numbering in brackets), I will give English verse numberings for this psalm.

6. Unless otherwise noted, my default Bible translation throughout this book will be the NRSV. Any emphases are, of course, my own.

7. Biblical scholars typically also list *address to God* (where God is named at the start of the prayer) as part of the lament form. Not all lament psalms have all of these components; when they do occur, they are not always neatly separated from each other, nor do they necessarily follow any particular order (though the vow of praise, if present, tends to come last). The classic analysis of the lament form is found in Claus Westermann, *Praise and Lament in*

Psalm 88 is one of a few that omits the vow of praise.[8] Since the psalm contains no explicit expectation of God's intervention, this would seem to be a prayer devoid of hope.[9]

Yet that appearance would be deceptive.

Psalm 88 as a Door to Hope

Although Psalm 88 is dominated by complaint, with no articulated expectation of God's intervention and only one slender confession of trust near the start (where the psalmist names YHWH "God of my salvation" [88:1]), I found this psalm generative of hope because of its radical honesty.

As Martin Bertman puts it, "The Hebrew attitude towards the apparent existence of evil in the world has generally been to adopt the principle that the individual ought not to deny his own experience."[10] I found this psalm's honest articulation of darkness appropriate to express the depths of my own experience. Anything more explicitly hopeful might have seemed Pollyannaish.

And, having prayed Psalm 88 (and meditated upon its words), I found my own faith beginning to be reawakened. Indeed, it began to undergo a process of deepening.

This reawakening and deepening is certainly related to the sense of being part of a community, stretching back in time, of others who had analogous experiences to my own. Psalm 88 proved I wasn't alone.

Beyond joining the community of lament, hope was generated by the very presence (indeed, dominance) of this form of address to God in the prayer book of Israel and the church. Given this text's status as Scripture, lament prayer could be taken as a normative model or paradigm that was serviceable in approaching God. This psalm (and the presence of other laments in the Psalter) gave me permission to articulate pain and need to God, to question God's goodness, and even to accuse God of complicity in my disorientation.

---

the Psalms, trans. Keith R. Crim and Richard N. Soulen from the 1965 German ed. (Atlanta: John Knox, 1981). In my list of the components of lament, I am using not Westermann's terminology but my own.

8. In the case of communal laments (such as Pss. 44, 74, 89, 137), there is rarely a vow of praise or any positive statement of hope (an exception is the vow of praise in Ps. 80:18 [80:19 MT]).

9. For an in-depth study of Ps. 88, see Anthony R. Piles, "Drowning in the Depths of Darkness: A Consideration of Psalm 88 with a New Translation," *Canadian Theological Review* 1, no. 2 (2012): 13–28.

10. Martin A. Bertman, "The Hebrew Encounter with Evil," *Apeiron* 9, no. 1 (1975): 43 (entire article 43–47).

The existence of these prayers in Scripture suggests that God approves of, even desires, such vigorous interaction on behalf of the human covenant partner. Yet when God asks Abraham to offer up his son, the patriarch says nary a word. I have been perpetually puzzled by Abraham's silence.

Why Abraham's Silence Matters

But Abraham is not alone in his silence. Many in the church think that, like Abraham, they must bear (or submit to) all that befalls them as God's will. Indeed, church leaders often counsel believers to accept all suffering and setbacks as part of God's (often inscrutable) purpose for their lives.

Sometimes the story of Abraham in Genesis 22 is used to reinforce this point of view. Abraham's silent obedience thus becomes a model or paradigm of how to respond to suffering. After all, isn't Abraham's response to God evaluated positively—both in the story of the Aqedah and in later Jewish and Christian tradition? Although the uses to which the Aqedah is put in the history of interpretation are quite varied (and will be discussed later in this book), it is common in popular Christian thinking to view Abraham's silent obedience to God's will as an example for the faithful to follow; this includes bearing our troubles without complaint.

Even when the Aqedah is not explicitly used to justify suffering in silence, the valorization of Abraham's response to God in Genesis 22 can paralyze people of faith in the face of evident evil. If even Abraham, the ancestor of both Jews and Christians, was silently submissive to God in the face of what he must have experienced as an unbearable, crushing reality, how could ordinary believers challenge God over what he brings us in our daily lives? The result is often a stance of passivity in the face of suffering, whether our own or that of others.[11]

Now, I do not mean to disparage the reality of suffering that sometimes must simply be endured. Many faithful Christians and Jews have prayed for deliverance from intolerable situations of suffering only to find that the

11. Although my context is the Christian church, and so I cannot speak authoritatively about contemporary Jewish experience of the Aqedah, it is clear that in earlier times the Aqedah had a prominent place for Jews as a paradigm of martyrdom in the face of persecution. And the fact that the Aqedah is central to Jewish liturgy (especially during Yom Kippur and the Days of Awe) suggests that my analysis may be relevant also to contemporary Jewish experience of this formative text. Indeed, writing out of her Jewish tradition, Tikva Frymer-Kensky notes, "In its stark horror and ambiguous statements, the story of the *Akeda* remains the central text in the formation of our spiritual consciousness." Frymer-Kensky, "Akeda: A View from the Bible," in *Beginning Anew: A Woman's Companion to the High Holy Days*, ed. Gail Twersky Reimer and Judith A. Kates (New York: Touchstone, 1997), 144 (entire chapter 127–44; nn. 345–46).

suffering continues. In Scripture we have the example of the apostle Paul, who three times asked God to remove his "thorn in the flesh," and three times was told that God's grace was sufficient for him (2 Cor. 12:7–9).[12]

I am particularly struck by the comments of biblical scholar Walter Moberly, who positively values Abraham's response to God in his many writings on Genesis 22.[13] Moberly admits that his interpretation of the Aqedah has been significantly impacted by his own "existential struggles with illness and bereavement"; specifically, he notes that his wrestling with God in the context of situations that he could not change (an autoimmune disease and the death of his first wife) has "informed my repeated writing on Genesis 22." Indeed, Moberly notes, "I have, in my own limited way, been to Moriah, as it were."[14]

Walter Moberly is a biblical scholar of the highest order and a Christian of deep faith and integrity. I, therefore, want not only to affirm my respect for this point of view but to acknowledge that there may well be situations of long-term suffering where God's will seems inscrutable and the best we can do is live through the suffering.

But I wonder if we are meant to bear even such suffering in silent acceptance. Or is the path of vigorous prayer open to us?[15] Indeed, how will we know if this is a case of suffering that cannot be changed unless we grapple with God over it? More importantly, how will we sustain a relationship with God if we are reduced to silence? I can attest that my own silence contributed to a shriveling of the relationship—which was reinvigorated only once I started praying (vigorously) again.

Job the Vocal Sufferer

Sometimes the story of Job, the sufferer par excellence, is used to reinforce the importance of bearing suffering submissively.

The typical attitude to the story of Job, in both the church and the academy, is complex. Many readers (whether laypeople, clergy, or scholars) are

12. The meaning of Paul's "thorn" has been greatly debated. I have found the most satisfying answer, both textually and contextually, to be J. Gerald Janzen's proposal in "Paul's 'Robust Conscience' and His Thorn in the Flesh," *Canadian Theological Review* 3, no. 2 (2014): 71–83.

13. Moberly's positive interpretation of Abraham in Gen. 22 (developed over a period of thirty years of writing on the Aqedah) will be addressed in a later chapter.

14. R. W. L. Moberly, "Learning to Be a Theologian," in *I (Still) Believe: Leading Bible Scholars Share Their Stories of Faith and Scholarship*, ed. John Byron and Joel N. Lohr (Grand Rapids: Zondervan, 2015), 205 (entire chapter 201–10).

15. Note that Moberly speaks of wrestling with God (presumably in prayer), which would have preceded his coming to terms with a life situation that couldn't be changed.

initially attracted to Job's bold protest of his innocence, in contrast to the condemnation of his friends, who claim he must have sinned to deserve such terrible suffering. This attraction is enhanced by the fact that both YHWH and the narrator validate Job's innocence in the first two chapters of the book.

Some readers are, however, put off by Job's outrageous curse against the day of his birth (Job 3) and especially by the abrasive way he defends his innocence while impugning God's justice, telling the Creator that he has ordered neither the cosmos nor Job's own life well (especially in his final discourse in chaps. 29–31). Then, when they get to YHWH's speeches from the whirlwind at the end of the book, they are convinced that God has definitively put Job in his place and shut him down for his arrogance in challenging divine justice.

Even those readers (perhaps a minority) who stick with Job all the way, cheering him on in his searing honesty in the face of opposition from his friends and even in his challenge to God, are typically confounded by God's counterchallenge in the speeches from the whirlwind, and agree (reluctantly) that Job has been bullied into submission by an overbearing deity, who has judged the bold protest of this puny human to be unseemly and inappropriate.

True, there are dissenters from this point of view, but the overriding interpretation of Job throughout history, right to the present day, is that the book ends with God's ringing reprimand of Job, which leads to Job admitting, "I . . . repent in dust and ashes" (42:6).

Having studied and taught the book of Job for many years, I have become convinced that this is a fundamental misreading of the message of the book. I have joined the ranks of the dissenters, having learned from—and contributed to—a reading of YHWH's speeches from the whirlwind as a positive affirmation of Job's protest.

Alternative Readings of Job and Abraham

That Job could be read differently, based on close attention to the text, has led me to wonder if we have also been reading Genesis 22 wrongly. Just as it is possible to show that Job's response to his suffering is validated by God, could it be that Abraham's response to God is not exalted as a paradigm for us to follow? This is a much more complicated question, given the overwhelming history of the exaltation of Abraham in Genesis 22, in both Jewish and Christian traditions.

It is especially complicated because I take seriously the warnings of contemporary biblical scholars Walter Moberly and Jon Levenson (from Christian and Jewish perspectives, respectively) about suspicious readings of the Aqedah. Both scholars have been at pains to critique recent interpretations of Abraham (as a child abuser) or of God (as arbitrary and unethical in demanding that Abraham sacrifice his son) in favor of what might be called a traditional, trusting (though complex and nuanced) reading of the text.

Moberly and Levenson both claim that negative evaluations of Abraham's actions in Genesis 22 tend to be arbitrary and extrinsic critiques, based on modern assumptions or predilections of the interpreter, which are simply juxtaposed with the ancient text.[16] In response to these warnings, I will attempt to show how an intrinsic reading of the Aqedah, in its own context (the Abraham story), may be understood to generate criticism of Abraham.

Reading Abraham with Job and the Lament Tradition

At one level, then, this book is an exercise in exegesis, attempting to explore the meaning of the Aqedah (Gen. 22) through close reading of the text in its context (this is known in the Jewish tradition as a *peshat* reading).[17] Along the way, I will also propose a coherent interpretation of the book of Job as a model of biblical lament. Although I will interpret these texts in their own right, I will also attend to their possible relationship to each other—an exercise in intertextuality.

My interest in relating Abraham and Job is not arbitrary. Rather, there are well-established connections between them. For example, the Babylonian Talmud (Baba Batra 15b–16a) contains a discussion among the sages comparing Abraham and Job for their piety and righteousness. But long before that, the book of Jubilees (ca. 160–150 BCE) juxtaposed the testings of Abraham and Job. Jubilees 17–18 retells a version of the Aqedah in which Prince Mastema (Satan) challenges God to test Abraham's devotion to him in much the same way that the book of Job begins.[18] Following Jubilees, there has been such a

16. For example, R. W. L. Moberly, "Abraham and God in Genesis 22," in *The Bible, Theology, and Faith: A Study of Abraham and Jesus* (Cambridge: Cambridge University Press, 2000), 76–78 (entire chapter 71–131); and Jon D. Levenson, "The Test," in *Inheriting Abraham: The Legacy of the Patriarch in Judaism, Christianity, and Islam*, LJI (Princeton: Princeton University Press, 2012), 108 (entire chapter 66–112; nn. 219–23).

17. In general terms, Jewish interpretation of biblical texts can range from peshat (exegetical or literary-contextual readings of the Bible) to midrash (readings that go beyond—often far beyond—the intent of text, in order to explore some aspect of contemporary significance).

18. Whereas Abraham is explicitly said to be tested by God in Gen. 22:1, the Prologue of Job frames the entire book as a test. Yochanan Muffs, in a famous study of vigorous prayer in the Jewish tradition, writes of "the tests to which God subjects Abraham and Job," admitting

pervasive tradition of connecting the stories of Abraham and Job that one scholar has coined the term *Jobraham* to convey the intrinsic connection of these two characters in the interpretive tradition.[19]

Beyond Exegesis to a Theology of Prayer

My interest in the meaning of Genesis 22, the book of Job, and how they may both be read in light of the lament tradition is not simply antiquarian. Rather, this exegetical exploration has a definite theological—even a pastoral—aim. As a biblical scholar, I love the in-depth exploration of biblical texts. Yet my purpose in this book is ultimately to help people of faith recover the value of lament prayer as a way to process our pain (and the pain of the world) with the God of heaven and earth—for the healing both of ourselves and of the world.

Although some might want to keep academic biblical study separate from theological and pastoral reflection, I have always found the existential and the exegetical to be fundamentally intertwined.[20]

On the one hand, I have never experienced what some think of as the ivory tower of academia. My study of Scripture has consistently been a matter of personal involvement, even when attending to technical matters of the Hebrew language, literary rhetoric, or ancient Near Eastern contexts. Indeed, serious engagement with Scripture has always been for me a matter of spiritual discipline, an important aspect of my formative spirituality. And beyond my own formation, I have found significant overlap between my scholarship in the academy, my teaching in the classroom, and my ministry in the church.[21]

On the other hand, my growth in the life of faith and the development of my theology have always been precisely *through* my grappling with biblical

---

that both tests seem arbitrary. Muffs, however, distinguishes between the responses of Abraham and Job in that he evaluates Job's questioning of God as positive. Muffs, *The Personhood of God: Biblical Theology, Human Faith and the Divine Image* (Woodstock, VT: Jewish Lights, 2005), 72, 184.

19. Nicholas J. Ellis, "The Reception of the Jobraham Narratives in Jewish Thought," in *Authoritative Texts and Reception History: Aspects and Approaches*, ed. Dan Batovici and Kristin de Troyer, BibInt 151 (Leiden: Brill, 2016), 124–40.

20. For an illuminating example of the integral combination of exegesis/peshat with an emphasis on contemporary theological and ethical significance, see Shai Held, *The Heart of Torah*, 2 vols. (Philadelphia: Jewish Publication Society, 2017).

21. I address the intersection of academic biblical studies and the lived context of the interpreter in my 2021 presidential address to the Canadian Society of Biblical Studies, "Beyond Eurocentrism: Envisioning a Future for Canadian Biblical Studies," *Canadian-American Theological Review* 10, no. 1 (forthcoming).

texts. I would be at a loss to develop a meaningful theology of lament prayer except by way of interaction with Scripture.

The argument of this book thus proceeds primarily through engagement with a series of biblical texts, in three movements or parts.

Part 1: Models of Vigorous Prayer in the Bible

Part 1 addresses models of vigorous prayer in the Bible, specifically the psalms of lament and prophetic intercession.

Chapter 1: "Voices from the Ragged Edge" takes an introductory look at the lament psalms as a resource for helping us address suffering with a view to renewal and hope in God. It is not a systematic introduction to the lament psalms, but it draws on specific examples from the Psalter to illustrate how existentially powerful these voices from the ragged edge are. The chapter concludes by suggesting how lament prayer fits into the normative pattern of the biblical story—specifically, the exodus, the cross, and the eschaton—and reflects on the relevance of lament prayer for living in a broken world.

Chapter 2: "God's Loyal Opposition" focuses on Moses as the paradigmatic prophet, who boldly challenges God, first at Sinai, when he convinces God to spare Israel after the idolatry of the golden calf, and then later at Kadesh-Barnea, when he appeals to the golden calf episode as a precedent for God to pardon Israel again. The chapter then proceeds to the memory of Moses's intercession in the Old Testament and later Jewish literature, including Moses-like intercession in the prophetic books of Amos, Micah, Jeremiah, and Ezekiel. The fact that God is the one who invites such bold intercession shows that this God positively values vigorous dialogue partners.

Part 2: Making Sense of the Book of Job

Part 2 addresses the meaning of the book of Job, with a focus on Job as someone who embodies the biblical affirmation of vigorous prayer.

Chapter 3: "The Question of Appropriate Speech" explores the book of Job as a thought experiment in wisdom, where the central question is: What should a wise or righteous person say (especially about/to God) in the face of terrible suffering? The book of Job takes the reader on a journey through a sequence of responses: Job's initial praise; his fatalistic silence; his vocal protest; and the responses of Job's friends, who try to defend God's ways;

to Job's responses to his friends; Elihu's interjection; and YHWH's response from the whirlwind.

Chapter 4: "Does God Come to Bury Job or to Praise Him?" explores the significance of YHWH's speeches from the whirlwind as an answer to Job, which addresses the question posed by the book about appropriate speech. In this context, YHWH's first speech can be seen as correcting Job's misunderstanding of divine justice or governance, which has been evident in much of Job's protests throughout the book. This correction, by means of a cosmic and zoological tour of creation, reduces Job to silence, which God did not intend—which is why God speaks again.

In the second speech from the whirlwind, YHWH affirms the validity of Job's protest. The core of the second speech is God showing off to Job two "chaotic" monsters, Behemoth ("which I made along with you"; 40:15) and Leviathan (Job 41)—both of which have powerful mouths and whom no one can tame. Having been compared (implicitly) to untamable monsters, in whom God exults, Job is "comforted about dust and ashes" (a better translation than the traditional "repent in dust and ashes"; 42:6).

Part 3: Unbinding the Aqedah from the Straitjacket of Tradition

Following the analysis of Job, we begin to examine the Aqedah proper, first in the history of interpretation, then by careful exegesis of the text itself. Here my focus is specifically on whether it is legitimate to read Genesis 22 against the grain of tradition—that is, without valorizing Abraham.

Chapter 5: "Is It Permissible to Criticize Abraham or God?" clarifies my own rationale for attempting a critical reading of Abraham's response to God in Genesis 22 and grapples with the nuanced versions of an exemplary reading of the Aqedah advanced by Jon Levenson and Walter Moberly—including their claim that all criticisms of Abraham are invalid since they are mounted from a position extrinsic to the biblical text and to biblical assumptions. The chapter then traces Jewish attitudes to Genesis 22 before the modern period, noting one strand of early Jewish tradition that came to view protest to God explicitly as sin, alongside the alternative tradition of questioning God. Yet even in this alternative tradition we do not find explicit questions raised about the Aqedah. But could the questions be implicit?

Such implicit questions are suggested by the ways that many ancient Jewish interpreters picked up on details in the text in order to address their profound unease with the story. While the majority of premodern writers (both Jewish and Christian) do not explicitly criticize God for testing Abraham and instead affirm the exemplary nature of Abraham's obedience, many in the ancient and medieval Jewish commentary tradition moderated their praise of God and Abraham by midrashically filling in details of the story in ways that suggest they were uncomfortable with the Aqedah. Although this is a far cry from the boldness of Moses or Job in their direct challenge to God, it opens the way for a more considered critical interpretation of the Aqedah.

Chapter 6: "Reading Rhetorical Signals in the Aqedah and Job" begins by exploring a range of rhetorical clues in the text of Genesis 22 that tip the reader off that something is not right here. These clues raise significant questions about whether Abraham is to be understood as a normative figure in this particular instance. The chapter then highlights various thematic and intertextual links between the Aqedah (and the wider Abraham story) and the book of Job. These links suggest that the book of Job was intended to be read in relation to the Aqedah. Indeed, Job's vocal protests could be thought of as an implicit critique of Abraham's silence in Genesis 22.

This *might* mean that the book of Job is at loggerheads with the assumed validation of Abraham's response to the test given by the author of Genesis 22 (especially as articulated by the angel of YHWH). However, it is also possible that we have misread the perspective of the author of Genesis 22 (and the angel's supposed validation of Abraham). Could it be that the book of Job and Genesis 22 are in fundamental agreement about the validity of protest to God? Could it be that *even Genesis 22* does not affirm Abraham's silence as exemplary?

The next chapter addresses this question head-on.

Chapter 7: "Did Abraham Pass the Test?" evaluates Abraham's response to God by engaging in a reading of the Aqedah in the context of the wider Abraham story, especially Abraham's changing understanding of God and his relationship with his family in the narrative arc of Genesis 12–25. This contextual reading suggests an entirely different reason for the test than is commonly proposed, one that makes more sense of the entire Abraham story. This reading effectively challenges the standard opinion that Abraham's response to God was exemplary—but it does so by trying to understand the story *on its own terms*, rather than from an extrinsic perspective. In this, it attempts to respond to the concerns of both Levenson and Moberly.

Having proposed an alternative reading of the purpose of the test (and Abraham's less-than-exemplary response), the chapter concludes by examining the two angel speeches, which are typically taken as praising Abraham's response. This examination shows that an alternative, critical reading of Abraham's silence is not only possible but eminently plausible.

A reflection on "The Gritty Spirituality of Lament" concludes the book. Having connected the purpose of Abraham's test in Genesis 22 with the book of Job, the lament psalms, and other biblical prayers of protest, I conclude the book by exploring the dialectic of submission and resistance implied in such texts. This dialectic not only has implications for vigorous prayer in situations of suffering but is essential for the development of a healthy spirituality and the renewal of our life and walk with God in the context of a violent and polarized world.

Facing the Difficulty of Scripture and Life—with Hope

For many years my ruminations concerning Abraham, Job, and lament have functioned like a great underground river, watering the soil of my life and work as a biblical scholar. More and more, however, this powerful underground flow has bubbled to the surface, forcing me to wade into the current and address more explicitly the difficulty of the life of faith and the complexity of these often baffling biblical texts.

It is my hope that the exploration of these biblical texts will be helpful in developing an honest, yet trustful spirituality that might empower God's people with hope in their daily lives, as they face a world full of chaos and pain.

PART 1

MODELS OF VIGOROUS PRAYER IN THE BIBLE

1

Voices from the Ragged Edge

In the movie *The Princess Bride* there is a conversation between the princess, who has been kidnapped, and her rescuer (the Dread Pirate Roberts), in which she says: "You mock my pain." To which he replies, "Life *is* pain, highness; anyone who says differently is selling something."[1]

Without being quite as cynical as that, most of us can affirm that pain or suffering is an indelible fact of human existence, as we know it. We live in a world racked by suffering.

A Multifaceted World of Suffering

Many marriages, despite our best intentions, fall apart. Close friends die of suicide or cancer. And we're confronted in our inner cities with hollow-eyed people living on the street, casting furtive glances in our direction, in the hope of a handout.[2]

---

1. *The Princess Bride*, scene 20, directed by Rob Reiner, screenplay by William Goldman, Twentieth-Century Fox, 1987. The movie is based on William Goldman's novel *The Princess Bride: S. Morgenstern's Classic Tale of True Love and High Adventure* (New York: Harcourt Brace, 1973).

2. This chapter is the fruit of many Bible studies, class lectures, and talks I have given on the lament psalms since the late 1980s. The title ("Voices from the Ragged Edge") was developed in dialogue with John Garner, pastor of Harbour Fellowship Church, St. Catharines, ON, when he invited me to preach on the lament psalms in 1993. I summarized that sermon in a short meditation, "Voices from the Ragged Edge: How the Psalms Can Help Us Process Pain," *Canadian Theological Society Newsletter / Communiqué de la société théologique canadienne*

Meanwhile the victims of terrorism and political violence continue to pile up as so many dead bodies in the streets of city after city, and country after country—every decade the names change, but the suffering continues. This violence leads to millions of displaced persons—refugees from their own nations and homes—living in destitute circumstances.

And the refugee crisis is accompanied by a world that is becoming increasingly tribalistic, desensitized to the suffering of others, even callously demonizing those viewed as enemies (whether for economic, national, political, or religious reasons).

And beyond inter-human violence, the planet groans in the thrall of our pollution of air, water, and land, with huge floating continents of plastic in the Pacific, widespread rainforest depletion, and the destruction of species at an alarming rate in our own time. As earth's climate warms (precipitated by human action), we are overwhelmed by massive and more frequent tsunamis, earthquakes, and hurricanes, which wreak destruction all over the globe, with a devastating loss of life.

The suffering of the world is multifaceted, and it is massive.

Tragic as this massive suffering is, the tragedy is compounded by our paralysis, often alternating with anger directed at those we perceive as our enemies. Despite God's call on our lives to respond in compassion to the pain of others, we find, if we are honest, that we lack the energy for this mission. We are too spent just coping with the ordinary crises of life to give much of ourselves to the needs of others. So we pull back self-protectively into a defensive posture, avoiding even eye contact with the street person, unable to bear such exposure to the world's wounds. Or we circle the wagons of our tribe and vehemently denounce anyone who threatens our sense of security and identity.

I believe that the roots of both our paralysis and our misdirected anger lie in our own pain that has never been adequately processed. Religious people have a very hard time dealing with pain. We prefer to accentuate the positive. But the positive—praise and celebration—isn't always appropriate.

14, no. 1 (November 1994): 4–7, reprinted in the bulletin of the Institute for Christian Studies, as "Voices from the Ragged Edge: How the Psalms Can Help Us Process Pain," *Perspective* 29, no. 1 (March 1995): 4–5. This short piece was then expanded into the current chapter. A preliminary version of this chapter was published as Middleton, "Voices from the Ragged Edge: The Gritty Spirituality of the Psalms," in *A Sort of Homecoming: Pieces Honoring the Academic and Community Work of Brian Walsh*, ed. Marcia Boniferro, Amanda Jagt, and Andrew Stephens-Rennie (Eugene, OR: Pickwick, 2020), 90–108. Used by permission of Wipf & Stock Publishers.

When Praise Is Inappropriate

Imagine barely surviving a car crash, perhaps being the only survivor, badly injured and lying in a hospital bed; then your pastor or rabbi comes to visit you and reads Psalm 150.

> Praise the LORD!
> Praise God in his sanctuary;
> > praise him in his mighty firmament!
> Praise him for his mighty deeds;
> > praise him according to his surpassing greatness!
>
> Praise him with trumpet sound;
> > praise him with lute and harp!
> Praise him with tambourine and dance;
> > praise him with strings and pipe!
> Praise him with clanging cymbals;
> > praise him with loud clashing cymbals!
> Let everything that breathes praise the LORD!
> Praise the LORD! (150:1–6)

That would, of course, be manifestly inappropriate.

Or suppose you are in the middle of a tragic divorce; or you've just lost your job and you're not sure how your family is going to survive, given the mortgage payments and other bills. And someone says to you (as a friend of mine used to say in every situation): *Just praise the Lord anyway, brother!*

But how *can* you praise God when you're suffering from the shock of disorientation? How could you, if you were an Israelite, newly exiled to Babylon, sing one of the songs of Zion? Psalm 46 is a classic Zion song, celebrating God's presence in the midst of Jerusalem. It opens with this confident assertion: "God is our refuge and strength, / a very present help in trouble" (46:1 [46:2 MT]). Because God is in the midst of the city, the psalmist affirms that it shall never be moved (46:5 [46:6 MT]). Except the city now lies in ruins.

So a later psalmist, writing in the midst of the exile, sings not a Zion song but a lament—a communal complaint: "By the rivers of Babylon—/ there we sat down and there we wept / when we remembered Zion" (Ps. 137:1). Psalm 137 goes on to ask, How can we sing YHWH's song (like Ps. 46 or Ps. 150) in a strange, alien land? (137:4). And this psalm is relevant well beyor original historical context, since when we are in a state of suffering, in an alien land, alienated from the reality of flourishing that God intends for this good creation.

In the song "These Plastic Halos," alternative Christian artist Mark Heard describes the struggle of many churchgoers to be honest about their pain. Heard uses the metaphor of "plastic halos" to describe the masks Christians often wear in church, behind which "lurks a scarred and fragile face." These masks serve to hide our pain because we "think our tears / would provoke holy wrath." The result of our "stone-gray silence" (our inability to "face our fears") is that "we press on / with feeble cheer," "refusing comfort unawares."[3]

In the final stanza Heard characterizes this approach to masking suffering as a "protocol" that we learn, in which we praise optimism and denigrate sorrow. The song ends with these words: "As we watch / the world turn to dust / the tears of God fall for us."

I believe that the lament psalms provide an *alternative* protocol for addressing suffering, a protocol that is both existentially healing and deeply rooted in the redemptive sweep of the biblical narrative.

The "Problem" of (Explaining) Evil

Sometimes it isn't a focus on praise and celebration that prevents our dealing with pain. Sometimes well-meaning people stop us short from hosting disorientation, from being fully honest about our suffering, by providing a quick (and ultimately superficial) *explanation* for suffering—much like Job's comforters did.[4]

Even if we have never pondered the philosophical "problem of evil" (also known as the "theodicy" problem), sensitive people of faith intuitively understand its basic contours.[5] This is the "problem" laid out in its simplest form.

---

3. Mark Heard, "These Plastic Halos," recorded July–September 1982, side 2, track 3 on *Eye of the Storm*, Home Sweet Home Records, 1983.

4. The categories of *orientation*, *disorientation*, and *new orientation*, which pervade this chapter, are based on Walter Brueggemann's insightful analysis in *The Message of the Psalms: A Theological Commentary*, Augsburg Old Testament Studies (Minneapolis: Augsburg, 1984). These categories are derived from the work of Paul Ricoeur, and Brueggemann uses them to connect the psalms to human experience. My metaphor of "hosting" disorientation is meant to suggest that it is not optimal for the disorientation caused by suffering to invade the "house" of our lives in a permanent takeover; but neither should we slam the door on disorientation, since it ends up coming in the back window anyway. Rather, we need to be *hospitable* to our disorientation, addressing it through the protocol of the psalms, until it is ready to leave, and we begin to shift to a new, transformed, orientation.

5. The term *theodicy* (derived from the Greek words for God [*theos*] and justice [*dikē*]) was coined by Gottfried Wilhelm von Leibniz (1646–1716) at the end of the seventeenth century to speak of God's general will as showing his benevolence. Although Leibniz's *Essais de théodicé*

1. We believe that God is good and loving (God *doesn't want* evil and suffering).
2. We believe God is sovereign or all-powerful (God *could remove or prevent* evil and suffering).
3. Yet evil exists.

This certainly seems like a contradiction.[6] And there are various ways to resolve it.

We could say, *There is no God* (that would certainly solve the logical problem, but it doesn't help those of us who believe in God). Or we could say, *God isn't totally good or trustworthy* (we could deny the first premise).[7] Or we could say, *God isn't totally sovereign*; God just can't do anything about it (we could deny the second premise).[8]

We could even say, *Evil doesn't really exist*; it is an illusion—which is affirmed by some Eastern religions.

However, by far the most common solution in the history of Christian thought is to claim that God has a "good reason" for allowing evil and suffering.[9] Or, to use different terminology, there is a "greater good" that God has in mind that could not be accomplished without all the evil and suffering in the world.[10] This is a Christian version of denying the third premise. In other

---

was published in 1710, he mentioned the title of his proposed work in a letter in 1695. For an English translation, see Leibniz, *Theodicy: Essays on the Goodness of God, the Freedom of Man and the Origin of Evil*, trans. E. M. Huggard, ed. Austin Farrer (Le Salle, IL: Open Court, 1985). In *Candide* (French original, Paris: Nilsson, 1759), Voltaire satirizes such optimism in his famous response to the tragedy of the 1755 Lisbon earthquake, related tsunami, and fires.

6. The above three points are based on the famous statement of the problem in David Hume, *Dialogues concerning Natural Religion*, ed. Martin Bell (1779; repr., London: Penguin, 1990), part 10, esp. pp. 108–9 (Hume here refers to an earlier formulation by the Greek philosopher Epicurus). J. L. Mackie states the problem in similar terms in "Evil and Omnipotence," *Mind* 64, no. 254 (1955): 200–212. Sometimes a fourth point is added—namely, that God is omniscient, knowing all things. I don't believe this contributes anything essential to the issue.

7. This position is advanced by David Blumenthal, *Facing the Abusing God: A Theology of Protest* (Louisville: Westminster John Knox, 1993).

8. This position is advanced by Harold S. Kushner, *When Bad Things Happen to Good People* (New York: Schocken Books, 1981). It is also the position of process theology and philosophy, which is based on metaphysical analysis of the nature of God and reality.

9. The terminology of God having a "good reason" for allowing evil can be found in Alvin Plantinga, *God, Freedom, and Evil* (Grand Rapids: Eerdmans, 1977), 26, 31. Before Plantinga, Nelson Pike had spoken of God having a "morally sufficient reason" for evil; see Pike, "Hume on Evil," *Philosophical Review* 72, no. 2 (1963): 183 (entire article 180–97).

10. This way of putting things goes back to at least Augustine (except that he did not think that suffering was technically evil; see *De libero arbitrio*, 1.11.22; 3.9.25). In an early work

words, what we *think* is "evil" is not really, ultimately evil, since it is necessary for the best of all possible worlds. This keeps God technically blameless, since God needed to allow all the evil and suffering that has actually happened in order to accomplish this greater good (whatever it is).

But to claim that every evil in the world contributes to some equal or greater good, which would be otherwise unattainable, means quite simply that there is no genuine evil. Genuine evil, as David Ray Griffin has cogently argued, requires, as a minimum, the criterion that without it the universe could be a better place. Otherwise it would not be genuine but only prima facie evil.[11]

There are many examples of prima facie evils that actually do serve a greater good. For example, there are times I have had to work hard on a lecture or a talk when on the surface it seemed like an "evil" to me; I would much prefer to be out walking in the woods or riding my bicycle. But I've buckled down to write the talk, since I judged it was a greater good that couldn't be accomplished if I slacked off.

Or suppose a soldier is wounded on the battlefield, with no antibiotics available, and the wound becomes infected with gangrene. Perhaps his leg has to be amputated to save his life. Normally, amputating a leg would not a good thing; but in this case it serves a greater good (saving someone's life), which could not be accomplished without it.

The trouble with the greater good defense as a global solution to the problem of evil is that it requires us to say that *all* the evil and suffering that happens in the world (every bit of it) is necessary for some greater good that God couldn't accomplish without it.[12] The problem with such claims is that they have the potential to undercut motivation for both petitionary prayer and active opposition to evil. After all, if I really believed that God had a greater good in mind that could not be produced without the particular "evil" situation I have encountered (and the greater good argument claims

---

Augustine claimed that whatever moral evil is committed by humans is immediately counterbalanced by God's just punishment, so that the world is made no worse by human evil (*De libero arbitrio*, 2.16.43; 3.9.25). In a later work Augustine claimed that God counterbalances the evil humans do so that the result is *better* than it was prior to human evil: "God judged it better to bring good out of evil than not to permit any evil to exist." *Augustine: Confessions and Enchiridion*, trans. and ed. Albert C. Outler (Philadelphia: Westminster, 1955), 355.

11. David Ray Griffin, *God, Power, and Evil: A Process Theodicy* (Philadelphia: Westminster, 1976), 21–26.

12. For my formal analysis and critique of the greater good defense, see Middleton, "Why the 'Greater Good' Isn't a Defense: Classical Theodicy in Light of the Biblical Genre of Lament," *Koinonia* 9, nos. 1 & 2 (1997): 81–113.

to justify all cases of evil in light of God's purpose), then why would I ask God for deliverance from this particular situation? Indeed, why would I ever resist evil? Believing a greater good approach to evil could, therefore, generate ethical paralysis.[13]

Free will is perhaps the primary example of a greater good that has been proposed to explain why God allows suffering. The free will version of the greater good defense claims that God values free will so much that even if it results in terrible evil—including terrorist bombings, the Holocaust, ethnic cleansing in Rwanda and Bosnia, and the ovens of Auschwitz and Dachau—then, so be it. It is all required (and worth it, from God's perspective) for us to have free will.

My point is not to discuss the merits of the free will argument but to note that we find many examples of this greater good *approach* among Christians who attempt to give an explanation for why someone suffers. For example, someone at a funeral might comment that God had a reason for taking the person. Even if we couldn't state what that reason is, it is very common for Christians to claim that there must be some purpose for our suffering.[14]

C. S. Lewis's Change of Mind about the Greater Good Defense

C. S. Lewis articulated a variant of the greater good defense in his famous book *The Problem of Pain*, originally published in 1940.

At one point in the book Lewis explains that people often are not aware that they are in a state of rebellion against God, especially if all is going well with them. "But pain," he notes, "insists upon being attended to." This leads to his famous statement: "God whispers to us in our pleasures, speaks in our conscience, but shouts in our pain: it is His megaphone to rouse a deaf

13. I am aware that simply affirming some version of the greater good argument would not necessarily lead a person to acquiesce to whatever comes their way, since all sorts of psychological motivations to resist evil come into play. But I am thinking here of the *logic* of the position, and especially the pressure of this logic on someone who actually *believes* the greater good argument.

14. Alvin Plantinga (*God, Freedom, and Evil*, 26–28) is famous for claiming that a free will *defense* (which he proposes) should be distinguished from a free will *theodicy* (thus, by implication, a greater good *defense* should be distinguished from a greater good *theodicy*). Whereas a defense attempts to show only the *logical possibility* that God has good reasons for allowing evil (in order to refute the claim that the existence of evil contradicts God's goodness and power), a theodicy argues for *specific reasons* why God allows evil. This distinction, while valid, does not affect my point about the greater good *approach* to evil or its consequences for the life of faith. My use of the term *defense* goes beyond Plantinga's technical usage.

world."[15] What happens once we find that pain has "roused" us from our slumbers, when we become aware that we are "not in accord with the universe," that there is a reality that impinges upon us, which we do not control? Lewis suggests we have two options: we might begin a process of turning to God or we might rebel against God (with the possibility of repentance later on).

"No doubt," Lewis admits, "pain as God's megaphone is a terrible instrument; it may lead to final and unrepented rebellion. But it gives the only opportunity the bad [person] can have for amendment. It removes the veil; it plants the flag of truth within the fortress of a rebel soul."[16] Pain, or suffering, in other words, is a wake-up call. It is needed in the world since it shocks at least *some* people into turning to God (which is the greater good). Of course, not all repent. But the implicit argument Lewis is making here is that there is a reason for suffering that justifies it.

That was in 1940.

Yet twenty-one years later (in 1961) Lewis wrote a book called *A Grief Observed*. He wrote it under the pseudonym N. W. Clerk because he couldn't come right out and contradict (in his own name) what he had said in *The Problem of Pain*. But contradict it he did. In this new book he rejected entirely the greater good argument to explain evil.

At one point Lewis wonders about God's presence—or rather God's felt *absence*.

> Meanwhile, where is God? This is one of the most disquieting symptoms. When you are happy, so happy that you have no sense of needing Him, so happy that you are tempted to feel His claims upon you as an interruption, if you remember yourself and turn to Him with gratitude and praise, you will be—or so it feels—welcomed with open arms.
>
> But go to Him when your need is desperate, when all other help is vain, and what do you find? A door slammed in your face, and a sound of bolting and double bolting on the inside. After that, silence.
>
> You may as well turn away. The longer you wait, the more emphatic the silence will become. There are no lights in the windows. It might be an empty house. Was it ever inhabited? It seemed so once. And that seeming was as strong as this.[17]

15. C. S. Lewis, *The Problem of Pain* (London: Centenary Press, 1940), 83.
16. Lewis, *Problem of Pain*, 83.
17. C. S. Lewis, *A Grief Observed* (1961; repr., Greenwich, CT: Seabury, 1963), 9.

Lewis concludes this line of thought with two questions. First, he asks simply, "What can this mean?" But then, alluding ironically to Psalm 46:1 (much as Job 7:17–18 may be an ironic comment on Ps. 8:4 [8:5 MT]), Lewis asks, "Why is He so present a commander in our time of prosperity and so very absent a help in time of trouble?"[18]

This is certainly far removed from any version of a greater good argument. So what happened between *The Problem of Pain* and *A Grief Observed*?

Many know the story of Lewis experiencing the joy of marriage (having been a bachelor for over fifty years). Shortly after this, his new and beloved wife, Joy Davidman, was diagnosed with cancer. There was a time of remission; then the cancer returned, and she died three years after the original diagnosis.

When Explaining Suffering Is Unacceptable

It is one thing to articulate a theoretical position about suffering serving a greater good; it is quite another to still believe this when suffering (and death) hits someone you know and love.

This is vividly portrayed in the 1993 movie *Shadowlands*, which depicts the life of C. S. Lewis with a focus on his marriage to Joy Davidman; the movie draws on *A Grief Observed*.[19]

There are three illuminating scenes (one right after another) that illustrate the shift that Lewis (known as Jack to his friends) went through after his wife died.

In the first scene, after Joy's funeral is over and Lewis is walking out of the church, the priest who just conducted the service says, "Thank God for your faith, Jack; it's only faith makes any sense of times like these." Without uttering a word, Lewis's body language speaks volumes. He briefly glances at the priest and continues walking, with his jaw set, as if he simply can't countenance this attempt at comfort.

In the second scene, Lewis is at home after the funeral, with his older brother, Warren (known as Warnie). After a time of silence, he muses: "So afraid of never seeing her again, thinking that suffering is just suffering after all—no cause, no purpose, no pattern." His brother answers, "I don't know

18. Lewis, *A Grief Observed*, 9.
19. *Shadowlands*, directed by Richard Attenborough, screenplay by William Nicholson, Savoy Pictures, 1993. The 1993 movie (Anthony Hopkins plays Lewis, and Debra Winger plays Joy Davidman) was a remake of the original 1985 made-for-TV movie and a 1989 play, both by the same name.

what to tell you, Jack." To which Lewis responds, "There's nothing to say; I know that now. I've just come up against a bit of experience, Warnie. Experience is a brutal teacher, but you learn, by God you learn."

In the third scene, Lewis re-enters the academic society at Cambridge University. When asked by a sympathetic colleague, "Anything I can do?" he responds, "Just don't tell me it's all for the best, that's all."

The priest (Harry) who had conducted Joy's funeral is there and offers a pious comment: "Only God knows why these things have to happen." Lewis responds, getting to the crux of the matter, "God knows, but does God care?" The dialogue then comes fast and furious.

"Of course, we see so little here. We're not the creator," says Harry.

"No, we're the creatures, aren't we?" rejoins Lewis. "We're the rats in the cosmic laboratory." At this point Harry shakes his head, but Lewis won't be stopped. "Have no doubt the experiment is for our own good, but that still makes God the vivisectionist."

Harry tries to interject, "Jack . . ." But Lewis responds by shouting, "NO! It won't do. It's a bloody awful mess and that's all there is to it."

The Honesty of the Psalms

What Lewis articulates in *A Grief Observed* (and what his movie character articulates in *Shadowlands*) places him squarely in the chorus of voices from the ragged edge, against those who would "explain" evil. He thus comes close to the lament or complaint psalms of many psalmists, the anguished prayers of the prophet Jeremiah (for example, Jer. 20:7–18), and the protests of Job the sufferer throughout the book that bears his name.

Lament psalms, which make up over one-third of the Psalms (compared to hymns of praise, which compose less than a quarter), are honest, abrasive prayers, which squarely face up to the dark side of human experience; and so they can provide us guidance (a "protocol") for how to "host" and process disorientation.

I will focus on two psalms—Psalm 30 (a thanksgiving psalm) and Psalm 39 (a psalm of lament). These psalms illustrate well the process of coming to lament and the nature of lament.[20]

20. Although I began to develop my understanding of lament psalms through a course on the Psalms, which led to my encounter with Ps. 88 (mentioned in the introduction to this book), this understanding was considerably deepened through a weekend workshop on the Psalms that Walter Brueggemann led at St. Andrew's Presbyterian Church in Kitchener, ON, in April

Although today we use terms like *thanksgiving*, *praise*, and *worship* often interchangeably, the genre of thanksgiving psalms is somewhat different from the genre of hymns of praise in the Psalter. Hymns of praise describe what God typically does. Thus they praise God in more general ways for characteristic attributes or actions—usually in the present tense. Take, for example, Psalm 103:

> Bless the LORD, O my soul,
>> and do not forget all his benefits—
> who forgives all your iniquity,
>> who heals all your diseases,
> who redeems your life from the Pit. (103:2–4a)

Another example is Psalm 117:

> Praise the LORD, all you nations!
>> Extol him, all you peoples!
> For great is his steadfast love toward us,
>> and the faithfulness of the LORD endures forever.
> Praise the LORD! (117:1–2)

Whereas hymns of praise (like Pss. 103 and 117) describe God's typical actions, a thanksgiving psalm tells a story in the past tense. It thus looks back on an event in which God did something wonderful for the psalmist.

Up from the Abyss—a Story of Deliverance (Ps. 30)

Psalm 30 is a psalm of new orientation. The psalmist has experienced a renewal, an encounter with God that has brought significant life transformation. That is why he praises God at the beginning of the psalm, essentially summarizing the story of rescue that generated the psalm.

> I will extol you, O LORD, for you have drawn me up,
>> and did not let my foes rejoice over me.
> O LORD my God, I cried to you for help,
>> and you have healed me.

1989. As part of that workshop, Brueggemann explored the meaning of Ps. 39. My thanks also to Brian Walsh for an insightful Bible study he led on Ps. 30, connecting it to Brueggemann's analysis of Ps. 39, which sparked my interest in exploring them further.

O Lord, you brought up my soul from Sheol,
> restored me to life from among those gone down to the Pit.
>> (30:1–3)[21]

Given that this last line could be translated as, "You spared me from going down to the pit" (NIV; see also NJPS, NASB, NAB, NLT, KJV), it may sound like a contradiction to say, as the previous line does, "You brought up my soul from Sheol." Which one is it? Spared or brought up? But this is not literal description. This is poetry. The psalmist is bursting with gratitude. The point is: God rescued him. He doesn't say from what, precisely. It could be from sickness, from war, from persecution, from poverty—we don't know exactly what the problem was. He also says that God protected him from enemies, but doesn't expand on it.

The psalms are full of images including the grave (or Sheol), the pit, the miry ground, the psalmist's enemies (also described as dogs or bulls) who have the psalmist surrounded. But the psalms rarely get more specific than that. It is almost as if the psalmist (and the God who inspired these psalms) wants the language open and porous enough so that we (whoever we are) can read *our own* troubles through these prayers, so they can be serviceable for our encounters with God.

The story of a thanksgiving psalm usually has two parts—what went wrong in the psalmist's life (the disorientation) and how God intervened to bring healing or deliverance (the new orientation or renewal).

A lament psalm is really half of a thanksgiving psalm. A lament psalm is a prayer for help from the bottom of the pit; but a thanksgiving psalm is a prayer of gratitude offered once the lamenter is back on solid ground.

On Top of the World—Orientation

Psalm 30 is slightly different from most thanksgiving psalms in that it doesn't just tell the story of disorientation and the subsequent renewal; it goes back *before* the disorientation, to the prior orientation that got "dissed."

> As for me, I said in my prosperity,
> > "I shall never be moved."

---

21. Ps. 30:2–4 MT. From here on I will give only English (NRSV) verse numberings for this psalm; the Hebrew (MT) is consistently one verse different.

By your favor, O LORD,
    you had established me as a strong mountain. (30:6–7a)

Those are words of assurance, security, and confidence. And we all need orientation, a secure sense of place and direction in the world. C. S. Lewis had an orientation in *The Problem of Pain* (this allowed him to explain why we suffer).

Psalm 1 (a Torah psalm, a psalm that instructs us in how to live) is a classic example of a psalm of orientation, which is probably why it has been put at the beginning of the Psalter. Its message is very simple: Blessed are those who walk in the way of righteousness; they shall be secure and fruitful, like a tree planted by streams of water. But the wicked (and those who follow their path) are not so. They are unstable and transitory, like the chaff the wind blows away.

Nothing could be simpler. There are two moral or religious directions in life: good and evil. You follow one path, you are secure and blessed by God. You follow the other, and you don't last. That's the covenantal structure of life; that's the basic "orientation" of Scripture. That's kid's stuff. In the good sense of the term, that's Sunday school faith. Every child (indeed, every adult) needs a clear-cut sense of what life is all about, a basic orientation that makes sense of things.

And it often *does* work that way. You work hard in school, and you may get good grades and even a scholarship, perhaps a good job after graduation. You apply yourself on the job, and you get a raise and maybe a promotion (which, of course, you deserve).

You work hard at a relationship and it turns into a marriage. And you work hard at marriage, and it endures. And you put a lot of energy into your kids, and they turn out alright. You work hard at a church, you're as faithful as you can be, and you have church growth (numerical and spiritual) and church unity.

"Orientation" works. Sometimes. And when it does, you feel on top of the world.

From Confidence to Dismay–Disorientation

But this psalmist's world came crashing down; or, to continue the psalmist's own metaphor, *he* came crashing down from the mountaintop. His memory of

God's favor (30:6–7a) is pervaded by a profound sense of loss. The psalmist tells of the withdrawal of God's presence and the disorienting fall from the heights into the abyss: "You hid your face; / I was dismayed" (30:7b).

He gives no specific details, but it felt like God was gone. This is exactly what C. S. Lewis experienced in *A Grief Observed*.

Like the psalmist (and like Lewis), many in the church and in our society at large have *experienced* the absence of God and are consumed by a sense of betrayal, with neither hope for the future nor energy for significant living. Pain has overwhelmed joy. Although this pain is often caused by large family or personal crises, much of it is the result of the accumulated frustrations of a life that does not seem to work out as it is supposed to. And this certainly amounts, in the end, to a large crisis.

What are we supposed to *do* when the "orientation" doesn't work the way it's supposed to? What was Lewis supposed to do? Say, "It's all for the best. God has a greater good that required this"? Is *that* what we should tell victims of a terrorist bombing or a natural disaster? Or the survivors of the Shoah (the Nazi Holocaust)?

Let us be clear about the reality of evil. This is Elie Wiesel's description of arriving at Birkenau, an extermination camp in the Auschwitz complex. The year was 1944 and he was an adolescent (fourteen or fifteen years old) at the time. "In front of us, those flames. In the air, the smell of burning flesh. It must have been around midnight. We had arrived. In Birkenau."[22]

Then, three days later, come Wiesel's famous words about never forgetting, which were forged of experience.

> Never shall I forget that night, the first night in camp, that turned my life into one long night seven times sealed.
> Never shall I forget that smoke.
> Never shall I forget the small faces of the children whose bodies I saw transformed into smoke under a silent sky.
> Never shall I forget those flames that consumed my faith forever.
> Never shall I forget the nocturnal silence that deprived me for all eternity of the desire to live.
> Never shall I forget those moments that murdered my God and my soul and turned my dreams to ashes.

22. Elie Wiesel, *Night*, trans. Marion Wiesel (New York: Hill and Wang, 2006 [French original 1958]), 28.

Never shall I forget those things, even were I condemned to live as long as God Himself.

Never.[23]

What can you say to an experience like that? Certainly not, "It's all for the best; God has a greater good that requires this." Instead, we need to take seriously the famous words of Irving (Yitz) Greenberg: "No statement, theological or otherwise, should be made that would not be credible in the presence of the burning children."[24]

What, then, *can* you say? Perhaps a psalm of lament would be appropriate.

From Silence to Speech (Ps. 39)

We will come back to Psalm 30. But first we turn to Psalm 39, an individual lament prayer, told from the bottom of the pit.

Whereas Psalm 30 is instructive for us because it goes back before the disorientation to the prior orientation, Psalm 39 is also instructive for us, but in a different way, because the psalmist tells us the story of how he came to lament.

The Difficulty of Honest Speech

This psalmist's first impulse is to silence.

> I said, "I will guard my ways
>> that I may not sin with my tongue;
> I will keep a muzzle on my mouth
>> as long as the wicked are in my presence." (39:1)[25]

Voicing his pain honestly in public, and especially to God, seems inappropriate. So he decides to keep quiet about his suffering and "muzzle" his

23. Wiesel, *Night*, 34. The repetitive (almost liturgical) nature of this description has been insightfully compared to the similar pattern found in Ps. 150, with the difference that "Praise him" has been replaced with "Never shall I forget." Sparknotes, *Night* by Elie Wiesel, "Important Quotations Explained," https://www.sparknotes.com/lit/night/quotes.

24. Irving Greenberg, "Cloud of Smoke, Pillar of Fire: Judaism, Christianity, and Modernity after the Holocaust," in *Auschwitz—Beginning of a New Era? Reflections on the Holocaust*, ed. Eva Fleschner (New York: KTAV, 1977), 27 (entire chapter 7–55).

25. Ps. 39:2 MT. As with Ps. 30, the Hebrew verse numbering for Ps. 39 is one higher than the English. From here on I will give English verse numberings.

mouth since "the wicked" are around and he wants a good testimony. He says, in effect, "I was taught that a truly spiritual person should speak only nice, edifying words." Presumably he did not want to display a lack of trust in the presence of unbelievers. So he said, "My lips are sealed!"

The Difficulty of Prolonged Silence

But the longer he kept quiet, the more agitated he became.

> I was silent and still;
>   I held my peace to no avail;
> my distress grew worse,
>   my heart became hot within me.
> While I mused, the fire burned. (39:2–3a)

Like many in the church (and in our society), this writer bottles up his pain until it grows into a raging fire within and he is ready to explode. "Then I spoke with my tongue" (39:3b). But it doesn't come out all at once.

Step 1: Testing the Waters

This is what he starts with:

> LORD, let me know my end,
>   and what is the measure of my days;
>   let me know how fleeting my life is.
> You have made my days a few handbreadths,
>   and my lifetime is as nothing in your sight.
> Surely everyone stands as a mere breath. *Selah*
>   Surely everyone goes about like a shadow.
> Surely for nothing they are in turmoil;
>   they heap up, and do not know who will gather. (39:4–6)

Perhaps he's not sure what God can handle. So he tests the waters, musing in a general way about human mortality and asking a safe, disinterested question about how long he has to live. I've noticed that people die, he says; none of us is more than a breath. So, I was wondering if you could (maybe) tell me how long I've got.

Step 2: What Is Really at Stake

And God doesn't strike him down. So he gets bolder. From safe musings and disinterested inquiry, he moves to an honest admission of need. "And now, O Lord, what do I wait for?" (39:7a). Not, How long am I going to live? But, What do I *really* wait for? What do I *really* hope for? "My hope is in *you*" (39:7b). And he pleads for deliverance.

He addresses seven imperatives to God, telling God what to do:[26]

- Deliver me. (39:8a)
- Don't make me the scorn of fools. (39:8b)
- Remove your stroke from me. (39:10a)
- Hear my prayer. (39:12a)
- Give ear to my cry. (39:12a)
- Don't hold your peace at my tears. (39:12a)
- Turn your gaze away from me. (39:13)

Why couldn't the psalmist have *started* with this? What held him back? In his newfound honesty, he tells God why. "I was silent; I would not open my mouth, / for *you* are the one who has done this" (39:9 NIV). The problem is that his pain came from God; he perceived his suffering as *God's fault* and was, understandably, slow to voice this. But whereas Psalm 30 faults God for abandonment, Psalm 39 goes considerably further. "Remove your stroke from me; / I am worn down by the blows of your hand" (39:10). The psalmist says, in effect, "Stop hitting me! I'm exhausted." He accuses God of violence against him and pleads for an end to the pain because he can't take it anymore.

The Power of Honest Speech

Now, it certainly isn't "theologically correct" to accuse God of doing evil, as this psalmist has done. This is a statement made in extremity, out of desperation. But it is not unique in the Psalter. Many psalms of lament make similar statements. From Psalm 22, which Jesus prayed on the cross ("My God, my God, why have you forsaken me?"; 22:1), to Psalm 88, which of all

---

26. Technically, there are no negative imperatives in Hebrew, so the grammatical form for the second and sixth items is slightly different. But they have the force of imperatives or commands.

the psalms seems most bereft of hope ("I suffer your terrors; I am desperate"; 88:15 [88:16 MT]), we are bombarded with voices from the ragged edges of life that articulate pain honestly to God. These abrasive prayers all complain about suffering as intolerable and implore God for deliverance. Indeed, many lament psalms, along with portions of the books of Jeremiah and Job, are prayers in which life is experienced as so raw and so fickle, where the pain and suffering are so massive, that the supplicant ultimately experiences *God* as fickle and dares to voice this in prayer.[27]

I think we can learn from the honesty of the psalmists. For when the pain and disorientation are that great, we have only three options.

Bottle It Up

We can bottle it up inside, nursing it until we self-destruct and it explodes into violence and abuse against those around us, especially those most vulnerable. A great deal of spousal and child abuse may well be rooted in accumulated suffering that, instead of being articulated, is kept within and has nowhere to go. Indeed, a great deal of vehement political and religious discourse today may have its origin in accumulated pain that has been bottled up, rather than dealt with appropriately. And when we have nowhere to direct our pain except at those around us, we can't even perceive—much less begin to respond to—their suffering.

Denial

Or, we can piously deny the pain and maintain the theologically correct status quo. We can sing hymns of praise in church and say, "God is good— all the time," though we don't, in our bones, believe a word of it. And then we become numb to our pain, and numb to God. And we certainly become numb to the pain of others.[28]

27. Just as it is inappropriate to bad-mouth someone behind their back, yet important to directly confront them, letting them know how they have let you down (for the sake of the relationship), so there is an important distinction to be made between general claims about God's character (say, in a theology book) and speech addressed directly to God in prayer. These are fundamentally different sorts of speech acts.

28. "God is good—all the time" is a common refrain in many contemporary churches. A more classical version of this statement is the Gloria Patri, often recited in liturgical churches: "Glory be to the Father, and to the Son, and to the Holy Spirit; as it was in the beginning, is now, and ever shall be—world without end." As someone committed to classical liturgy, I understand that these words are meant to refer to the glorification of God throughout all time. But

Lament–Supplication with an Edge

Or, following the lead of the psalmists, we can take our anger, our doubt, and all the dismay and the terror of life, and we can put it at the feet of the Most High. We can bring our pain to the throne of God and say, "You're supposed to be faithful, but I don't see it! You're supposed to be good, but I don't experience it."

And, contrary to appearances, that desperate, honest voicing of pain to God is not blasphemous, but is a holy, redemptive act. Prayers of lament are radical acts of faith and hope because they *refuse*, even in the midst of suffering, to give up on God.

Notice how desperate—even childish and regressive—the speech of the psalmist becomes in Psalm 30:

> What profit is there in my death,
>> if I go down to the Pit?
> Will the dust praise you?
>> Will it tell of your faithfulness? (30:9)[29]

Here the psalmist mounts an argument for why God should save him. I'm going down for the count, he says. I'm about ready to die, and they don't praise you in the grave. Don't you want me to praise you? Then save me quickly!

This childish, desperate outburst is actually a radical confession of faith; the psalmist, even in his desperation, knows that help lies in God alone. None other can deliver.

That is why Psalm 39 is peppered with imperatives, commands addressed to God. You have to be desperate to address imperatives to the Creator, to tell God what to do. That is the inherent boldness of supplication or petitionary prayer. And lament is supplication *with an edge*.

---

the words "as it was in the beginning, is now, and ever shall be—world without end" are often heard as a statement that nothing ever changes (partially because it is often sung in churches that seem stuck in a particular era). I can testify that singing the Gloria Patri while in a state of deep pain only intensified the pain and plunged me further into depression; the words I sang discouraged lament. I am, therefore, grateful for the words of Bob Marley in "One Love / People Get Ready" (recorded 1977, side 2, track 10 on *Exodus*, Tuff Gong), which articulate a future that is different from the present: "As it was in the beginning, so shall it be in the end—Alright." Given that the present is often at odds with God's original and ultimate purposes, Marley's lyrics affirmed for me the possibility of dissent from the status quo and encouraged me to bring my concerns to God in lament.

29. Note the similar strategy in Ps. 6:4–5 (6:5–6 MT) and Ps. 88:10–12 (88:11–13 MT).

The fact is that silence will not get us through the pain. Only speech addressed to God gets us through—speech that summons God into our suffering, which says to God, as the writer of Psalm 30 did, "Hear, O LORD, and be gracious to me! / O LORD, be my helper!" (30:10). Or, even as the writer of Psalm 39 did in his impropriety, "Turn your gaze away from me, that I may smile again" (39:13a). It doesn't have to be theologically correct speech. But it has to be gut-honest speech.

The Biblical Story as Paradigm

When we have the audacity to lay our pain at God's feet, to summon the Most High into our suffering, something remarkable happens. God comes.

The Exodus

Lament psalms have their roots, ultimately, in the exodus, the central and founding event of the Old Testament, when YHWH delivered the Israelites from Egyptian bondage. Central to the story as it is told in the Bible is the Israelites' primal scream of pain to God. Between centuries of accumulated suffering and God's decisive intervention, we find this remarkable statement:

> The Israelites groaned under their slavery, and cried out. Out of the slavery their cry for help rose up to God. God heard their groaning, and God remembered his covenant with Abraham, Isaac, and Jacob. God looked upon the Israelites, and God took notice of them. (Exod. 2:23b–25)

This agonized cry of pain at the heart of the exodus echoes resoundingly throughout the psalms of lament. Lament is redemptive, therefore, not simply because the supplicant clings to God in desperate faith. More fundamentally, lament is rooted in the very pattern of the biblical story, at the hinge—even the fulcrum—between bondage and deliverance.[30] This is true both in the Old Testament and in the New.

30. I am grateful to Melody Knowles, who challenged me to move beyond the metaphor of lament as the *hinge* between bondage and deliverance (which I proposed in Middleton, "Why the 'Greater Good' Isn't a Defense," 103). Knowles insightfully noted that laments have "causational power" for "the transformation of God's heart," which is what moves God to action. See Melody D. G. Knowles, "Lament and the Transformation of God: Response to J. Richard Middleton," *Koinonia* 9, nos. 1 & 2 (1997): 118 (entire article 114–19). Perhaps the metaphor of lament as *fulcrum* conveys this point.

Jesus

As Jesus faced his time of disorientation in the garden of Gethsemane, he cried out in sorrow, sweating blood (Luke 22:44), and pleaded with his Father to "remove this cup from me" (22:42). And on the cross, in the midst of his disorientation and agony, he cried out, quoting Psalm 22, "My God, my God, why have you forsaken me?" (Matt. 27:46; Mark 15:34).

The disorientation represented by the death of Jesus was so massive, says the New Testament, that when he died the earth shook (Matt. 27:51); creation itself reeled in a kind of cosmic sympathy with the Son of God. And Jesus was plunged into the abyss of disorientation, even death. He was crucified, dead, buried, says the Apostles' Creed; he descended into hell, into Hades, into Sheol, into the pit. But his cry, even of abandonment, went up to God. And three days after his disorientation and his agonized cry, God answered his cry and raised him from the dead.

All Creation

But more than this, the cross itself was God's response to the lament of all creation. For creation itself, says Paul, is groaning in its bondage to corruption, subject to futility, and yearning eagerly for redemption (Rom. 8:19–22). And we ourselves groan inwardly, says the apostle (8:23). I submit that our articulation of these groanings into prayer, even ragged prayers on the boundary of propriety, has the potential to unleash the power of the resurrection, leading to new creation.

But we have to cry out. What unites these three pivotal events (groaning before the exodus, Jesus's cry to God, and creation's groaning) is the pattern of *calling on God*. The watchword of lament prayer could well be the words of Joel 2:32 (3:5 MT): "Everyone who calls on the name of the LORD shall be saved." That these words are quoted by Peter on the day of Pentecost in Acts 2:21 and by Paul in Romans 10:13, which suggests that lament, in the form of supplication, also finds a home in the New Testament.[31]

31. Patrick D. Miller, *They Cried unto the Lord: The Form and Theology of Biblical Prayer* (Minneapolis: Augsburg Fortress, 1994), shows that lament is found also in the New Testament, esp. in chap. 3: "'They Cried to You': Prayers for Help" (55–134). Although the focus of that chapter is the Hebrew Bible / Old Testament, Miller cites dimensions of lament in the New Testament. He continues the discussion in chap. 10: "'Teach Us to Pray': The Further Witness of the New Testament" (304–35).

Jesus's Teaching on Prayer

The importance of calling on God for help is nowhere more evident than in the Lord's Prayer, taught by Jesus as a model for his disciples (Matt. 6:9–13; Luke 11:2–4).[32] This prayer is constituted purely by supplication or petition from start to finish (this excludes the doxology added to Matt. 6:13 in later manuscripts and used in the church's liturgy). Although the opening petitions are explicitly God-oriented ("May your name be sanctified," "May your kingdom come," "May your will be done on earth as in heaven"), such petitions are not purely disinterested, since the granting of them will positively affect the supplicant, who is associated with God's name and lives on earth.[33] And the prayer continues with requests for daily bread, forgiveness, preservation from testing, and deliverance from evil—all of which affirm the legitimacy of articulating human needs to God.

This focus on petition is congruent with two parables about prayer ascribed to Jesus, both of which fit the pattern of biblical laments.

In the parable of the importunate widow (Luke 18:1–8), prayer is compared to a widow who badgers a judge who has refused to give her justice (presumably because she is a relatively powerless person, without much status or influence). Her boldness and persistence in bringing her case to the judge until he enacts the justice due her is analogous, says Jesus, to the steadfastness (and I would add, audaciousness) required in asking God to meet our needs.

In the parable of the friend at midnight (Luke 11:5–8), prayer is compared to knocking on the door of a neighbor's house late into the night in order to ask for food to feed a visitor. The persistence required to get the neighbor to come to the door at that hour is analogous, says Jesus, to the steadfastness (and also the audaciousness) required in intercessory prayer.[34]

Both of these parables about prayer combine complaint with petition or supplication—the articulation of need with a request for help. The combination of humility and boldness required for such prayer is fundamentally

---

32. The resonance of the Lord's Prayer with phrasing from classic Jewish liturgy is fruitfully explored by Chuck Day in "The Lord's Prayer: A Hebrew Reconstruction Based on Hebrew Prayers Found in the Synagogue," *Conspectus* 17 (2009): 27–37.

33. The translations of the petitions in Matt. 6:9–10 are my own. Thanks to Rev. David Biberstein for his profound teaching on the Lord's Prayer when he was my pastor during my undergraduate theological studies in Jamaica.

34. This parable follows immediately on the Lukan version of the Lord's Prayer and is itself followed by the exhortation to ask, seek, and knock, with the assurance that God wants to give his children good gifts (Luke 11:9–13 // Matt. 7:7–11).

an expression of trust in God (and leads to further trust, when practiced regularly).

Jesus himself embodies the lament tradition on the cross (Matt. 27:46), when he prays Psalm 22:1 from the depths of his suffering ("My God, my God, why have you forsaken me?"). But his lament prayer began earlier, in Gethsemane before his arrest. That Jesus can both honestly express his desire not to die ("Father, . . . remove this cup from me"), yet still affirm submission to God's purposes ("Not my will but yours be done") suggests the requisite combination of boldness and trust characteristic of lament (Luke 22:42).[35]

The Psalms as Models for Processing Pain

Silence about pain in our society and in the church conveys the message that God simply doesn't care about suffering. Too many churchgoers have had to suppress their pain to sing glib hymns of praise and thanksgiving, when what was really needed was closer to a primal scream of rage. And hurting visitors are effectively excluded from participation in worship by invocations that enjoin the congregation to put aside their problems and come and worship God.

But if the church took seriously the psalms of lament as model modes of speech (an alternative "protocol") in its communal life and processed the pain of its members in liturgy and public worship, it would convey the quite radical message that our suffering matters to God. Indeed, it matters so much that he bore it in his own body on the tree.[36]

And if our suffering matters to God, then we might begin to believe—and feel—that the suffering of others matters too. Voicing our pain to God might then be redemptive not only for ourselves but ultimately for the world. As the hinge or fulcrum, which unleashes the power of the resurrection, lament has the potential to generate genuine thanksgiving for the grace of God, thus energizing God's people for their vocation in a suffering world.

35. For an in-depth exploration of lament in the New Testament, see Rebekah Ann Eklund, *Jesus Wept: The Significance of Jesus' Laments in the New Testament*, LNTS 515 (London: Bloomsbury T&T Clark, 2015).

36. Here I allude to the language of 1 Pet. 2:24 (KJV); though many modern translations (such as NRSV) have replaced "tree" (KJV) with "cross."

2

God's Loyal Opposition

In the movie *Stardust Memories*, Sandy Bates (played by Woody Allen) quips, "To you, I'm an atheist. To God, I'm the loyal opposition."[1] A few years before the movie, biblical scholar George Coats described Moses in Exodus 32–34 as "The King's Loyal Opposition" because of his bold and vigorous challenge to God.[2] But although Moses objected to the judgment that God was going bring on Israel after the idolatry of the golden calf, essentially saying no to the divine King (32:11–12), he was certainly no atheist. In fact, in the midst of this very narrative we are told that whenever Moses would enter the tent of meeting, the Shekinah glory would descend on the tent (33:9) and YHWH would "speak to Moses face to face, as one speaks to a friend" (33:11). Even a friend of God may talk back to God without jeopardizing that friendship.[3]

It turns out that when Moses talks back to God, he is responding to God's own invitation to intercede on Israel's behalf. In this, Moses is the precursor of the later prophetic tradition, where various prophets implore God to withhold bringing judgment on Israel for their sins.

---

1. *Stardust Memories*, directed by Woody Allen, screenplay by Woody Allen, United Artists, 1980.
2. George W. Coats, "The King's Loyal Opposition: Obedience and Authority in Exodus 32–34," in *Canon and Authority: Essays in Old Testament Religion and Theology*, ed. Burke O. Long and George W. Coats (Philadelphia: Fortress, 1977), 91–107.
3. This, of course, raises the question of why Abraham, whom God calls "my friend" (Isa. 41:8; see also James 2:23), does not talk back in Gen. 22. I address this question in the final chapters of this book.

We typically think of the prophet, standing between God and the people, as someone who brings a word of judgment or salvation (depending on the situation). But sometimes the prophet also speaks back to God. Having delivered God's word of judgment for the people's disobedience, some prophets turn to this same God and plead for a delay or postponement of the promised judgment in order to give the people time to repent.[4]

Here we should clarify the relationship between intercessory prayer and lament. The previous chapter (on lament psalms) described lament as supplication *with an edge*, in view of the honesty of the complaint. The complaint in a lament psalm is that portion of the prayer that brings some dire situation to God's attention, even accusing God of complicity in the problem. But lament prayer involves more than complaint. Having got God's attention, the lament psalms call upon God to act, in order to remedy the situation. Supplication or petition is thus an important part of lament. And intercession is a particular form of supplication; it is supplication or petition on behalf of another.

The Paradigm of Moses's Intercession

The great exemplar of prophetic intercession is Moses, who is regarded as the paradigmatic prophet in the Bible. Moses predates the formal office of prophet, as found in the writing prophets of the eighth century and later (Isaiah, Jeremiah, Ezekiel, and the Twelve), or in the stories of Elijah and Elisha, set in the ninth century (1–2 Kings), or even in the stories of Samuel and Nathan, set in the eleventh and tenth centuries (1–2 Sam.). Yet Deuteronomy regards Moses as the first in a line of prophets who will later arise, who are therefore said to be "like" Moses (Deut. 18:15–18).

Moses certainly functions like a prophet in that he brings the word of God (in his case, the Torah) to Israel. But Moses also models intercession on behalf of Israel.[5] Although Moses intercedes on behalf of Israel on various

---

4. Here it is important not to overstate the case for prophets as intercessors, since not all prophets are presented in Scripture as interceding for the people. Samuel E. Balentine goes further than this observation and concludes, from his study of the terminology of intercession in the prophets, that intercession was not an expected "characteristic function" or "routine or regular activity" of prophets in the Bible. Balentine, "The Prophet as Intercessor," *JBL* 103, no. 2 (1984): 171 (entire article 161–73). Nevertheless, I will give examples later in this chapter of intercession by Amos, Micah, Jeremiah, and Ezekiel.

5. Abraham is also called a prophet because of his intercession—initially on behalf of Sodom (Gen. 18), but also on behalf of Abimelech, king of Gerar (20:7). I will explore the significance of Gen. 18 in chap. 7.

occasions, the first and most important episode is his extended prayer at Sinai/ Horeb in the aftermath of the idolatry of the golden calf (Exod. 32–34).[6] We, therefore, need to spend some time unpacking this episode.

The Idolatry at Sinai—the Setting for Moses's Intercession

According to the narrative, Moses was up on Mount Sinai for forty days and forty nights (Exod. 24:18), where he received the tablets of the law, written by God's own finger (31:18). While Moses was on the mountain, the people convinced Aaron to make them a golden calf—a molten image by which they intend to worship YHWH, something expressly prohibited in the Ten Commandments:

> You shall not make for yourself an idol, whether in the form of anything that is in heaven above, or that is on the earth beneath, or that is in the water under the earth. You shall not bow down to them or worship them. (20:4–5a)

Whereas the preceding commandment prohibited the worship of any deity besides YHWH (20:3), this commandment goes further in prohibiting the use of a humanly constructed image in worship (this applies even to the worship of YHWH).[7]

This distinction between the commandments requires us to reflect on the function of idols or images in the ancient Near East. Most fundamentally, an image of deity was intended to facilitate the mediation of the presence, blessing, and favor of the deity to the worshipers.[8] In a certain sense, then, Moses

6. For a classic study of this key text, see R. W. L. Moberly, *At the Mountain of God: Story and Theology in Exodus 32–34*, JSOTSup 22 (Sheffield: JSOT, 1983); also Michael Widmer, *Moses, God, and the Dynamics of Intercessory Prayer: A Study of Exodus 32–34 and Numbers 13–14*, FAT 2 (Tübingen: Mohr Siebeck, 2004). Interestingly, while the first volume was Moberly's doctoral thesis, the second was Widmer's doctoral thesis, written under Moberly's supervision. Widmer has also addressed Exod. 32–34 in chap. 3 of his more recent *Standing in the Breach: An Old Testament Theology and Spirituality of Intercessory Prayer*, Siphrut 13 (Winona Lake, IN: Eisenbrauns, 2015).

7. The Ten Commandments (known in the Jewish tradition as the "Ten Words," since Exod. 20:1 begins with "God spoke all these *words*") are counted differently by Jewish and Christian traditions. Jewish tradition counts verse 2 ("I am the LORD your God, who brought you out of the land of Egypt, out of the house of slavery") as the first "word," so that verse 3 is the second "word." Protestant and Orthodox Christian traditions regard verse 2 as a preamble to the commandments proper, so that verse 3 ("You shall have no other gods before me") is the first commandment and verses 4–5 are the second. The Roman Catholic tradition treats verses 2–3 (including YHWH's self-identification) as the first commandment.

8. This is the basic conceptual background to humanity as *imago Dei* (Gen. 1:26–28). For my own exposition of the role of images in the ancient Near East (especially its application

took the place of the image in the early religion of Israel, since Moses himself functioned as the divinely authorized mediator between Israel and YHWH on their journey from Egypt to the Promised Land. So it is understandable that the people become anxious during Moses's long absence on the mountain (32:1–2, 23), since they now have no guaranteed way to connect with God.

In Moses's absence they decide to construct their own form of mediation, which (paradoxically) leads to the loss of divine favor. By their idolatry, the people of Israel have broken one of the key commandments of the Sinai covenant (Moses symbolizes this covenant breaking when he smashes the tablets of the law in 32:19). The covenant they have made with God (24:7–8) is now, in effect, null and void.

The prohibition of images in Exodus 20 is accompanied by a "motive clause," a reason given to motivate Israel to keep the commandment. The motivation is twofold, including both a negative warning and a positive incentive:

> For I the LORD your God am a jealous God, punishing children for the iniquity of parents, to the third and the fourth generation of those who reject me, but showing steadfast love to the thousandth generation of those who love me and keep my commandments. (20:5b–6)[9]

The prohibition of images is grounded explicitly in the fact that YHWH will not tolerate rivals; and this jealousy will result in clear negative consequences. But paired with the warning is a reference to God's "steadfast love" (*ḥesed*) as a positive motivation to obey.[10] Whereas judgment was prom-

---

to human imaging), see Middleton, *The Liberating Image: The* Imago Dei *in Genesis 1* (Grand Rapids: Brazos, 2005), 43–90 (esp. 74–90); Middleton, "The Role of Human Beings in the Cosmic Temple: The Intersection of Worldviews in Psalms 8 and 104," *Canadian Theological Review* 2, no. 1 (2013): 44–58; and Middleton, *A New Heaven and a New Earth: Reclaiming Biblical Eschatology* (Grand Rapids: Baker Academic, 2014), 37–56 (esp. 37–50), 155–76 (esp. 163–76).

9. This motive clause is also found in Deut. 5:9b–10, the parallel passage where Moses rearticulates the Ten Commandments for the new generation who are about to enter the Promised Land (see 5:1–22 for the Ten Commandments plus Moses's framing comments).

10. This Hebrew word is subject to many different translations, often varying from passage to passage. In Exod. 20:6, it is rendered "mercy" (KJV), "lovingkindness" (NASB 95), "kindness" (NJPS), "faithful love" (NJB), "steadfast love" (NRSV, ESV), and "love" (NIV). The classic study of this word is Katharine Doob Sakenfeld, *The Meaning of Hesed in the Hebrew Bible: A New Inquiry*, HSM 17 (Missoula, MT: Scholars Press, 1978; repr., Eugene, OR: Wipf & Stock, 2002). See also Sakenfeld's more recent *Faithfulness in Action: Loyalty in Biblical Perspective*, OBT 16 (Philadelphia: Fortress, 1985).

ised for three or four generations (possibly referring to one extended family living in the same household, as was common in ancient times), God's *ḥesed* is for a *thousand* generations of those who love YHWH and keep his commandments.[11]

However, by their disobedience, the people have just demonstrated that they *don't* love YHWH, since they have broken the commandment about images.[12] Judgment will, therefore, inevitably follow. And we find that God immediately begins to distance himself from the people, using that distancing tactic well known to many parents, as when one parent angrily asks their spouse, "Do you know what *your* son has just done?"

God tells Moses, "Go down at once! *Your* people, whom *you* brought up out of the land of Egypt, have acted perversely; they have been quick to turn aside from the way that I commanded them; they have cast for themselves an image of a calf, and have worshiped it and sacrificed to it, and said, 'These are your gods, O Israel, who brought you up out of the land of Egypt!'" (Exod. 32:7–8). God puts the responsibility for the people—who have just broken the second commandment—squarely on Moses's shoulders. And, initially, Moses doesn't know how to respond.

We can infer this because the very next verse has what is effectively a speech resumption formula: "the LORD said to Moses" (32:9). But God has just been speaking in the previous verse, so there is technically no need to start verse 9 with "the LORD said to Moses," unless God had finished speaking in verse 8, then waited for a response, but got none.

So God speaks again, informing Moses about his anger: "The LORD said to Moses: 'I have seen this people, how stiff-necked they are. *Now let me alone*, so that my wrath may burn hot against them and I may consume them; and of you I will make a great nation'" (32:9–10).

Having received no response from Moses after his statement in 32:7–8, God signals to Moses that he is angry with the people for their idolatry, *but not angry enough* to destroy them yet. So he (somewhat ironically) tells Moses

11. The Hebrew of Exod. 20:6 simply says that God will show his *ḥesed* to "thousands" (reflected in KJV, NASB, ESV, NJB), but in context this may mean a thousand *generations* (reflected in NRSV, NIV, NJPS, NLT).

12. Although the use of the term *love* for Israel's commitment to God takes on emotional connotations in later Jewish and Christian tradition, it was used in ancient Near Eastern political covenants for allegiance to a sovereign, the opposite of which is treason. See William L. Moran, "The Ancient Near Eastern Background of the Love of God in Deuteronomy," *CBQ* 25 (1963): 77–87.

to leave him alone so that his anger may grow sufficiently for that purpose, which gives Moses the dialogical space to intercede for the people.

Moses Finds His Voice and Steps into the Breach

Moses, who was initially speechless, discerns an opening, in two senses. First, a breach has opened between God and his people—a tragic parting of the ways. But Moses senses another sort of opening. God seems to have intentionally left him a space for intervening. So Moses steps into the opening; he stands in the breach. Although God said two things to Moses—let me alone so I can get angry enough to destroy the people *and* I will start over again with you— Moses ignores the second point (for the time being) but homes in on the first.

Just as the commandment against idolatry has motive clauses attached to it, and just as lament prayers give God reasons to act, so Moses provides God with a threefold motivation not to destroy Israel. He starts with a question, which is a safe way to start praying; it's difficult to go wrong with a question. "O Lord," he asks, "why does your wrath burn hot against *your* people, whom *you* brought out of the land of Egypt with great power and with a mighty hand?" (32:11).

Note what Moses has just done under the guise of asking an innocent question. God described the people to Moses as "*your* people, whom *you* brought up out of the land of Egypt" (32:7). But Moses won't have it; he turns the tables: these are "*your* people," says Moses, "whom *you* brought out of the land of Egypt." Moses places the burden of responsibility back on God. The first motivation for not destroying them is that they are God's own people, and Moses reminds God of this in no uncertain terms (you might say that he throws this back into God's face).

Then Moses immediately asks another question (which includes his second motivation): "Why should the Egyptians say, 'It was with evil intent that he brought them out to kill them in the mountains, and to consume them from the face of the earth'?" (32:12a). In other words, Moses tells God to finish what he started—the redemption of God's own people from Egypt—otherwise God will get a bad reputation.

And if we think that God would not be swayed by this sort of reasoning, then Moses's final motivation may count for more. "Remember Abraham, Isaac, and Israel, your servants, how *you* swore to them by *your own self*, saying to them, 'I will multiply your descendants like the stars of heaven, and all this land that I have promised I will give to your descendants, and they shall inherit it forever'" (Exod. 32:13). Moses here reminds God that he made a promise, he swore a solemn oath (presumably a reference to Gen. 22:16–18 or possibly to 15:13–16); and he calls God to be true to his own commitments.[13]

Sandwiched between the second and third motivations is Moses's petition or request: "Turn from your fierce wrath; change your mind and do not bring disaster on your people" (Exod. 32:12b). "Change your mind" is a translation of the Hebrew verb *nāḥam*, referring to God's "repentance," while "disaster" translates *rā'â*, a general Hebrew word referring to all sorts of "evil" (from moral evil to injury and harm). Moses, in other words, tells God that he is in the wrong and needs to change. In the classic words of the KJV, Moses says to YHWH: "*Repent* of this *evil* against thy people."

Does God take offense that Moses dares to ask him (actually, to *tell* him) to change his mind, to take a different course—as if Moses knows better than God what he should do? Not at all. In fact, God's response is almost anticlimactic: "And the LORD changed his mind about the disaster that he planned to bring on his people" (Exod. 32:14). Just like that, without rejoinder, God simply accepts what Moses asks. It is as if this is what God wanted all along.

God's positive response emboldens Moses. He goes on to make a series of further requests or petitions.[14] Having successfully convinced God not to destroy the people (32:11–14), Moses next persuades God to forgive (or bear) Israel's sin (32:31–32) so that the covenant relationship can be maintained.[15]

When God first articulates his desire to wipe out the people, he proposes to start over with Moses as, in effect, a new Abraham (32:10). At the time, Moses simply ignores that proposal. But we find Moses's delayed response to that proposal linked to his request for God to forgive the people's sin. He effectively ties himself to the fate of the people when he declares that if God will not forgive their sin, "blot me out of the book that you have written" (32:32).

God agrees to Moses's request for forgiveness, with two caveats. First, those who rebelled will be punished (and God, indeed, sends a plague), but God accepts that Moses will lead the people to the Promised Land (32:33–34),

13. I will address the significance of the Gen. 22 oath, which God swears to Abraham after the Aqedah, in chap. 7.

14. Although I have divided Moses's intercessions into four distinct requests, a careful reader of Exod. 32–34 will note that there is some overlap between the requests. There may even be more than four requests, depending on how they are counted; multiple sources have evidently been used in this composite account.

15. The verb Moses uses is *nāśā'*, meaning "to lift up" or "to bear." When used in connection with sin it is typically translated as "forgive."

which implies that they have been forgiven. Second, God says that he will send an angel to guide them on the wilderness journey, which is portrayed as a distancing tactic due to divine anger, since this anger might break out if God's presence were too near (33:2–3).

But Moses refuses to accept this; he appeals to his cachet (his "street cred") with God ("You have said, 'I know you by name, and you have also found favor in my sight'"; 33:12); he uses this as leverage to argue that God should personally accompany them on the journey. Moses actually asks something both for himself ("Show me your ways") and for the people ("Consider too that this nation is your people"; 33:13). Indeed, Moses may be reminding God that his "ways" are ways of mercy and faithfulness to his covenant with Israel.

And God responds positively to Moses's request: "My presence will go with you, and I will give you rest" (33:14). But *who* exactly will God go with and give rest? The NRSV's phrase "with you" (33:14) is not in the Hebrew; it is supplied by translators. God just says, "My presence will go [with you], and I will give you rest." So we need to focus on the "you" in "I will give you rest." But that "you" is singular in Hebrew. Does it refer to Israel or to Moses alone?[16]

Moses clearly isn't satisfied with the ambiguity of this response. So he presses his case once again: "If your presence will not go, do not carry *us* up from here. For how shall it be known that I have found favor in your sight, *I and your people*, unless you go with *us*?" (33:15–16).

Note the emphasis on *us*. Moses tells God that he and the people are a package deal; if God wants to show his commitment to Moses, he needs to include the people in the bargain. And the tactic works. "The Lord said to Moses, 'I will do the very thing that you have asked; for you have found favor in my sight, and I know you by name'" (33:17).

Finally, Moses comes back to his personal request to see God's "ways," phrased now as seeing God's "glory," or *kābôd* (33:18).[17]

---

16. By contrast, the singular "you" in Exod. 33:3 refers to the singular noun "people" ("for you are a stiff-necked people"), so it is, in effect, plural.

17. Biblical theophanies often use *kābôd* in reference to God's visible form. Various studies have examined the manifestations of God in ordinary human form (in the ancestral stories of Genesis) and other, more numinous appearances (elsewhere in the Pentateuch and the prophetic books). See Benjamin D. Sommer, *The Bodies of God and the World of Ancient Israel* (New York: Cambridge University Press, 2011); and Mark S. Smith, "The Three Bodies of God in the Hebrew Bible," *JBL* 134 (2015): 471–88.

The New Revelation of the Divine Name YHWH–beyond Exodus 3

Once again God agrees to Moses's request, telling him that all God's "good-ness" (which seems to be equivalent to "glory") will pass before him, with the caveat that he cannot see this manifestation full on (God's "face"). So God will place Moses in a cleft of the rock face of the mountain (presumably a small cave) and cover him so that he sees God's "back" (Exod. 33:19–23)—which is enough to cause Moses's face to shine when he comes down the mountain (34:29–35).[18] As God passes before Moses, he proclaims the meaning of the name YHWH.

This is something YHWH had done on a previous occasion, at the burn-ing bush (Exod. 3). The prompt on that occasion was that Moses asked God what his name was, in preparation for going down to Egypt to deliver the Israelites from bondage. God's response is the famous *'ĕyeh 'ăšer 'ĕyeh*—"I am who I am," or (better) "I will be who I will be" (3:14). God then adds that his name is YHWH (3:15), which seems to be derived from the verb "to be" in Hebrew (it might mean "He causes to be").[19]

Although Exodus 3:14–15 is a particularly dense text, the main point seems to be that the character of this God named YHWH would be actively and dynamically revealed in the exodus from Egypt, which is future (so "I will be who I will be"). In particular, God *will be* revealed as the one who cares about his people's suffering in subjugation to the most powerful empire of the ancient Near East. YHWH *will be* revealed as a powerful actor on the stage of world history, who confronts Pharaoh and breaks the bonds of the empire to set Israel free.

This was a new revelation, something that could not have been gleaned about YHWH from his relationship with the ancestors in Genesis 12–50, when he entered into covenant with Abraham and his descendants, promising to protect and prosper them. In those texts YHWH was more like a family or

18. The Hebrew for God's "back" in Exod. 33:23 is *'āḥôr*, from the root for "behind" or "after." Diana Lipton, through an astute study of terminology, suggests that what Moses was given a glimpse of was not God's "back" but the future (that which comes "after"), since the Hebrew Bible typically envisions a person facing the past, with the future "behind" them. See Lipton, "God's Back! What Did Moses See on Sinai?," in *The Significance of Sinai: Traditions about Sinai and Divine Revelation in Judaism and Christianity*, ed. George Brooke, Hindy Najman, and Loren Stuckenbruck, TBN 12 (Leiden: Brill, 2008), 287–311.

19. This is the classic proposal of Frank Moore Cross, *Canaanite Myth and Hebrew Epic: Essays in the History of the Religion of Israel* (Cambridge, MA: Harvard University Press, 1973), 65.

clan deity (though there were hints of more to come). This contrast between the God of the ancestors and this same God's appearance on the stage of world history becomes explicit in Exodus 6, when God explains to Moses, "I appeared to Abraham, Isaac, and Jacob as God Almighty [El Shaddai], but by my name 'The LORD' [YHWH] I did not make myself known to them" (6:3).[20] Although this is sometimes taken to mean that the name YHWH was not known to the ancestors (thus the multiple occurrences of YHWH in Genesis are anachronistic), this is not a necessary inference. Rather, something new was being revealed about God in the exodus—namely, the *meaning* of the divine name (at least, the initial meaning, appropriate to the exodus).[21]

But what is revealed about the meaning of the name YHWH in Exodus 34:6–7, when God "passed before" Moses, goes significantly beyond what was revealed about the meaning of the name in Exodus 3. This new revelation of the divine name at Sinai is tailored specifically to the idolatry of the golden calf, and it addresses how Israel would go forward after this serious setback.

As YHWH "passed before" Moses, he proclaimed:

> The LORD, the LORD [YHWH, YHWH],
> a God merciful and gracious,
> slow to anger,
> and abounding in steadfast love and faithfulness,
> keeping steadfast love for the thousandth generation,
> forgiving iniquity and transgression and sin . . . (34:6–7a)

20. For a profound study of the meaning of "El Shaddai" and God's covenant with the ancestors in relation to YHWH and the Sinai covenant, see J. Gerald Janzen, "Israel's Default Position before God," in *At the Scent of Water: The Ground of Hope in the Book of Job* (Grand Rapids: Eerdmans, 2009), 15–36. Janzen likens the Sinai covenant to a computer's customized operating system, while the Abrahamic covenant is the default or factory operating system. This analogy makes sense of a great deal of the Old Testament, including the golden calf episode and the book of Job. *At the Scent of Water* is, as a whole, so good that I hesitate to single out any particular part. But chap. 2 is so brilliant that, as the saying goes, it is by itself worth the price of the book.

21. I am not disputing that Exod. 3 and 6 might come from different literary traditions (usually thought of as J and P, the Yahwist and the Priestly sources), which allows them to be read as alternative accounts of the call of Moses. On this reading, the Priestly source (represented by Exod. 6) claims that the name YHWH was unknown to the ancestors, while the Yahwist (anachronistically, by P's reckoning) inserts the name YHWH into the Genesis narratives. Whatever the truth of this hypothesis as an explanation of the origin of these two texts, Exod. 3 and 6 have been edited together into the canonical narrative as two phases of Moses's dialogue with God.

But with love comes judgment, since God adds:

> yet by no means clearing the guilty,
> but visiting the iniquity of the parents
> upon the children
> and the children's children,
> to the third and the fourth generation. (34:7b)

Here we find language similar to the motive clause for the earlier prohibition of idolatry in Exodus 20, which came before the episode with the golden calf:

> For I the LORD your God am a jealous God, punishing children for the iniquity of parents, to the third and the fourth generation of those who reject me, but showing steadfast love to the thousandth generation of those who love me and keep my commandments. (20:5b–6)

Although these two statements are similar, there are significant changes between Exodus 20 and 34. In Exodus 20 God's warning of dire consequences preceded the positive motivation. In Exodus 34, however, this is reversed; the positive motivation (the promise of God's *ḥesed*) comes first. But beyond the reordering of these two elements, the positive motivation is exponentially expanded. There is a piling up of terms related to love. YHWH is merciful (*raḥûm*) and gracious (*ḥannûn*), abounding in love (*ḥesed*) and faithfulness (*'ĕmet*).

Indeed, this love is so abundant that it overflows into forgiveness, a new element not mentioned in Exodus 20. And forgiveness is said to cover multiple categories of wrongdoing—iniquity (*'āwôn*), transgression (*pešaʻ*), and sin (*ḥaṭā'â*).[22] Although showing love to a thousand generations is repeated from Exodus 20, the conditional element is gone. God's love is not here limited to those who love God and keep his commandments. It is given unconditionally, to a thousand generations (or possibly to thousands).[23]

This does not mean there are no consequences for disobedience. But those consequences no longer cancel the covenant. The momentous change signaled by this new revelation of the divine name is that from here on the Sinai covenant is no longer conditional. It is now an unconditional covenant. How else

---

22. These are the same categories of wrongdoing covered by the Yom Kippur ritual (Lev. 16:21).

23. As in Exod. 20:6, so here in 34:6 the word "generations" is missing. But it is plausible that "thousands," in this context, means a thousand generations.

could Israel have continued with God after the golden calf episode, which involved flagrant idolatry—unfaithfulness to the God of the covenant?[24]

God's Love as the Basis for Moses's Intercession

But while the text says clearly that Moses changed God's course of action, should we infer that Moses precipitated a change in God's character? Was God primarily a God of judgment *before* Moses interceded? And then became a God of mercy and love *after*? Or, was it that Moses's intercession brought out—and made clear—what was already there?

One of the things Moses learns about YHWH when God passes by is that YHWH is "slow to anger" (Exod. 34:6). But this was not something new, since Moses was able to pray in the first place—indeed, he was invited to pray—because God was *not yet* angry enough to make an end of the people. Even back before Moses's intercession, YHWH was already slow to anger.[25]

In fact, that core summary of God's character that Moses receives in the cleft of the rock turns out to be the *ground* and *basis* for God inviting Moses's intercession in the first place. YHWH was always a God of love and forgiveness. This is a God of overflowing love, who desires, and actively invites, vigorous, honest prayer on the part of the human covenant partner.

The Memory of Moses's Intercession at Sinai/Horeb—in the Bible

Yet, while such prayer is made possible by God's gracious character, we should not downplay Moses's role. Indeed, it is not too much to say that if Moses

24. Here Janzen's analogy (in "Israel's Default Position before God") between the Abrahamic and Sinai covenants, on the one hand, and the default and customized operating systems of a computer, on the other, come into play. If the computer crashes, the only hope for recovery is to reboot it from the default system. The idolatry of the golden calf would thus be a massive computer failure that requires a significant reboot. So Israel's new relationship with God, symbolized by the Sinai covenant, reverts to the original relationship, represented by the Abrahamic covenant (perhaps we could say that the Sinai covenant is itself transformed into an expanded Abrahamic covenant). Janzen's argument has interesting intersections with Jon D. Levenson's analysis of the relationship of the conditional and unconditional covenants that God makes with Moses and David; see Levenson, *Sinai and Zion: An Entry into the Jewish Bible* (New York: HarperOne, 1987).

25. The phrase "slow to anger" (Exod. 34:3) translates the Hebrew *'erek 'appayim*, which means literally "long of nose." The dominant metaphor for anger in the Hebrew Bible is *heat*, which is thought to originate inside a person and to come out through the nostrils. This is the basis for the vivid description of God's anger at the Egyptians (mentioned in Exod. 15:7), which results, in the next verse, in the parting of the sea by "the blast of your nostrils" (15:8). But God's (metaphorical) long nose means that it takes a long time for the heat to build up enough to be manifest in judgment. To use a modern metaphor, God does not have a "short fuse."

had not interceded for Israel, there would no longer have been an Israel. And the history of salvation would be very different.

Later, in Numbers 14, Moses appeals to precisely what he learned about God from this disclosure at Sinai, when he cites God's mercy and forgiveness in his prayer for the people after they refuse to enter the land at Kadesh-Barnea (14:13–19). When the spies bring back a report of giants in the land (13:25–33) and the people refuse to enter (14:1–4), God wants to wipe them out, as he had wanted to at Sinai, and he proposes to start again with Moses (14:11–12).

Once again, Moses refuses. He appeals, as he did at Sinai, to God's reputation among the nations (14:13–16) and he insightfully asks God to show his power in mercy: "And now, therefore, let the power of the LORD be great in the way that you promised when you spoke, saying, 'The LORD is slow to anger, / and abounding in steadfast love, / forgiving iniquity and transgression'" (14:17–18).[26]

Having quoted God's words from Exodus 34 back to him, Moses then pleads, "Forgive the iniquity of this people according to the greatness of your steadfast love, just as you have pardoned this people, from Egypt even until now" (Num. 14:19). And, as before, YHWH accepts Moses's request: "I do forgive, just as you have asked" (14:20).

The indispensable role of Moses as intercessor on behalf of Israel is highlighted in Psalm 106, which recounts multiple examples of Israel's rebellion against YHWH, both during the wilderness trek and after they entered the Promised Land (Ps. 106:6–46), including specifically the episode with the golden calf (106:19–22). The psalmist explains that, after the idolatry at Sinai/Horeb,

> He [God] said he would destroy them—
>   had not Moses, his chosen one,
>   stood in the breach before him,
>   to turn away his wrath from destroying them. (106:23)

26. Moses's prayer in Num. 14:17–18 for God's power to be shown in mercy may have influenced the wording of Proper 21 in the Anglican *Book of Common Prayer* (New York: Church Publishing, 1979): "O God, *who declarest thy almighty power chiefly in showing mercy and pity*: Mercifully grant unto us such a measure of thy grace, that we, running to obtain thy promises, may be made partakers of thy heavenly treasure; through Jesus Christ our Lord, who liveth and reigneth with thee and the Holy Spirit, one God, for ever and ever. Amen." Thanks to J. Gerald Janzen for this insight.

This psalm then proceeds to draw on the revelation of the overflowing of God's *ḥesed* (Exod. 34:6) as the basis for God's deliverance of Israel in the time of the judges. Although the people continually disobeyed YHWH (Ps. 106:34–39), resulting in their being given into the hands of their enemies (106:40–42), and continued to rebel even after each episode of God's deliverance (106:43),

> Nevertheless he [God] regarded their distress
>   when he heard their cry.
> For their sake he remembered his covenant,
>   and showed compassion according to the abundance
>   of his steadfast love. (106:44–45)[27]

This psalmist, writing from the context of the exile, is motivated to implore YHWH for help because of the example of Moses, who in an earlier time decisively changed the outcome for Israel by his prayer.

The memory of Moses's intercession after the golden calf incident, and the subsequent revelation of God's mercy in Exodus 34:6–7, is strong in Psalm 51, which appeals to God for forgiveness and restoration after sin. It is significant that the first verse of the psalm alludes to the description of YHWH's core character as revealed to Moses. The opening plea asks God to "be gracious to me" (*ḥānnēnî*; my translation), according to God's steadfast love (*ḥesed*), and pleads for sins to be blotted out according to God's abundant mercies (*raḥămîm*). This language echoes God's self-revelation to Moses as "a God merciful [*raḥûm*] and gracious [*ḥannûn*], . . . abounding in steadfast love [*ḥesed*]" (Exod. 34:6).[28]

---

27. The example of Moses's intercession may have even inspired the opening and closing prayers of the psalm, both of which call on God for help. Near the start, the psalmist pleads: "Remember me, O LORD, when you show favor to your people; / help me when you deliver them" (Ps. 106:4). And the psalm ends with this plea: "Save us, O LORD our God, / and gather us from among the nations, / that we may give thanks to your holy name / and glory in your praise" (106:47). Verse 48 is technically the doxology that closes book four of the Psalter (Pss. 90–106), rather than the last verse of the psalm.

28. The decisive revelation of God's character in Exod. 34:6–7 has long been recognized as a sort of creedal statement, which shows up in later Old Testament texts in even clearer forms than its echoes in Ps. 51. Beyond Num. 14:18, the most obvious citations include Neh. 9:17b, 31; Pss. 86:5, 15; 103:8; 145:8; Jer. 32:18; Joel 2:13; Jon. 4:2; Mic. 7:18; and Nah. 1:2–3 (which draws on the Exod. 20 formulation). Phyllis Trible provides a brief account of such texts in *God and the Rhetoric of Sexuality*, OBT (Philadelphia: Fortress, 1978), 1–5. For a profound study of the explicit citations and possible echoes of Exod. 34:6–7 throughout Old and New Testaments, the Apocrypha, the Dead Sea Scrolls, later Jewish tradition (including the Talmud),

Beyond this, the same three words for categories of wrongdoing (iniquity, transgression, and sin) that God forgives according to Exodus 34:7 are found in Psalm 51:1–2 (51:3–4 MT) and recur throughout the psalm in both nominal and verbal forms.

These allusions to Exodus 34 make it plausible that the psalmist's pledge in Psalm 51:13 [51:15 MT] to teach transgressors "your ways" is also an allusion to the golden calf narrative. The psalmist's pledge may hark back to Moses's request to God in Exodus 33:13 to "show me your ways" (which turn out to be ways of mercy).[29]

When these allusions to the golden calf episode are taken together, they suggest that the psalmist is appealing to this paradigmatic example of YHWH's forgiveness in the past as the basis for being forgiven in the present. He is asking God to act in accordance with the divine character as revealed to Moses and forgive an individual's sin as he did the sin of the community.[30] Like Moses's vigorous interaction with God, this psalmist boldly makes his requests known to God, with the confident expectation of being heard.

The Memory of Moses's Intercession at Sinai/Horeb—in Midrash and Talmud

The indispensable role of Moses as Israel's intercessor forms the basis of a Jewish midrash on Moses's death, found in the collection of medieval texts known as Midrash Tanḥuma. At one point, Metatron the archangel finds God weeping. In perplexity, Metatron tells God that just as the life of Moses was in God's hand, so was his death (in other words: Wasn't his death your own decision? Why, then, are you crying?).

In response God proposes the following parable:

---

and even the Qur'an, see Michael P. Knowles, *The Unfolding Mystery of the Divine Name: The God of Sinai in Our Midst* (Downers Grove, IL: IVP Academic, 2012).

29. Beyond the specific linguistic connections between Ps. 51 and the golden calf episode, there is the similarity of the thematic focus on the forgiveness of serious sin (idolatry in the Exodus text, unspecified sin in Ps. 51), for which there is no sacrifice possible. And since the superscription links the psalm to the story of David's sin and its aftermath in 2 Sam. 11–12, the death of David's son despite the forgiveness of David's sin (2 Sam. 12:13–14, 18) might reflect Exod. 34:7, which combines forgiveness with "visiting the iniquity of the parents upon the children" (my translation).

30. For my analysis of this psalm, see Middleton, "A Psalm against David? A Canonical Reading of Psalm 51 as a Critique of David's Inadequate Repentance in 2 Samuel 12," in *Explorations in Interdisciplinary Reading: Theological, Exegetical, and Reception-Historical Perspectives*, ed. Robbie F. Castleman, Darian R. Lockett, and Stephen O. Presley (Eugene, OR: Pickwick, 2017), 26–45.

To what is the matter comparable? To a king who had a son. Now on each and every day, his father was angry with him and sought to kill him because he did not maintain respect for the father; but his mother rescued him from his hand.

One day his mother died and the king wept. His servants said to him, "Our lord king, why are you weeping?" He said to them, "It is not over my wife alone that I am weeping, but for my son; for [how] many times when I was angry with him and wanted to kill him, did she rescue him from my hand?"

Then God explains to Metatron:

It is not over Moses alone that I am weeping, but over him and over Israel, for look at how many times that they angered Me, and I was angry with them; but he stood in the breach before Me to turn back My anger from destroying them.[31]

Another rabbinic text, from the Talmud, views the revelation of God's character in Exodus 34 as the ground of prayer for later Israel, even without Moses. As Rabbi Yoḥanan is reported to have said (in Bereshit Rosh HaShanah 17b),

Were it not written in the text, it would be impossible for us to say such a thing; this verse teaches that the Holy One, blessed be He, drew his robe round Him like the reader of a congregation and showed Moses the order of prayer. He said to him: Whenever Israel sins, let them carry out this service before Me, and I will forgive them.[32]

The Prophetic Tradition of Intercession after Moses

Moses's bold intercession on behalf of Israel becomes part of the prophetic tradition. Various prophets stand in the breach between God and the people, bringing a divine word of challenge and repentance while defending the people

31. *Midrash Tanḥuma* (S. Buber ed.), vols. 1–3, trans. J. T. Townsend (New York: KTAV: 1989–2003), Va'etchanan, section 6.
32. *The Babylonian Talmud*, vol. 4, *Seder Mo'ed*, ed. and trans. Isidore Epstein (London: Soncino, 1938), 68. This midrash is based on (among other things) the statement in the text that God "passed before" Moses; in later rabbinic tradition a person leading prayers was said to "pass before" the leader's stand.

before God in prayer in an attempt to avert judgment for as long as possible.[33] Here the examples of Amos and Micah (eighth century), Jeremiah (seventh century), and Ezekiel (sixth century) are illuminating.

Amos, after two parallel visions he is given of God's impending judgment on Israel (7:1, 4), cries out to God for mercy (7:2, 5), and each time God relents of the judgment (7:3, 6). The first vision is of a locust plague (7:1–2a).

When they [the locusts] had finished eating the grass of the land, I said,

> "O Lord God, forgive, I beg you!
> > How can Jacob stand?
> > He is so small!"
> The Lord relented concerning this;
> > "It shall not be," said the Lord. (7:2–3)

The second vision is of a devastating fire (7:4).

> Then I said,
> > "O Lord God, cease, I beg you!
> > > How can Jacob stand?
> > > He is so small!"
> > The Lord relented concerning this;
> > > "This also shall not be," said the Lord God. (7:5–6)

In a different context (likely the eighth-century Assyrian invasion of Israel), we find the prophet Micah imploring YHWH:

> Shepherd your people with your staff,
> > the flock that belongs to you,
> which lives alone in a forest
> > in the midst of a garden land;
> let them feed in Bashan and Gilead
> > as in the days of old. (7:14)

33. See Yochanan Muffs's classic study "Who Will Stand in the Breach? A Study of Prophetic Intercession," in Muffs, *Love and Joy: Law, Language, and Religion in Ancient Israel* (New York: Jewish Theological Seminary of America, 1992), 9–48.

And the basis for this plea of restoration is precisely the revelation of YHWH's character in Exodus 34:

> Who is a God like you, pardoning iniquity
> > and passing over the transgression
> > of the remnant of your possession?
> He does not retain his anger forever,
> > because he delights in showing clemency.
> He will again have compassion upon us;
> > he will tread our iniquities under foot.
> You will cast all our sins
> > into the depths of the sea.
> You will show faithfulness to Jacob
> > and unswerving loyalty to Abraham,
> as you have sworn to our ancestors
> > from the days of old. (Mic. 7:18–20)[34]

Later, in the context of the impending Babylonian conquest of Judah, Jeremiah cries out to YHWH, both on his own behalf (given that his message has largely been rejected, and he has been persecuted as a result) and on behalf of the people, for whom he has compassion. Although Jeremiah's prayers are unusual in the prophetic literature in that they focus on the crisis in his own prophetic vocation, the prophet also expresses his anguish over the desolate state of the people and land:

> How long will the land mourn,
> > and the grass of every field wither?
> For the wickedness of those who live in it
> > the animals and the birds are swept away,
> > and because people said, "He is blind to our ways." (12:4)

On another occasion, when he is being persecuted for his message of judgment, Jeremiah reminds God that these were the very people on whose behalf

---

34. This oracle begins with the question "Who is a God like you?" (*mî-'ēl kāmôkā*), a reference to the incomparability of YHWH. This question is related to the name of the prophet, given as *mîkâ* in Mic. 1:1 and in fuller form as *mîkāyâ* in Jer. 26:18. The name means "Who is like YAH?"

he had interceded: "Remember how I stood before you / to speak good for them, / to turn away your wrath from them" (18:20).[35]

Although we do not have a record of many of Jeremiah's intercessions, he is so persistent in pleading on behalf of the very people that he has been challenging with the prophetic word that God has to warn him three times *not* to intercede any more. The first warning occurs in Jeremiah 7:16: "As for you, do not pray for this people, do not raise a cry or prayer on their behalf, and do not intercede with me, for I will not hear you." The reason is that the people have not repented and continue to trust in lies, so judgment has become inevitable (in the form of the approaching Babylonian armies). And when Jeremiah doesn't stop praying for the people, God has to tell him to refrain from intercession on two other occasions (11:14; 14:11–12).

One of Jeremiah's intercessory prayers is found in chapter 14, a few chapters after God's second instruction to desist from praying. Here is Jeremiah's plea, which leads to God's third instruction to stop praying:

> O hope of Israel,
> > its savior in time of trouble,
> why should you be like a stranger in the land,
> > like a traveler turning aside for the night?
> Why should you be like someone confused,
> > like a mighty warrior who cannot give help?
> Yet you, O LORD, are in the midst of us,
> > and we are called by your name;
> > do not forsake us! (14:8–9)

But God responds, "Do not pray for the welfare of this people. Although they fast, I do not hear their cry, and although they offer burnt offering and grain offering, I do not accept them; but by the sword, by famine, and by pestilence I consume them" (14:11–12).

These prohibitions of prayer in response to Jeremiah's continuing intercessions are not simply a statement of God's firmness or wrath in the face of the people's recalcitrance. Rather, they testify to the power of prophetic

---

35. Although not all prophets are viewed as intercessors in the Bible, Samuel Balentine admits that Jeremiah is definitely portrayed in this way. Indeed, he views Jeremiah as the primary example of prophetic intercession (after Moses). Balentine discusses multiple indicators in the text of Jeremiah that describe his intercessory role. Balentine, "Prophet as Intercessor," 169–70; also Balentine, "Jeremiah, Prophet of Prayer," *RevExp* 78 (1981): 331–44.

prayer, which appeals to YHWH's *predisposition* to show mercy. And they are intertwined with expressions of God's own grief and pathos over the coming judgment (as in 14:17–18).

The prophet Ezekiel was among the first wave of deportees to Babylon at the beginning of the sixth century. In response to a vision of the massive destruction of God's people that was coming, Ezekiel falls on his face, crying out, "Ah Lord God! will you destroy all who remain of Israel as you pour out your wrath upon Jerusalem?" (9:8). God responds that it is too late; the people are too far gone, so judgment will come (9:9–10).

Later, in response to the partial fulfillment of his own prophecy against the leaders of Jerusalem, Ezekiel cries out, "Ah Lord God! will you make a full end of the remnant of Israel?" (11:13). Although the exile can't be staved off, God's response focuses on divine presence in the midst of judgment, with restoration to follow. Not only has God been a sanctuary for the exiles (11:16), but God promises to gather them and return them to the land (11:17), giving them a new heart to enable them to do God's will (11:19–20).

Although Ezekiel's prayer comes too late to prevent the exile, intercession is so crucial to the prophetic vocation that Ezekiel 13 lists *lack* of intercession (13:5) as part of the accusation against false prophets (13:1–16). Later in the book (22:25–29) we have further indictment against the prophets of Judah (along with other leaders, including priests), followed by God's own lament (using language from Ps. 106:23): "I sought for anyone among them who would repair the wall and stand in the breach before me on behalf of the land, so that I would not destroy it; but I found no one" (Ezek. 22:30).

Elijah as Anti-Moses—a Study in Prophetic Contrasts

In the light of the tradition of prophetic prayer, Elijah's point-blank refusal to intercede for the people after the Mount Carmel episode stands out in high relief. This episode is instructive for the text's contrast between Elijah and Moses.

Having defeated the prophets of Baal in the famous contest (1 Kings 18:20–40), Elijah then flees for his life after a threat from Queen Jezebel (19:1–3). When he arrives in the wilderness near Beersheba, he prays that he might die (19:4). Succored by an angel with food for the journey to Horeb (another name for Sinai), he arrives forty days later and spends the night in a cave

(19:5–9a).[36] To be in a cave at Sinai/Horeb already begins to have resonances of Exodus 34.[37]

Twice God asks him, "What are doing you *here*, Elijah?" (1 Kings 19:9b, 13b)—that is, why are you at Horeb? And twice Elijah gives the identical reply. "I have been very zealous for the LORD, the God of hosts; for the Israelites have forsaken your covenant, thrown down your altars, and killed your prophets with the sword. *I alone am left*, and they are seeking my life, to take it away" (19:10, 14).[38]

Moses, by associating himself with the people, despite their idolatry, refused to allow God to destroy Israel and begin again with him (Exod. 32:10–14, 31–32; Num. 14:12–20). In Exodus 33:16, Moses twice uses the phrase "I and your people" to make it clear he stands with the people. Elijah, however, *disassociates* himself from the people ("I alone am left"), thus opening the way for their destruction. Indeed, Elijah's myopic vision has to be corrected by God, who explains that there are *seven thousand* who have not bowed the knee to Baal (1 Kings 19:18) and who will therefore be spared destruction—but not because of Elijah's intercession, which is simply absent.[39]

But there are other, equally significant contrasts between Moses and Elijah in the two episodes at Sinai/Horeb.

Right after Elijah's first response of "I alone am left" (1 Kings 19:10), God tells him to come out of the cave "and stand on the mountain before the LORD" because God is about to "pass by" (19:11), a clear allusion to God causing his goodness to "pass before" Moses in Exodus 33:19 (the identical verb is used: *ʿābar*). Whereas in Exodus 33 *Moses* is the one who asked God to show him his glory, in 1 Kings 19 it is *God* who offers the manifestation of his presence to Elijah.

36. Horeb is the typical name for Sinai in the book of Deuteronomy. Although "the mountain of God" (Exod. 3:1) is usually called Sinai in the book of Exodus, it is called Horeb in 3:1; 17:6; and 33:6.

37. We are not told why Elijah is going to Horeb, nor whether it was by his own decision or at God's instruction.

38. YHWH does not bother to correct Elijah that it was Jezebel, and not the Israelites, who had thrown down his altars.

39. For an illuminating study of Elijah in 1 Kings 19, see Mark A. Throntveit, "1 Kings 19: Lead, Follow, or Get Out of the Way?," *LTJ* 50, no. 2 (August 2016): 125–35. For a comprehensive study of ways in which Elijah may be a deficient prophet, given the standard of Deuteronomy, see Roy L. Heller, *The Characters of Elijah and Elisha and the Deuteronomistic Evaluation of Prophecy: Miracles and Manipulation*, LHBOTS 671 (London: Bloomsbury T&T Clark, 2018).

Then there is the difference in the way God's presence was manifested. I won't decide here how best to translate *qôl dəmāmâ daqqâ* (whether "a still small voice" [KJV], "a soft murmuring sound" [NJPS], "a gentle whisper" [NIV], or "a sound of sheer silence" [NRSV]; 1 Kings 19:12). The point is that God was present in a mode different from the theophany at Horeb/Sinai that Moses witnessed (that one had been accompanied by fire, earthquake, and storm).

But beyond the difference in the manifestation of God's presence, we find contrasting attitudes of Moses and Elijah to the event. When Moses asked God to show him his glory, God placed him in a cleft of the rock and granted Moses only a partial vision (God's "back").

But not only does God tell Elijah to come *out* from the cave, when Elijah hears the *qôl dəmāmâ daqqâ*, which signified YHWH's presence, he did come out, at least to the *entrance* of the cave, but "he wrapped his face in his mantle" (1 Kings 19:13), in essence averting his eyes. Could Elijah's lack of intercession for the people be related to his inability to face God?

Whereas initially, at the burning bush, "Moses hid his face, for he was afraid to look at God" (Exod. 3:6), by the time we get to Sinai we are told that God regularly spoke to Moses "face to face," as one speaks to a friend (33:11); later we are told that God speaks to Moses "mouth to mouth" and that Moses sees the form of YHWH (Num. 12:8).[40]

Elijah, it turns out, lacks the requisite boldness to stand up either to Jezebel or to YHWH. As Reuven Kimelman explains, Elijah is therefore decommissioned from being a prophet and told to appoint a successor.[41]

The Authentic Israelite Attitude of Boldness toward God

The requisite boldness in approaching God is addressed in a ninth-century rabbinic midrash on Proverbs that recounts the Queen of Sheba testing Solomon for his wisdom. In one of the tests she devises, as Simon Chavel puts it, "Solo-

40. Although Num. 12:8 says literally that God speaks to Moses "mouth to mouth" (see ESV, KJV, and NASB), this is translated as "face to face" in the NIV, NRSV, NLT, and NJB.

41. On Elijah's failure at Horeb in the context of the prophet's dual loyalty (to God and to the people), see Reuven Kimelman, "Prophecy as Arguing with God and the Ideal of Justice," *Int* 68 (2014): 17–27 (esp. 25–26). For a consideration of the larger context of the proper attitude of anyone who would enter the divine presence and "see God" (namely, proper boldness combined with genuine humility), see Simeon Chavel, "The Face of God and the Etiquette of Eye-Contact: Visitation, Pilgrimage, and Prophetic Vision in Ancient Israelite and Early Jewish Imagination," *JSQ* 19 (2012): 1–55 (38 on Elijah).

mon must distinguish between Israelites and non-Israelites in a homogeneous-looking group. To do so, he rolls back the curtains of the Holy of Holies to reveal before their eyes the ark of God. The non-Israelites prostrate themselves face-down entirely, but the Israelites bow at the waist *so they can crane their necks and see.*"[42]

Based on this midrash, Moses is the true Israelite, while Elijah's reticence may be thought of as falling short of the Israelite ideal. But the point of wanting to *see God* does not hinge on the question of divine visibility. It has more to do with the courage required to come into the presence of the King of the universe, to boldly approach the throne of grace (Heb. 4:16).

If we are preconditioned to view submission to God as the essentially pious posture, Moses's bold challenge after Israel's idolatry may seem, on the surface, to be an act of rebellion, or at least arrogance. Yet the purpose of Moses's challenge is, as George Coats puts it, "to persuade God to pursue the initial aim, to act in consistency with his own promise."[43] Moses's boldness is thus rooted in a discernment of God's fundamental character and intent.

A similar paradox—of bold challenge rooted in faithfulness—is found in the lament psalms (discussed in the previous chapter), which have been described by Samuel Balentine as "holding to God against God."[44] Likewise, Job's passionate protests to the very God whose unjust treatment he has received (which I will address in the next chapter) leads Claus Westermann to say that Job "clings to God against God."[45]

These formulations all converge on the paradox that genuine piety allows for challenging God in the name of God, a paradox rooted in God's own desire for boldness on the part of his servants. Whether it is lament psalms, prophetic intercession, or Job's passionate protests about his suffering, Scripture affirms in multiple ways that the God of Abraham positively desires vigorous dialogue partners.

---

42. Chavel, "Face of God," 52 (emphasis added). This episode is found in Midrash Mishle. See Burton L. Visotzky, *The Midrash on Proverbs: Translated from the Hebrew, with an Introduction and Annotations,* YJS 27 (New Haven: Yale University Press, 1992), 19.

43. Coats, "King's Loyal Opposition," 98.

44. Samuel E. Ballentine, *Prayer in the Hebrew Bible: The Drama of Divine-Human Dialogue,* OBT (Minneapolis: Augsburg Fortress, 1993), 146.

45. Claus Westermann, "The Role of Lament in the Theology of the Old Testament," *Int* 27, no. 1 (1974): 32 (entire article 20–38).

PART 2

MAKING SENSE OF THE BOOK OF JOB

3

The Question of
Appropriate Speech

The book of Job has attracted and fascinated readers for two and a
half thousand years. Contemporary readers are especially attracted to
Job's honesty about his suffering and his challenge to God for vindication, especially in the face of his friends' claim that his suffering is deserved.
However, not all readers have been attracted to Job's honesty. Especially in
earlier times, many readers, though interested in the theme of innocent suffering that the book explores, have thought that Job's abrasive speech was
rebellious, and thus inappropriate.

The book itself seems ambiguous on this point.

The Simplicity, yet Complexity of the Book of Job

At one level, the book of Job is quite easy to understand. It has a clearly
delineated structure, consisting primarily of a series of speeches by Job, his
three friends (Eliphaz, Bildad, and Zophar), a fourth persona named Elihu,
and YHWH—all cast into Hebrew poetry (3:1–42:6). This lengthy poetic
section is framed by a prose narrative, which consists of a short prologue
(chaps. 1–2) and an even shorter epilogue (42:7–17). In the prologue, the main
characters are Job, YHWH, and the Adversary or Accuser (*haśśāṭān*), though
Job's children and servants are mentioned, his wife has a brief speaking part,
and Job's three friends are introduced at the end of chapter 2. In the epilogue,

the Accuser drops out from the story and the characters are Job, YHWH, the three friends, and new children that are born to Job.[1]

But this simple structure reveals a complex story, whose point is not entirely clear. Here is a righteous man, who suffers extreme tragedy (the loss of his wealth and children, followed by terrible sickness); yet his friends accuse him of having sinned in some way to deserve his tragic fate. The back-and-forth dialogue between Job and his friends, in which he maintains his integrity and denies that his suffering is justified, leads him to direct his complaint to God and plead for God's vindication, or at least for an explanation of why he is suffering. Following Job's dialogues with his friends (chaps. 4–27) and an interlude on Wisdom (chap. 28) comes a lengthy set of speeches in which Job affirms his innocence, while critiquing God for being unjust (chaps. 29–31).

Job's complaints to God about his suffering clearly link the book to the honesty of the lament psalms, thus making Job a prime example of vigorous prayer in the Bible. Job's prayers, however, are more abrasive than most laments in the Psalter.[2]

After Job's final speeches, a new speaker appears on the scene. Elihu is a younger man, who critiques both Job and his friends for misrepresenting God (chaps. 32–37), though it is not clear what new insight he brings to the discussion. The book of Job reaches a climax with God's powerful and mysterious appearance in a storm or whirlwind, from which God addresses Job (chaps. 38–41). Although the main point of God's speeches is disputed by interpreters, it is common to think that God attempts to verbally bully Job into submission, which leads to his repentance "in dust and ashes" (42:6). Yet, paradoxically, the epilogue to the book has God condemning Job's friends and affirming that Job had spoken of him what was right (42:7–8). This fascinating book is also a perplexing book.

1. The divine name YHWH is used almost exclusively in the prologue and epilogue and to introduce God's speeches and Job's response to God (the only exception is the phrase "the hand of the LORD [YHWH]" in 12:9). The rest of the book tends to use other names for God, including El, Eloah, and Shaddai. This avoidance of the name YHWH is appropriate since none of the speakers is portrayed as an Israelite (although all of the speakers seem to be monotheistic).

2. Will Kynes notes that Job "follows the models for relationship with God that the psalms depict, pressing them to their breaking point" (Kynes, "Reading Job Following the Psalms," in *The Shape of the Writings*, ed. Julius Steinberg and Timothy J. Stone, Siphrut 16 [Winona Lake, IN: Eisenbrauns, 2015], 142 [entire chapter 131–45]). In this article, Kynes addresses the intertextual connections between Job and various psalms, as well as the rabbinic decision to place Psalms before Job so these connections would be recognized. See also Kynes, *"My Psalm Has Turned to Weeping": Job's Dialogue with the Psalms*, BZAW 437 (Berlin: de Gruyter, 2012).

In this chapter I will propose a particular focus for the book of Job, along with a reading strategy for coming to grips with its message. This will require a quick tour through the entire book—from the opening chapter through the speech of Elihu, which prepares us for God's first speech—in order to understand the development of the book's plot in light of my proposed focus. In the next chapter, I will zero in on God's speeches to Job from the whirlwind, with a focus on the second speech, in order to address the question of whether, and in what sense, God approves of Job's vocal response to his suffering.

The Role of "Satan" in Job

Perhaps a word of explanation is needed about the Accuser (*haśśāṭān*). Although most Bibles translate *haśśāṭān* in Job 1–2 as "Satan," the Hebrew has the definite article ("the"), which means it is a title, not a proper name.[3] The Hebrew word *śāṭān* typically refers in the Bible to a person who opposes someone (hence "adversary"), as when the Philistine commanders worry that David may turn against them and become their *śāṭān* (1 Sam. 29:4) or when David says that the sons of Zeruiah have become his *śāṭān* (2 Sam. 19:22 [19:23 MT]). Initially, we are told that there was no *śāṭān* opposing Solomon (1 Kings 5:4 [5:18 MT]), but later YHWH raised up Hadad (11:14) as his *śāṭān*, and then Rezon (11:23, 25).

Although in the above passages *śāṭān* is best translated as "adversary" or even "attacker," the opposition might take the form of verbal assault or accusation, as seems to be the case in Psalm 109. There the psalmist laments that wicked and deceitful people are lying about him and attacking him with words (109:2–5); indeed, they plan to appoint a *śāṭān* to accuse him falsely in court (109:6). In this psalm *śāṭān* is best translated "accuser." This is also the case in Job 1–2, where *haśśāṭān* questions Job's motives for being a God-fearer, accusing him of compromised loyalty to God (dependent on the material blessings he has received).

The Accuser (*haśśāṭān*) in Job is not a human being, but neither is he the full-fledged figure of Satan or the devil found later in Jewish and Christian

---

3. This does not mean that translations always need to use the definite article ("*the* Accuser"). English translations typically do not translate *hā'ĕlōhîm* as "the God" when it refers to YHWH (as it does in the story of the Aqedah), but simply as "God" (it can sometimes mean "the gods"). However, whether or not the article is translated, neither *haśśāṭān* nor *hā'ĕlōhîm* is a proper name.

thought (i.e., a fallen angel directly opposed to God).[4] The Accuser is, rather, one of the heavenly court, a group referred to in Job 1:6 and 2:1 as "the sons of God" (equivalent to what we typically call angels). He is not a fully independent entity, since he reports to God about his "going to and fro on the earth" and "walking up and down on it" (1:7; 2:2).

A possible precursor to this use of *śāṭān* in Job is found in Numbers 22, where an angel or messenger of YHWH is said to be a *śāṭān* ("adversary") to Balaam (22:22, 32). But the use of *śāṭān* in Numbers 22 is not yet a title and simply designates an emissary sent to do God's will—to stop Balaam from cursing Israel. The Accuser in Job, while clearly a member of the heavenly court, functions as a sort of prosecuting attorney on the lookout for cases to report to the divine Judge.[5]

There are only two other places in the Bible beyond Job 1–2 where the term *śāṭān* is used of an angelic being with a quasi-independent status—Zechariah 3 (where he opposes or accuses the high priest Joshua) and 1 Chronicles 21 (where he incites David to commission a census).[6] This suggests that we

---

4. The fully formed idea of Satan or the devil as a fallen angel, which we find in later (medieval) tradition, is not even explicit in the New Testament. There he is described as a tempter, an accuser, an adversary, a liar and deceiver, and called "the ruler of the power of the air, the spirit that is now at work among those who are disobedient" (Eph. 2:2). But he is never explicitly said to be a fallen angel (in the traditional sense), although his fall from power/heaven is mentioned in Luke 10:18 and Rev. 12:7–10, as the kingdom of God advances. Neither is he explicitly a fallen angel in either the Apocrypha or the Dead Sea Scrolls. In the Apocrypha, Wisdom 2:24 (dating to about 100 BCE) says that "through the devil's envy death entered the world, and those who belong to his company experience it." There is also a reference in the Dead Sea Scrolls (4Q543, manuscript C, dating to perhaps 200 BCE) to two non-human figures fighting over someone. One figure is identified as the archangel Michael, who explains that he is empowered to "rule over all Light," while the other, who looks like a viper or serpent, is called Belial, the Prince of Darkness, and the King of Evil, and is "empowered over all Darkness." For a translation of this text, see Robert H. Eisenman and Michael Wise, *The Dead Sea Scrolls Uncovered: The First Complete Translation and Interpretation of 50 Key Documents Withheld for over 35 Years* (New York: Penguin, 1992), 151–56. The earliest reference to the notion of fallen angels (in the classical sense) is found in 1 Enoch 6–9 (possibly third century BCE), where they are called "Watchers," a term taken from Dan. 4:13 and identified with the "sons of God" in Gen. 6:1–4 (the idea of fallen angels may come from Gen. 6:4, which notes that the "Nephilim" or "fallen ones" were on the earth in those days). The earliest explicit reference to the fall of Satan or the devil (though neither term is used) is 2 Enoch 29, which recounts events on the second day of creation. In the text, God explains that he created the various divisions of angels on that day, but that one of the archangels thought to exalt his throne so as to be equal to God; so God cast him from the height, together with his angels, and he ended up flying in the air over the bottomless abyss (all this happened on the second day of creation).

5. Marvin H. Pope calls him a "roving investigator." Pope, *Job: A New Translation with Introduction and Commentary*, 3rd ed., AB 15 (Garden City, NY: 1973), 10.

6. The prophet Zechariah (writing after the exile) reports a vision of "the high priest Joshua standing before the angel of YHWH, and standing at his right hand was *haśśāṭān* to

should be careful in taking the figure of the Accuser in the book of Job as representing a clearly delineated theology. Given that he shows up only in the prologue, it may be that the Accuser is no more than a literary figure meant to get the story going.[7]

The Extremes of Righteousness and Suffering

The prose prologue opens with a brief introduction to Job in which the narrator asserts that Job is "blameless [*tām*] and upright [*yāšār*], a God-fearer [*yîrē' 'ĕlōhîm*] who turned away from evil" (1:1; my translation).[8] YHWH repeats this description almost verbatim in his conversations with the Accuser in chapters 1 and 2. But when YHWH speaks to the Accuser, he goes further than the narrator in affirming the extraordinary extent of Job's righteousness, by prefacing his statement with the claim: "There is no one like him on the earth" (1:8 and 2:3). In other words, Job is not just righteous; he is uniquely righteous. In Ezekiel 14:12–20 (which may predate the book of Job), Job is

---

śāṭan [accuse] him [i.e., the high priest]. And YHWH said to *haśśāṭān*, 'YHWH rebuke you, *haśśāṭān*!'" (3:1–2a; my translation). The context here suggests that *haśśāṭān* is best translated as "the Accuser" (as in Job) or simply as "Accuser" (when YHWH addresses him directly). Chronicles retells the story of David from 2 Sam. 24, where he numbers the people in a census (against God's will). In the Samuel text, which is earlier than Chronicles, it is YHWH himself who, paradoxically, initiates the census: "The anger of the LORD was kindled against Israel, and he incited David against them, saying, 'Go, count the people of Israel and Judah'" (24:1). Even up to the exile, Israel's theology often held that God was the underlying determining power in the world, evident in Isa. 45:7, where YHWH claims: "I form light and create darkness, / I make weal [lit. good] and create woe [lit. evil]; / I the LORD do all these things." But the postexilic book of Chronicles attests to a theological shift when it says, "*śāṭān* stood up against Israel, and incited David to count the people of Israel" (1 Chron. 21:1; my translation). It is possible that *śāṭān*, which is without the definite article here, should be understood as a common noun ("an adversary"); but it may be that this is the first reference in the Bible to Satan as a proper name. Either way, the context suggests an angelic adversary who takes the place of God's direct agency in inciting David to sin.

7. Ryan E. Stokes has made an impressive argument that in the cases of a human *śāṭān*, the sort of adversarial opposition in view is physical violence (he says in every case; though I am doubtful about Ps. 109). This leads him to suggest that when the *śāṭān* is an angelic figure he should be thought of as YHWH's Executioner, whose job it is to destroy the wicked (this is why he has to be given special permission to attack Job, who is righteous, and why YHWH has to tell him not to actually kill Job). See Stokes, "Satan, YHWH's Executioner," *JBL* 133, no. 2 (2014): 251–70. However, it isn't clear to me that the angelic *śāṭān* in Num. 22 was sent to kill Balaam or that the *śāṭān* in Zechariah is trying to kill the high priest. And the *śāṭān* in Job is both Job's accuser and (later) his attacker.

8. These are all standard terms for a righteous person in the book of Proverbs. Although many translations say that Job "fears God," the Hebrew literally says that he is a "God-fearer." This particular Hebrew adverbial construction ("God-fearer") is also found in the story of the Aqedah (more on that later).

mentioned as a legendary figure because of his righteousness, listed along with Noah ("a righteous [*ṣadîq*] man, blameless [*tāmim*] in his generation"; Gen. 6:9) and Danel (this is not the biblical Daniel, since the names are spelled differently and the book of Daniel is later than Ezekiel).[9]

Job is also uniquely blessed. He has many children—seven sons and three daughters (1:2)—and great wealth ("seven thousand sheep, three thousand camels, five hundred yoke of oxen, five hundred donkeys, and very many servants; so that this man was the greatest of all the people of the east"; 1:3). If the number of his flocks and herds seems a bit excessive, it does indicate that Job is not "everyman." He is a unique individual, who stands out from others both in his righteousness and in his material blessings (children, livestock, and servants).[10]

Yet Job loses all his livestock, his servants are killed, and his children are taken from him in terrible circumstances (in chap. 1). Then Job's body is afflicted with boils or sores from head to toe (in chap. 2). Just as Job is portrayed as an extreme example of blessedness, so the disasters that overtake him are extreme.

The highly stylized way in which the disasters or calamities of chapter 1 are recounted heightens their extreme character. This can be seen from the way they are reported to Job by four successive messengers. Four specific disasters are mentioned: an attack by the Sabeans, who carried off Job's oxen and donkeys and killed the servants who were tending them (1:14–15); "fire of God" that fell from the sky and burned up Job's sheep and servants (1:16); a raid by the Chaldeans, who carried off Job's camels and killed the servants (1:17); and a great wind from the desert that struck the house in which Job's children were feasting and killed them all (1:19–20).

In each case the account of the calamity is concluded with the messenger saying, "I alone have escaped to tell you" (which is itself quite remarkable), and in the case of the first three, this is immediately followed by: "While he was still speaking, another came and said . . ."

---

9. Scholars have come to recognize that Danel is the father of Aqhat, known from the Ugaritic epic of Aqhat, discovered (along with the Baal myths) in the excavations at ancient Ras Shamra.

10. August H. Konkel critiques the idea that Job represents everyman and suggests that Job may have been modeled on the author of the book himself, who was likely an educated, elite wisdom teacher in Israel; the author also seems to have been widely traveled. Konkel points out that the author of Job had knowledge of different geographical regions (including Egypt, deserts, mountains, and the ocean), meteorological phenomena, the constellations, mythology, the science of mining, and trapping (he refers to six different types of traps in Job 18:8–10). To this I would add that 4:10–11 uses five different Hebrew words for lions. This is clearly a learned author, who had extensive knowledge of the world, as well as great literary skill. See Konkel, *Job*, in *Cornerstone Biblical Commentary*, ed. Philip W. Comfort (Carol Stream, IL: Tyndale, 2006), 6:7–9.

I have sometimes had four different students read the parts of the four messengers, with the instruction that *while* the previous messenger is saying, "I alone have escaped to tell you," they must interrupt this and state emphatically (over those words), "*While he was still speaking*," and then continue with the rest of their part.

The effect is striking. It is clear that this is not historical reporting. This is a literary device to emphasize the extreme, hyperbolic character of the events in question. I suggest that these verses have analogies to the dramatic genre known as farce, which is characterized by improbable situations and hyperbolic exaggeration. The difference is that a farce typically has comedic value, but there is nothing humorous about Job's misfortunes. He is the epitome of a righteous man who suffers extreme (and undeserved) loss—both in chapter 1 (his livestock, his servants, and his children) and in chapter 2 (his bodily health).[11]

Job Suffers the Curses of the Covenant

Job is not an Israelite. He is from Uz, somewhere in the east (1:1, 3).[12] Although he is portrayed as a non-Israelite, the language describing Job's troubles reflects the consequences of unfaithfulness to YHWH (the so-called covenant curses) in Deuteronomy 28. The section on curses opens with this general statement: "The LORD will send upon you disaster, panic, and frustration in everything you attempt to do, until you are destroyed and perish quickly, on account of the evil of your deeds, because you have forsaken me" (Deut. 28:20). Among the consequences for unfaithfulness, the text lists the loss of livestock (28:31) and children (28:32)—both of which come true in Job's case.

Although the language of Deuteronomy 28 only approximates the description of Job's losses in chapter 1, the covenant curse concerning disease is different: "The LORD will strike you on the knees and on the legs with grievous boils [*šəḥîn rāʿ*] of which you cannot be healed, *from the sole of your foot to the crown of your head*" (28:35). This is almost identical to what

11. Indeed, his very name may be symbolic. The name Job (*'îôb*) seems to be derived from the verb *'āyab*, "to be hostile." Later in the book (13:24 and 33:10) Job will accuse God of treating him as an "enemy" (*'ôyēb*), a participle from this very verb.

12. There is no consensus concerning the location of Uz, beyond that it is not part of Israel. It is very common to think of Job as an Edomite. This is based partly on Lam. 4:21, which links the "land of Uz" with Edom, and the Septuagint ending of Job (42:17), which adds a note identifying Job as Jobab, a king living between Iduemea (= Edom) and Arabia. The Septuagint ending may have been influenced by Gen. 36:33, which mentions an Edomite king named Jobab (a descendant of Esau). Beyond being a gentile, however, it is unclear what specific nationality the book claims for Job.

Job experiences in chapter 2. With God's permission, the Accuser "inflicted loathsome sores [šəḥín rāʿ] on Job *from the sole of his foot to the crown of his head*" (2:7). He even suffers the social ostracism that results from skin disease, according to Leviticus 13–14, as "Job took a potsherd with which to scrape himself, and sat among the ashes" (Job 2:8). The language of Job's bodily affliction (along with the loss of his livestock and children) portrays him as suffering from the stated consequences of disobedience to God, even though both the narrator and God have affirmed his exemplary righteousness.

What Issue or Topic Does the Book of Job Address?

Given the opening description of Job's suffering, there have been a number of approaches to interpreting the book. One of the most common is to think that the book addresses the question of theodicy (the justice of God) in light of the suffering of the innocent, while another is to think that it addresses the question of disinterested allegiance to God (obedience without concern for reward). Both of these approaches, however, are significantly *under*determined by the content of the book.

Take the first approach. Many introductions to the book of Job suggest that it addresses the theodicy problem. The opening chapters certainly *raise* the question of the justice of God in the face of evident evil, especially the suffering of the innocent. Whereas Job's friends try to defend God's justice and accuse Job of sin (or at least hubris), Job continues to maintain his innocence (which agrees with the approval he receives both from the narrator and from God). Yet while the friends are criticized by YHWH in the epilogue, no solution is ever presented in the book that would reconcile Job's suffering with God's justice.[13] Indeed, YHWH's speeches in answer to Job seem to sidestep (and, on some interpretations, intensify) the problem.[14]

13. William P. Brown notes, "The book of Job offers no explanation for suffering, even as it provocatively sets up the problem." Brown, *Wisdom's Wonder: Character, Creation, and Crisis in the Bible's Wisdom Literature* (Grand Rapids: Eerdmans, 2014), 70. Konkel admits that "the book of Job does not resolve the rational question of the problem of innocent suffering"; however, he suggests that the focus of the book is "the mystery of evil" (the fact that humans cannot know or understand God's providential care of the world) and the existential or practical question of what we are to do in light of this mystery (Konkel, *Job*, 6:4, 11). Claus Westermann has also claimed that the book of Job addresses not the theoretical issue of evil but the existential question of how to respond to suffering. Westermann, *The Structure of the Book of Job: A Form-Critical Analysis*, trans. Charles A. Muenchow (Philadelphia: Fortress, 1981), 1–2.

14. James L. Crenshaw notes some of the ways interpreters have seen YHWH's speeches: "as irrelevant, sometimes irrelevance preceded by the adjective 'sublime'; irritating; empty; missing

Does the book, then, address the possibility of disinterested allegiance to God, without regard for reward? This is suggested by the question raised by the Accuser in the first chapter: "Does Job fear God for nothing?" (1:9). The full question continues: "Have you not put a fence around him and his house and all that he has, on every side? You have blessed the work of his hands, and his possessions have increased in the land" (1:10). Such blessing is what would be expected, according to Israel's Scriptures, as a consequence or reward of obedience.[15]

"But stretch out your hand," the Accuser continues, "and touch all that he has, and he will surely curse you to your face" (1:11; my translation). Later, the Accuser ups the ante, beyond "touching" Job's possessions and children, by stating, "Stretch out your hand and touch his bone and his flesh, and he will surely curse you to your face" (2:5; my translation).

Will Job, in other words, remain faithful to God without the material blessings (including health) that are supposed to accompany faithfulness, according to the Torah? The question "Does Job *fear God* for nothing?" plays on the opening description of Job by the narrator and by YHWH as a *God-fearer* who shuns evil. The connection between fearing God and shunning evil is found in texts in the wisdom tradition, such as Proverbs 3:7 and 16:6. This connection is also stated as the culmination of Job 28 (the interlude on wisdom): "Truly, the fear of the Lord, that is wisdom; / and to depart from evil is understanding" (28:28). In the first two chapters of the book, therefore, Job fits the description of a wise person. The question is, Will this continue?

However, the Accuser's question, which is introduced in the prologue—whether Job fears God for nothing—is never returned to later in the book. Furthermore, the figure of the Accuser simply disappears after the prologue; he is absent both from the poetic dialogues that form the bulk of the book and from the final scene that narrates Job's vindication (42:7–17).[16] So while

---

the point by stressing power, which was not an issue, and ignoring justice; and a three-hour lecture on natural science." Crenshaw, *Reading Job: A Literary and Theological Commentary* (Macon, GA: Smyth & Helwys, 2011), 148.

15. The blessing of family and children is also explicitly stated as a consequence of the fear of the LORD in Ps. 128:1–4.

16. David J. A. Clines, followed by William Brown, suggests that the Accuser's challenge in 1:11 ("Stretch out your hand and touch all that he has [his bone and his flesh; 2:5], and he will *surely* curse you to your face"; my translation) contains a self-imprecation (Clines, *Job 1–20*, Word Biblical Commentary 17 [Dallas: Word Books, 1989], 26; Brown, *Wisdom's Wonder*, 76). The word "surely" (which most translations have, but which is missing from the

the Accuser's question "Does Job fear God for nothing?" may get the story going, it is not clear that it is significant for the book as a whole.[17]

The Question of Appropriate Speech

Nevertheless, there is another, more promising approach to the book of Job, one that attends more carefully to the Accuser's words. The challenge put to God was not simply whether Job would remain faithful to God, but whether Job will curse God to God's face (1:11; 2:5). The issue raised by the Accuser is not simply faithfulness to God in the face of suffering, but what sort of *speech* such suffering would engender.

The issue of cursing God actually predates the Accuser's words. In the narrator's introduction to Job, we are told that Job would regularly present burnt offerings to God on behalf of his children, because of his worry that they may have sinned and "cursed God in their hearts" (1:5). Then, after the Accuser's second suggestion that Job will curse God (2:5), Job's wife encourages him to "curse God and die" (2:9).

Technically, Job's wife says, "*Bless* God and die." Likewise, Job wonders whether his children might have "blessed" God in their hearts (1:5), and the Accuser claims that if God afflicts Job, he will "bless" God to his face (1:11; 2:5).[18] It is clear that "bless" (*bārak*) is used in these cases as a euphemism, introduced into the text of Job every time a verb for "curse" would have *God* as its object. In contrast to this euphemistic use of "bless," Job genuinely blesses God in 1:21, after the first set of calamities.[19]

This emphasis on appropriate speech (blessing or curse) concerning God at the outset of the book finds a correlate in YHWH's words to Eliphaz and

---

NRSV) represents the Hebrew *'im-lō'*, which in other places functions as a self-curse. Clines renders it as "I'll be damned if . . ." (Clines, *Job 1–20*, 26), and Brown suggests that since Job remained faithful, this self-imprecation rebounded on the Accuser and so he disappears from the epilogue of the book (Brown, *Wisdom's Wonder*, 76n34).

17. Terence Fretheim makes a similar point when he suggests that the disappearance after the prologue of both the Accuser and the wager God makes with him indicate that they function as a "rhetorical setup." Fretheim, *God and World in the Old Testament: A Relational Theology of Creation* (Nashville: Abingdon, 2005), 224–25.

18. An analogous euphemism might be when Whoopi Goldberg exclaims, near the end of *Sister Act I* (directed by Emile Ardolino, written by Paul Rudnick, Touchstone Pictures, 1992): "Well, *bless* you!" The audience knows that she means a very different word.

19. The euphemistic use of the verb *bārak* in Job 1–2 has led some interpreters to overplay the difficulty of determining when it should be understood literally. See Tod Linafelt, "The Undecidability of BRK in the Prologue to Job and Beyond," *BibInt* 4 (1996): 154–72. The verb *bārak* is occasionally used euphemistically for cursing God outside of the book of Job, as in 1 Kings 21:13.

his friends in the epilogue: "You have not spoken of me what is right, as my servant Job has" (42:7, repeated in 42:8). In the beginning of Job, the emphasis on appropriate speech is limited to blessing and cursing—two opposite extremes. But there is a whole lot more speaking going on between the prologue and the epilogue, in the poetic section of the book, which does not clearly fit this simply binary. One way to understand the book of Job, therefore, is as a wisdom treatise that raises the question of what constitutes true fear of God—specifically, what sort of speech vis-à-vis God (either to or about God) exhibits such fear.

Here I draw on William Brown's suggestion to view the book of Job as a "thought experiment," reveling in "What if?" questions.[20] Although Brown suggests a number of such questions, I think it is fruitful to connect Brown's notion of a thought experiment to Gustavo Gutiérrez's proposal that the book addresses "the question of *how we are to talk about God*. More particularly: how we are to talk about God from within a specific situation—namely, the suffering of the innocent."[21] Choon-Leong Seow makes a similar proposal when he suggests that Job raises the question of "how one speaks of God in the face of chaos."[22]

So *what if* we take the most upright, righteous God-fearer imaginable (indeed, a person of legendary virtue, associated with Noah and Danel in Ezek. 14) and portray him as suffering a series of terrible calamities (the loss of goods and family, in four consecutive announcements, one piling up on the other, as portrayed in chap. 1, then his degradation through physical suffering and social ostracism, as portrayed in chap. 2)—what would constitute appropriate, God-fearing speech in that situation?[23]

This question does not depend on taking the book of Job as a historical account (even if Job is modeled on a legendary, possibly historical figure). Indeed, the book has been viewed as a parable (*māšāl*) as early as the Talmud and, like the parables of Jesus, its purpose is to stimulate reflection and wise

---

20. Brown, *Wisdom's Wonder*, 68. In a similar vein Terence Fretheim suggests that Job is "a let's-suppose-for-the-sake-of-argument book." Fretheim, *God and World in the Old Testament*, 221.

21. Gutiérrez, *On Job: God-Talk and the Suffering of the Innocent*, trans. Matthew J. O'Connell (Maryknoll, NY: Orbis Books, 1987), xviii (emphasis original).

22. C. L. Seow, *Job 1–21: Interpretation and Commentary*, Illuminations (Grand Rapids: Eerdmans, 2013), 108.

23. Despite the explicit affirmations of Job 1–2 and Ezek. 14, Job's righteousness has often been denied by premodern interpreters, both Jewish and Christian, who judge that his abrasive speeches are inappropriate and impious.

living, not to give an account of an actual situation.[24] Beyond this, most of the book—the dialogues between Job and his friends, the speeches of Elihu and YHWH—is in poetry. But people do not speak in poetry, especially in the highly stylized, well-crafted poetry of Job 3–41. So even if the book were based on an actual conversation (which is unlikely), the lengthy and complex speeches recounted in the book could not be verbatim.

Nor does the question of appropriate speech depend on viewing the suffering of Job as standing for Israel's exilic suffering (though that is a possible application), since right speech is a standard wisdom theme found throughout the book of Proverbs and is relevant to any historical era.[25] Right speech is also a focus in the New Testament wisdom book of James, which contains a discourse on the power of the tongue (James 3), by which we bless God and curse human beings made in God's likeness (3:9). The book of Job, however, opens with the question of whether Job will bless or curse *God*, given his extreme calamities.

To understand how the book may have functioned, let us imagine a discussion of the book in the wisdom schools of Israel, which focuses on the question of right speech vis-à-vis God in the face of suffering. The fact that the book is framed largely as a dialogue between different interlocutors, each with a different opinion of the matter, would certainly generate interest among those reading the text.

I myself remember participating in graduate seminars on the dialogues of Plato (*Phaedo, Phaedrus, Symposium, Theaetetus*), where the dramatic form Plato utilized was a boon to student interest and drew us in to listen carefully to the various voices, as we evaluated their articulated positions. Granted, we knew that the voice of Socrates was the definitive position for each dialogue, and some of the interlocutors were "yes-men," simply echoing Socrates's position (especially in *Phaedo*). However, the dialogue form has the benefit of not stating a clear position at the outset but developing various positions by means of the give-and-take of conversation.

Once we focus on the question of appropriate speech (especially speech in relation to God) in the face of suffering, the flow of the book of Job begins to unfold in a coherent way.

24. Moses Maimonides, writing in the twelfth century, cites various Talmudic sages who thought the book was a parable and also others who disagreed with this judgment. See Maimonides, *Guide for the Perplexed*, 3.22–23, https://www.sacred-texts.com/jud/gfp/.

25. The issue of appropriate speech is addressed in Prov. 10:18–21, 31–32; 11:9, 11–14; 12:6, 14, 17–19, 22; 13:2–3; 14:5, 25; 15:1–2, 4, 23; 16:1, 23–24, 27–28; 17:4, 7, 27; 18:4, 6, 13, 20–21; 19:5, 9; 20:19; 21:6, 23; 22:10; 25:11, 15, 23, 27; 26:20–28; 27:2; 28:23; 29:20.

The Movement of the Prologue through Various Speech Options

Although most of the speaking in the book of Job takes place in the poetic dialogues (Job 3–41), the prose prologue also contains speech. Both chapters 1 and 2 begin with a scene in heaven, where YHWH speaks with the Accuser (1:6–12; 2:1–6); the scene then shifts to earth, describing the troubles that come upon Job, along with his verbal responses (1:13–22; 2:7–10).

Option 1: Blessing God

After Job's first round of calamities (the destruction of his property and his children), "Job arose, tore his robe, shaved his head, and fell on the ground and worshiped. He said, 'Naked I came from my mother's womb, and naked shall I return there; the LORD gave, and the LORD has taken away; blessed be the name of the LORD'" (1:20–21). The narrator then evaluates Job's response: "In all this Job did not sin or charge God with wrongdoing" (1:22).

Contrary to the Accuser's claim that Job would curse God because of his calamities (1:11), Job accepts his fate as from God's hand, accompanied by physical signs of mourning and worship. He then explicitly blesses God (using the verb *bārak* in its non-euphemistic sense). And the narrator approves of this. However, some ambiguity is introduced by appending to the statement that "Job did not sin" the further statement that he did not "charge God with wrongdoing."[26] Are these meant to be equivalent, so that charging God with wrongdoing just *is* sin? Or are they two different things?

But matters get even more complicated when we note that the word the NRSV translates as "wrongdoing" (*tiplâ*) in Job 1:22, which occurs only three times in the Hebrew Bible (Job 1:22; 24:12; and Jer. 23:13), has the identical consonants as the Hebrew word for "prayer" (*təpillâ*).[27] Hebrew was originally written only with consonants and Choong-Leong Seow has shown that the book of Job is full of double entendres at the consonantal level (so that a given word may mean different things, depending on which vowel points are inserted).[28] It is thus entirely possible that the narrator's evaluation could be

26. David Clines translates this as "Job did not sin or speak irreverently of God." Clines, *Job 1–20*, 2.

27. This may be why the NRSV translates it as "prayer" in Job 24:12.

28. One famous example of this is the word translated as "day" (*yôm*) in Job 3:8 (based on the Masoretic vowel points), which many commentators (and some translations, like the NRSV) think should be the word "sea" (*yām*), since this fits the context better. Seow demonstrates that both meanings work well for 3:8, so that this could be an intended double entendre. Seow,

translated as "In all this Job did not sin or offer prayer to God" (the word for "charge" in the NRSV is the Hebrew verb for "give"). So the point here would be that although Job blessed God (which is appropriate speech), he did not address God directly (a point that will become important later on in the book).

However we interpret the details of Job 1:22, we know that the narrator evaluates the response of blessing God in a situation of suffering as a legitimate option for an upright and wise person.

Option 2: Cursing God

It is equally clear that cursing God is not a legitimate option. After Job's second round of trouble (his affliction with boils or sores), his wife encourages him to curse God and die (2:9), to which Job responds: "You speak as any foolish woman would speak. Shall we receive the good at the hand of God, and not receive the bad?" (2:10). The use of "foolish" (from *nābāl*) in a wisdom book to characterize a speech option is surely significant and clearly sets up cursing God as inappropriate speech.

Option 3: Passive Acceptance of Suffering

However, it is important to note that Job no longer blesses God.[29] His question "Shall we receive the good at the hand of God, and not receive the bad?" (2:10) reflects a posture similar to that of his earlier statement: "Naked I came from my mother's womb, and naked shall I return there; the LORD gave, and the LORD has taken away" (1:21). But, given the absence of any explicit word of blessing, his verbal response in chapter 2 feels much more like passive, even stoical acceptance of his fate. Perhaps he is so overcome by his suffering that he is simply unable to vocalize praise.[30] Yet, according to

"Orthography, Textual Criticism, and the Poetry of Job," *JBL* 130, no. 1 (2011): 74–76 (entire article 63–85). Seow does not explicitly address the possible double entendre of "prayer" and "wrongdoing" (1:22) in this article.

29. Job's words in 1:21 have been immortalized in a praise song that has been popular in many churches, called "Blessed Be Your Name," written by Matt and Beth Redman, recorded on the album by Matt Redman, *Where Angels Fear to Tread* (Thankyou Music, 2002). Although it is a beautiful song, it articulates a relatively superficial spirituality since it utilizes Job's response at the end of the first chapter as a paradigm for our attitude to suffering and ignores the complexity of the rest of the book. The song lyrics also directly address God ("Blessed be *your* name"), whereas Job does not speak directly to God until chap. 7.

30. I have had students tell me that Job's response in chap. 2 seems more honest than his response in chap. 1. Their suggestion is that although Job blessed God in 1:21, this feels like

the narrator, "In all this Job did not sin with his lips" (2:10). So far, so good: Job has not yet crossed the line to inappropriate speech.[31]

Option 4: Nonverbal Mourning, Followed by Silence

Then Job's three friends arrive and sit with him in silence for seven days (a precursor to the Jewish ritual of sitting shiva).[32] We are told that the friends came, each from their own home, to comfort and console him (2:11), but "when they saw him from a distance, they did not recognize him, and they raised their voices and wept aloud; they tore their robes and threw dust in the air upon their heads" (2:12). After this vocal, yet nonverbal, mourning, they lapsed into silence: "They sat with him on the ground seven days and seven nights, and no one spoke a word to him, for they saw that his suffering was very great" (2:13).

Although there is no specific evaluation from the narrator at this point, I take it that such weeping out of sorrow for someone's suffering is an appropriate response, as is sitting in silence with them.

The Movement of the Dialogues through Various Speech Options

Then chapter 3 opens with these ominous words: "After this [the seven days of silence], Job opened his mouth" (3:1). As Rick Moore aptly puts it, "The reader cannot help but lean forward to hear what came forth from these, until now, sinless lips."[33]

Option 5: Protest/Complaint about Suffering

When Job breaks his silence, he utters a torrent of audacious words. His outburst is like an X-rated lament psalm; yet it is different from a lament in that it is a soliloquy. Job doesn't address God (he certainly doesn't bless God), and he doesn't address his friends. "After this, Job opened his mouth

---

an automatic response of verbalizing what one is supposed to say, rather than an authentic response from the heart.

31. The statement that Job did not sin with his lips might raise in our minds the question of whether Job sinned in his heart (after all, he had earlier worried that his children might have sinned by cursing God in their hearts; 1:5), and some premodern commentators indeed claimed that Job sinned in his heart (evident by what he says in chap. 3, where the thoughts of his heart are articulated).

32. For details on this Jewish practice see Wikipedia, s.v. "Shiva (Judaism)," last modified April 7, 2021, https://en.wikipedia.org/wiki/Shiva_%28Judaism%29.

33. Rick D. Moore, "The Integrity of Job," *CBQ* 45, no. 1 (1983): 23 (entire article 17–31).

and *cursed the day of his birth*" (3:1).[34] Here we finally have the actual verb for curse (*qālal*). And here is where it gets interesting.

Job's pain that has been building up during seven days of silence finally explodes into a passionate malediction: "Let the day perish in which I was born, / and the night that said, / 'A man-child is conceived'" (3:3). Then Job expands on cursing the day:

> Let that day be darkness!
> > May God above not seek it,
> > or light shine on it.
> Let gloom and deep darkness claim it.
> > Let clouds settle upon it;
> > let the blackness of the day terrify it. (3:4–5)

Then Job curses the night that preceded his birth—he's trying to be comprehensive here:

> That night—let thick darkness seize it!
> > let it not rejoice among the days of the year;
> > let it not come into the number of the months.
> Yes, let that night be barren;
> > let no joyful cry be heard in it.
> Let those curse it who curse the Sea,
> > those who are skilled to rouse up Leviathan.
> Let the stars of its dawn be dark;
> > let it hope for light, but have none;
> > may it not see the eyelids of the morning—
> because it did not shut the doors of my mother's womb,
> > and hide trouble from my eyes. (3:6–10)

The final two lines of this extended curse state the *basis* for the curse—Job's desire to undo his own birth.

The rest of chapter 3 expands this desire into a series of pained questions, starting with "Why did I not die at birth, / come forth from the womb and expire?" (3:11). In all, Job asks three interconnected questions, which could

---

34. The text literally says that Job "cursed his day" (3:1). The immediate context suggests that this means the day of his birth (hence the NRSV and many translations), but since Job goes on to question why he is still alive, "his day" might refer to his entire life.

be summarized as follows: Why didn't I die at birth? (3:11–15); Why didn't I die *before* birth (in the womb)? (3:12–19); and Why am I still alive? (3:20–26). In these questions, which articulate Job's death wish, we catch a glimpse of his remarkable honesty about his suffering.

Job is in so much pain—physical, psychological, even theological pain (given that he doesn't understand what God is up to)—that he desires death, because then he could be at "rest," using the verb *nûaḥ* three times in the chapter, once each in connection with his three questions (3:13, 17, 26). Job ends his soliloquy honestly, stating, "I am not at ease, nor am I quiet; / I have no rest; but trouble comes" (3:26).[35]

How would ancient readers in a wisdom school respond to Job's outburst? Would they feel his pain, and be in sympathy with his complaint? Or would they judge that he has gone too far in his speech?

Job's abrasive outburst in chapter 3 raises for us today (as it would have for ancient readers) the question of the relationship between the existential reality of suffering and the appropriate way to respond verbally to this suffering. Has Job spoken of God what is right? Many readers have judged that he has not. There are two reasons for this.

First is his attitude toward creation (and thus toward the Creator).

Job's third question in this chapter is formulated in terms of God continuing to give him *light*, when darkness is what he really needs. "Why is light given to one in misery, / and life to the bitter in soul?" (3:20). "Why is light given to one who cannot see the way, / whom God has fenced in?" (3:23). Light also figures in Job's second question: "Why was I not buried like a stillborn child, / like an infant that never sees the light?" (3:16). And, of course, light is central to his opening malediction. He wants to reverse the day of his birth, to plunge it back into darkness; and he wants the night of his birth never to see the light of day.

In Job's desire to reverse God's gift of *his own* light/life, many readers have noticed an implicit rejection of the goodness of creation. Although Job's words focus on his own individual creation by God, doesn't he, in effect, reject God's creation of the world, which began with God proclaiming, "Let there be light" (Gen. 1:3)?[36] For many, this simply goes too far.

35. Given that Job's wife said, "Curse God and die" (2:9), the paradox of chap. 3 is that while Job resists cursing God, he now wants to die.

36. One of the classic studies of the relationship between Job 3 and Gen. 1 is Michael Fishbane, "Jer IV 23–26 and Job III 3–13: A Recovered Use of the Creation Pattern," *VT* 21 (1971):

Leo Perdue, for example, describes Job 3 as Job's "Assault on Creation" and suggests that "what Job desires is a return to oblivion, not only for himself but indeed for the entire creation. Job seeks by the power of his spoken word, formulated in lament and curse, to obliterate all existence."[37] Perdue suggests that the language of Job's curses ("Let x happen") is meant to be a reversal of God's creative speech in Genesis 1 ("Let there be x"), and he discerns seven specific curses or incantations in Job 3:3–10, corresponding to the seven days of creation in Genesis 1 (plus other, more detailed parallels).[38]

Even if we don't think that Job goes quite that far (and I don't), Job's attitude toward life expressed in chapter 3 reminds me of the words of Ivan to his friend Alyosha in Dostoevsky's novel *The Brothers Karamazov*. At one point Ivan says that the suffering of the world (especially of children) is too high a price to pay for the supposed harmony of the world (the reconciliation of evil with God's goodness):

> I don't want harmony, for the love of mankind I don't want it. . . . They have put too high a price on harmony; we can't afford to pay so much for admission. And therefore I hasten to return my ticket. . . . It's not that I don't accept God, Alyosha, I just most respectfully return him the ticket.
> "That is rebellion," Alyosha said softly, dropping his eyes.[39]

Many readers of Job have also thought that his outburst in chapter 3 is rebellion, or at least borders on rebellion. Job may not have explicitly cursed God; but his curse on the day of his birth, followed by his questioning of why God allowed his birth and why God continually gives him life, seems to express a fundamental ingratitude to his Creator.[40]

151–67. However, Fishbane may have overstated how close the relationship is between the two.

37. Leo G. Perdue, *Wisdom and Creation: The Theology of Wisdom Literature* (Nashville: Abingdon, 1994), 133. "The Assault on Creation" is the subtitle of Perdue's section on Job 3 (131–37); this title is derived from his earlier article "Job's Assault on Creation," *HAR* 10 (1987): 295–315.

38. Perdue, *Wisdom and Creation*, 133–34. Perdue goes so far as to say that "Job's earlier, enduring faith has crumbled, and now in angry rage he seeks to collapse all traditional theological meaning that creates and sustains the world" (Perdue, *Wisdom and Creation*, 137). While Rick Moore does not go quite that far, he thinks that Job has compromised his integrity by his assault on God, which "brings God's counter-assault on him" in the speeches from the whirlwind. "Job is rebuked for the line of questioning initiated by the theological suspicions of chap. 3." Moore, "Integrity of Job," 30.

39. Fyodor Dostoevsky, *The Brothers Karamazov: A Novel in Four Parts with Epilogue*, trans. Richard Pevear and Larissa Volokhonsky (New York: Farrar, Straus & Giroux, 1990), 245.

40. Although it is possible to see Job's rejection of his life as ingratitude to God, we should note that Job is at pains to avoid actually cursing God (which is prohibited in Lev. 24:15). And

But there is another reason for judging his speech inappropriate.

It is significant that Job does not address God directly here.[41] Whereas the lament psalms usually speak pain directly to God, Job's soliloquy in chapter 3 has been compared to the grumbling of the Israelites in the wilderness. Whereas God seems to accept the prayers of lament in the Psalter as appropriate speech (implied by the fact that they have been collected into the canon), the speech of the Israelites in the wilderness, in which they complain behind God's back about God's treatment of them, is deemed illegitimate in the narrative of Numbers, and so brings God's judgment. Shouldn't we judge Job's protests about his suffering here as likewise illegitimate?[42]

The book of Job itself gives us no hints at this point; there is no more evaluation of what Job says from here on, until we come to the epilogue. Instead, the poetry plunges us further into ambiguity via the response of Job's three friends.

Option 6: Defend God and Explain Suffering

Having sat with Job in silence for seven days, his friends finally speak. Job's outburst in chapter 3 was too much for them. Eliphaz begins with a question: "If one ventures a word with you, will you be offended? / But who can keep from speaking?" (4:2). After Eliphaz's speech (chaps. 4–5), Bildad speaks (chap. 8), then Zophar (chap. 11). Following the speech of each friend, we have Job's response (chaps. 6–7; 9–10; 12–14).

After the first round of speeches (chaps. 4–14), the friends speak again, in the same order—Eliphaz (chap. 15), Bildad (chap. 18), and Zophar (chap. 20), followed again by Job's responses (chaps. 16–17; 19; 21). Then comes a third round of speeches (chaps. 22–27)—at least, the beginning of a third round. There are speeches by Eliphaz (chap. 22) and Bildad (chap. 25), with

---

when he alludes to his parents (Job 3:3, 11–12), he also avoids cursing them for bringing him into the world (prohibited in 20:9). In this, Job stays within the bounds of the prohibitions of the Torah. Job is much like Jeremiah, who also curses the day of his birth and mentions his mother and father, yet does not curse them (Jer. 20:14–18).

41. Yet YHWH hears Job's outburst and responds in the speeches from the whirlwind to various points Job makes. On this, see Alex Breitkopf, "The Importance of Response in the Interpretation of Job," *Canadian Theological Review* 4, no. 1 (2015): 1–14. Thus, even if Job didn't specifically direct his words to God, the fact is that God treats his outburst in chap. 3 as a prayer.

42. For this interpretation, see Tremper Longman III, *Job*, BCOTWP (Grand Rapids: Baker Academic, 2012), 106–7.

responses from Job (chaps. 23–24; 26–27), but there is no third speech from Zophar.

Although there is no recorded third speech from Zophar, his second speech is longer than his first.[43] This contrasts with those of Eliphaz and Bildad, whose speeches tend to get shorter in the second round and shorter again in the third.[44] Not only are Job's speeches longer than those of his friends, but they often get longer within each speech cycle.[45]

Throughout the speech cycles, Job's friends reprimand him for speaking impiously and even seek to trace the cause of his suffering back to his sinfulness—he must have done something terribly wrong for these calamities to come upon him. Or, they try to convince him that God is trying to teach him something, so he should accept his suffering, quietly and piously, as God's discipline. And, he might as well repent anyway, since no human being can be righteous before God.

Here I have simply summarized the gist of what the three friends say, without trying to distinguish too clearly between them. If we had time, we could parse out their slightly different attitudes toward Job and the nuances of their arguments about God's goodness and Job's suffering. These attitudes and arguments are not quite the same, nor are they static. Instead, they develop somewhat throughout the dialogues. Tracing these nuances is the primary point of Susanna Baldwin's essay, "Miserable but Not Monochrome: The Distinctive Characteristics and Perspectives of Job's Three Comforters."[46] Baldwin distinguishes between Eliphaz, Bildad, and Zophar on the basis of the overall stance or tone of each speaker, the "argument" (or worldview) exhibited in their speeches, their justification (or source of truth) for their position, the specific accusation they level at Job, and the remedy they propose. For example, Eliphaz initially seems to be more patient with Job than

43. Zohpar's first speech is twenty-two verses long, while his second speech grows to twenty-nine verses.

44. Eliphaz's speeches go from forty-eight verses (round 1) to thirty-three verses (round 2) to thirty verses (round 3). Bildad's first two speeches are twenty-two verses each, but his third speech is a mere six verses.

45. In Job's first round of responses to his friends, his speeches increase from fifty-one verses (response to Eliphaz) to fifty-seven verses (response to Bildad), to seventy-five verses (response to Zophar). In his second round of responses, Job's speeches do not clearly increase (they go from thirty-eight, to twenty-nine, to thirty-four verses). In his third round of responses, Job's first speech is thirty-four verses, while his second speech is thirty-seven verses.

46. Baldwin, "Miserable but Not Monochrome: The Distinctive Characteristics and Perspectives of Job's Three Comforters," *Them* 43, no. 3 (2018): 359–75.

the other friends, and Zophar is more adamant than the others about Job's guilt (which may be why his second speech is longer than his first).

Although these differences in nuance are fascinating, it is the similarity between the three friends that is striking. All accept some version of a causal relationship between sin and suffering; all affirm that God is always in the right (no matter what happens); and all have a view of the human person as relatively insignificant in God's sight.

To be honest, reading this lengthy set of dialogues between Job and his friends can get a bit tedious, since the friends keep giving the same basic spiel over and over again (with variations). Could this be why Bildad's final speech is so short (six verses) or why there is no final speech from Zophar? Did they simply run out of steam? While this idea is sometimes floated in commentaries on Job, it is more common to think that part of the speech attributed to Job in chapters 26–27 is mislabeled and should be read as a continuation of Bildad's short speech or even as Zophar's missing speech. Yet since chapter 27 begins with a speech resumption formula ("Job again took up his discourse and said"; 27:1), this suggests that having finished his response to Bildad (in chap. 26), Job waited for Zophar's speech, but none was forthcoming. So Job spoke again (chap. 27).[47]

The shared assumptions of the three friends result in their unanimity in judging Job's speech—both about and to God—as inappropriate. Thus Bildad begins his first speech by asking Job, "How long will you say these things, / and the words of your mouth be a great wind?" (8:2). Zophar, likewise, opens his first speech with critical questioning of Job:

> Should a multitude of words go unanswered,
>   and should one full of talk be vindicated?
> Should your babble put others to silence,
>   and when you mock, shall no one shame you? (11:2–3)

47. J. Gerald Janzen mentions (without endorsing) the idea that the author may have "deliberately dissolved the otherwise orderly sequence of statements and counter-statements into a confused tangle of incoherent voices—a formal way of paralleling the argument of Job that the hedge against chaos has given way and that disorder and evil in the world make clear understandings impossible" (Janzen, *Job*, Interpretation [Atlanta: John Knox, 1985], 172). Janzen's own opinion, however, is based on the fact that Job often quotes and parodies what his friends have said. This leads Janzen to suggest that Bildad's third speech is cut short because Job interrupts him "with a sarcastic challenge . . . and then finishes his speech for him." And Zophar's third speech is missing because Job "concludes his engagement with his friends with a parody of what he might expect to hear from Zophar." Janzen, *Job*, 185.

Although Eliphaz may be somewhat more sensitive to Job's plight, at least at the start of the dialogues (as Baldwin notes), in his second speech he berates Job for his inappropriate words:

> Should the wise answer with windy knowledge,
>   and fill themselves with the east wind?
> Should they argue in unprofitable talk,
>   or in words with which they can do no good?
> But you are doing away with the fear of God,
>   and hindering meditation before God. (15:2–4)

But beyond critiquing Job's speech, all three friends engage in some form of theodicy, justifying God in the face of evident evil (that evil being Job's sufferings). So, in addition to blessing or cursing God, passive acceptance, mourning in silence, and protest, here we have another possible verbal response to suffering: the attempt to explain why suffering is appropriate, while defending the unimpeachable character of God.[48]

Is this a legitimate speech option in the face of suffering? No hint is given at this point. We can imagine a dispute between the readers of the book in the wisdom school, some siding with the friends (perhaps leaning toward Eliphaz or Bildad or Zophar), while others wondering if this is really the sort of "comfort" Job needs.

Option 7: Direct Protest/Complaint to God

In response to his friends, Job pleads his innocence and clearly articulates his pain as undeserved. Along the way, he often indicts God with responsibility for his suffering but also wonders if God would ever take his complaint seriously.

In most of his responses to his friends, Job addresses their prior speech to him, but at times he shifts his attention directly to God, addressing God in the second person ("you"). This shift begins in the first dialogue cycle, in

48. I have addressed the relationship of the book of Job and the lament psalms to classical Western theodicy in Middleton, "Why the 'Greater Good' Isn't a Defense: Classical Theodicy in Light of the Biblical Genre of Lament," *Koinonia* 9, nos. 1 & 2 (1997): 81–113. This essay testifies to my own shift from a Western philosophical stance concerning God's relationship to evil to what I consider to be a biblical approach to the subject. As I see it, the fundamental question is whether it is more appropriate to justify God and explain evil or to challenge God about the existence of evil.

the midst of responding to Eliphaz, where Job first speaks directly to God (7:11–21). He prefaces his "prayer" by adamantly stating that he will not restrain his mouth from speaking (7:11), and he opens with a question, which is really a challenge to God: "Am I the Sea, or the Dragon, / that you set a guard over me?" (7:12). Here Job wonders if God wants to restrain or muzzle him, like the chaos powers of Canaanite mythology (Sea and Dragon). Then Job goes on to accuse God of targeting him and directly causing his pain, using language from Psalm 8 about the special status of humanity (7:17–20).[49]

In his response to Bildad, Job again addresses God (9:27–31), and after a brief interlude where he speaks about God (presumably to Bildad), he resumes direct address to God (indicated by the "you" in 10:2):

> I loathe my life;
>> I will give free utterance to my complaint;
>> I will speak in the bitterness of my soul.
> I will say to God, Do not condemn me;
>> let me know why you contend against me. (10:1–2)

Job addresses his complaint directly to God throughout the entirety of chapter 10 (twenty-two verses). Then, in his response to Zophar, Job first explains, "I would speak to the Almighty, / and I desire to argue my case with God" (13:3). He then directly addresses God with his longest complaint yet (13:17–14:22). Here, in the first dialogue cycle, we find the clearest connection between Job's speech and the genre of lament psalms.

There is very little, if any, of Job's direct speech to God in the second and third dialogue cycles (an exception seems to be 17:4); instead, Job speaks about God, criticizing God's justice, claiming that God allows all sorts of evil in the world (beyond his own suffering), and oscillates between calling on God to answer him and wondering if God would ever take his complaint seriously.[50]

For those readers of Job (ancient or contemporary) who judge his outburst in chapter 3 as inappropriate speech, the question here is whether the fact that

49. In 7:12, Job draws on the Baal myth, where the goddess Anat says she has conquered the Sea and muzzled the Dragon, both of which represent the forces of chaos. We will come back to this important passage in the next chapter, addressing not only the mythological imagery Job uses, but also the view of humanity that Eliphaz proposes in chap. 4, to which Job responds in chap. 7.

50. Even when Job does not directly address God, his complaints are different from the grumbling of the Israelites in the wilderness, in that Job clearly wants an audience with God; indeed, he pleads for this (he is not just bad-mouthing God behind his back).

he takes his complaint directly to God (at least, in the first dialogue cycle) would change their opinion. Is it any more (or less) appropriate to protest directly to God's face, calling God personally to account for one's suffering?

The text of Job gives no clear answer at this point. But Job 28 gives the reader an opportunity to pause and reflect on the question.

An Interlude on Wisdom

After the dialogues between Job and his friends—each friend giving his opinion about the appropriate response to suffering, followed by Job's objections and complaint—and with no resolution in sight, we have an interlude on wisdom.

My choice of the term *interlude* makes no judgment about whether the chapter, which has a different, more elevated Hebrew style than the speeches so far, is a later addition to the book. Whether or not it was added later is not as important as the function it has in the book of Job as it stands. Some think it continues Job's speech, since Job has been speaking in chapter 27 and continues to speak in chapter 29. However, given the fact that 29:1 states, "Job again took up his discourse and said" (which implies that he had stopped speaking for a while), it makes more sense to treat chapter 28 as a pause for reflection on the various opinions voiced by Job and his friends.

Job 28 begins with a portrayal of someone searching out hidden treasures, even to the farthest corners or depths of the earth (28:1–11), followed by the question, "But where shall wisdom be found? / And where is the place of understanding?" (28:12).[51] This question leads to an affirmation of the difficulty of finding wisdom:

> Mortals do not know the way to it,
>> and it is not found in the land of the living.
> The deep says, "It is not in me,"
>> and the sea says, "It is not with me." (28:13–14)

Then the topic changes to the surpassing value of wisdom, in comparison to precious metals or jewels (28:15–19), after which the question is asked again:

---

51. Although it is typical to think that the dominant metaphor used in Job 28 is mining (digging deep for minerals), Scott C. Jones has shown that a closer parallel for the imagery is found in the legendary journey of Mesopotamian kings to the ends of the earth to seek out wealth in secret places (this may include mining but is broader than that). See Jones, *Rumors of Wisdom: Job 28 as Poetry*, BZAW 398 (Berlin: de Gruyter, 2009).

"Where then does wisdom come from? / And where is the place of understanding?" (28:20). After affirming that wisdom is hidden from both the living and the dead (28:21–22), we are told that "God understands the way to it, / and he knows its place" (28:23). This is because God utilized wisdom in creating the world, which suggests that wisdom is embedded in the created order (28:24–27). This may well be an anticipation of God's answer to Job, especially God's first speech, where he speaks at length about creation.

However, given Job 28's focus on the difficulty in finding wisdom, along with its placement after the speeches in chapters 3–27, we are warranted in taking the chapter as an implicit comment on these speeches. Wisdom is very difficult to find. Even persistent searching through the dialogues between Job and his friends may not lead to a definitive answer about appropriate speech in the face of evil. The chapter thus asks the reader, Who among the interlocutors might have approached wisdom? But it is a genuinely open question at this point.[52]

The interlude on wisdom (like the book of Job as a whole) is much less optimistic about the human ability to attain wisdom than is the book of Proverbs. In Proverbs, personified Wisdom calls out in the public square, inviting the simple to come and learn (1:20–33; 8:1–11; 9:1–6). The implication is that wisdom is available to anyone with ears to hear.[53] On the contrary, Job 28 affirms that only the Creator can access wisdom directly. Yet the chapter concludes that humans do have a certain access to wisdom, but it is the wisdom of an ethical stance, equivalent to a right relationship to God: "Truly, the fear of the Lord, that is wisdom; / and to depart from evil is understanding" (28:28).

Since these words basically quote the description of Job given by the narrator and YHWH in chapters 1 and 2, we are drawn back to the realization that Job started out wise. But we are left to wonder if this description continues to be true for Job in the poetic dialogues. Could Job's abrasive complaints be consistent with the fear of God?

---

52. Westermann (*Structure of the Book of Job*, 137–38) calls Job 28 a "resting point" after the dialogue of Job and his friends, which becomes the basis for God's later judgment (in 42:7–8) of their speech as inappropriate (that is, they have not been able to find wisdom). I am not sure it is a clear judgment on the friends (yet), or a condemnation of Job's responses, for that matter.

53. Even Proverbs, however, expresses that finding wisdom takes energy and intentionality. It must be desired and sought with all one's might (2:1–5; 4:1–8, esp. v. 7). Also, it is not only Wisdom who calls out in the public places; Folly also calls. So the simple need to discern whom to listen to. My thanks to Josef Sykora for reminding me of this latter point.

Job's Final Discourse

As if to make matters even more complicated, Job speaks again (Job 29–31). His lengthy concluding discourse does not address his friends. It is primarily a soliloquy (like his opening speech in chap. 3), though he addresses God directly at one point (30:20–23).

Job's discourse divides naturally into three parts, with each chapter focused on one topic or theme. In chapter 29, Job looks back to his former prosperity and blessing, when he was in tune with God. Then in chapter 30, he complains about his present calamities, including his sense that God has forsaken him. Finally, in chapter 31, Job utters a series of oaths of innocence, in which he affirms his continuing integrity.

One helpful way to understand Job's words in chapters 29–31 is to view them as Job's *interior* perspective on what was previously described *from the outside* in the opening narrative. Thus, his first speech corresponds to the opening description of Job's blessedness in 1:1–5; his second speech corresponds to the calamities that are described in 1:13–19 and 2:7–9; and his third speech corresponds to the narrator's positive comments about Job's responses in 1:20–22 and 2:10.[54]

Yet Job's speeches expand on these themes considerably beyond what is found in the prologue. In the first speech (chap. 29), which looks back longingly on his past, Job gives much more detail about his former blessedness, especially the fact that he was held in high regard on account of his righteous deeds toward the needy. Those were the days, he muses, "when the friendship of God was upon my tent; / when the Almighty was still with me" (29:4–5).

Job's description of his troubles in chapter 30 focuses less on his loss of property, children, and health than on the mockery and persecution he has endured as a result of these losses. He attributes all this to God, initially in the third person: "He has cast me into the mire, / and I have become like dust and ashes" (30:19). Then Job addresses God directly, accusing him of ignoring his pleas and causing his pain:

> I cry to you and you do not answer me;
> I stand, and you merely look at me.

54. I read this intriguing suggestion many years ago. However, I need to thank the author anonymously, since I can no longer remember the source.

> You have turned cruel to me;
>> with the might of your hand you persecute me. (30:20–21)

In the third speech (chap. 31), Job affirms his innocence, citing a long list of unethical behaviors he has avoided. These affirmations are framed as a series of if-then statements; if he has done any of these things, he willingly accepts the appropriate consequences.

In all of Job's speech, both here and in his prior dialogues with his friends, what Job *doesn't* say is significant. Nowhere does Job seek revenge on those who have mistreated him.[55] Nowhere does he ask for a return to his prior material prosperity. Instead, his underlying desire, which surfaces throughout his complaints, is to be vindicated by God. To that end, he wants God to hear his case and respond (powerfully stated in 23:1–7, among other places).

Yet Job often wavers between this desire and his despair over it ever coming to pass. Whereas his desire to be heard testifies to his trust in the divine Judge, he often admits that God seems absent or he lapses into doubt that God would take him seriously—due to his own insignificance or to God's transcendence of human affairs (in this, it looks like Job has absorbed the low estimate of humanity articulated by his friends). At one point, in the midst of despairing that God would ever answer him, Job says, "Look, he passes by me, and I do not see him; / he moves on, but I do not perceive him" (9:11). Job here desires the sort of encounter that Moses received (and that Elijah was offered) at Sinai/Horeb (Exod. 33:19; 1 Kings 19:11), using the same verb for God passing by (*'ābar*). But he wonders if it will ever happen.

Yet Job never quite gives up on his desire to be answered by God. Almost at the end of his final speech, Job interrupts his affirmations of innocence with a passionate statement of his desire to be vindicated by God:

> O that I had one to hear me!
> (Here is my signature! Let the Almighty answer me!)
> O that I had the indictment written by my adversary!

---

55. In a careful study of Job 19 and its intertextuality with Lam. 3, Amy Erickson has shown that while both Job and the speaker in Lamentations use similar imagery to describe their plight (including that their glory has been stripped away and their path forward has been blocked) and both challenge God for his attack against them, Job studiously avoids the call for vengeance on enemies that is found in Lam. 3:64–66. See Erickson, "Resistance and Surrender: The Self in Job 19," *JBHT* 1, no. 2 (2011): 1–32.

> Surely I would carry it on my shoulder;
>> I would bind it on me like a crown;
> I would give him an account of all my steps;
>> like a prince I would approach him. (31:35–37)

Does Job's desire for a meeting with the divine Judge affect our appraisal of his abrasive speech, which often accuses God of complicity in his suffering?

It isn't clear that Job 29–31 adds anything radically new to what Job has already said. It does not seem to add a new option for appropriate speech in the face of suffering. In these chapters, Job continues his complaint about his calamities, sometimes addressing God directly (option 7), sometimes not (option 5). We are left with the question of whether Job's protest about his suffering, whether addressed to God or not, is wise speech.

Without an answer to this question, the last line of chapter 31 states, "The words of Job are ended" (31:40).

Now, finally, we may receive an answer to our question—that is, if God will respond to Job's complaint.

Who the Heck Is Elihu, and What Does He Want?

But God's hoped-for response is interrupted by another speaker, named Elihu. Whereas Job's three friends had stopped answering Job "because he was righteous [ṣadîq] in his own eyes" (32:1), Elihu speaks because he is angry with Job for this very reason: "because he justified [the verbal form of ṣadîq] himself rather than God" (32:2). But he was also angry with Job's friends "because they had found no answer, though they had declared Job to be in the wrong" (32:3).

Elihu admits he is young, in contrast to Job and his friends, so he initially gives them deference, waiting until they had all finished speaking—something stated both by the narrator (32:4) and by Elihu himself (32:6–7, 11–12, 16). Yet he intimates that because of access to God's spirit, rather than the wisdom of age (32:8–10), he has a fresh perspective on the matter.[56] In the memorable words of Monty Python, "And now for something completely different!"[57]

56. This more personal and direct claim for access to God's wisdom is emphasized by the name Elihu, which means, "He is my God."

57. This is a catchphrase used by John Cleese in many episodes of the TV series *Monty Python's Flying Circus*. Four seasons (forty-five episodes) of the series aired on British TV between October 5, 1969, and December 5, 1974.

Will Elihu provide the definitive response to Job's complaint? Might his speeches suggest an answer to the question of what is wise speech in the face of extreme suffering?

Our expectation is built up by the narrative introduction to Elihu's speech (32:1–5) and by his lengthy opening words (32:6–22), which preface the four speeches that follow (chaps. 33–37). In his self-introduction, Elihu spends seventeen verses saying that he has been waiting to say something important. As Patrick Shekan ironically puts it, in this section "by way of introducing himself, the speaker says almost nothing at all, with a seeming maximum of repetition."[58]

Following his introductory comments (32:6–22), Elihu addresses his words to Job (chap. 33), then to his friends (chap. 34), then to Job again (chap. 35), before concluding with a final lengthy speech (chaps. 36–37), which seems to be addressed to Job (37:14). This final speech reads like an add-on, given how it is introduced: "Elihu continued and said, 'Bear with me a little, and I will show you, / for I have yet something to say on God's behalf'" (36:1–2).

What is the substance of Elihu's speeches? What is so important that he has to say?

First of all, Elihu continuously points out, both directly to Job and to the friends, that Job has been speaking wrongly of God (32:8–13; 34:5–9, 35–37; 35:16); at one point, he even challenges Job to be silent and listen to his wisdom (33:31–33). But this is nothing new, since the friends have been critiquing Job's speech throughout the prior dialogues.[59] Beyond that, Elihu claims that God is so transcendent that the good or evil humans do is insignificant to him (35:5–8; 36:10–16)—again similar to what the friends had said.

Perhaps, then, Elihu seeks to provide a better interpretation of Job's suffering than Job's friends have, by focusing on suffering as God's discipline or correction of those (presumably like Job) who are too proud (33:16–19). But this is a point the friends had (intermittently) made in their speeches. Plus, Elihu does not limit suffering to God's discipline but also views it as punishment for sin (34:10–27). Strangely, Elihu addresses this latter point to the friends (34:10), as if it is something they need to learn. But this had been one of their main points all along.

58. Patrick W. Shekan, *Studies in Israelite Poetry and Wisdom*, CBQMS 1 (Washington, DC: Catholic Biblical Association of America, 1971), 85. Shekan suggests that Elihu might be intended as a (gentle) caricature.

59. What is different about Elihu's critique is that it often quotes Job's words verbatim from his prior speeches, in order to refute them.

So Elihu's claim to present a new perspective is ultimately disappointing. There is nothing radically new in what he says, despite his long discourses. There are certainly new emphases, such as Elihu's stress on God's revelatory power in contrast to the ossified wisdom of the ages (32:8–10; 33:4, 14–15). But there is no new explanation of Job's sufferings on offer. And, like the friends, Elihu thinks that Job's complaint about his suffering has been inappropriate.

So, despite a minority of interpreters who think that Elihu's speeches are important for the book of Job—even that they are the key to the book—I judge that they exhibit nothing more than variations on a theme we have already heard. Nothing new is added to the point of view of Job's friends.[60] Elihu is best understood, therefore, as simply another representative of option 6 (defend God and explain suffering).[61]

I tend to agree with the dominant scholarly opinion that the Elihu speeches are a later addition to the book of Job, since nowhere in the book is Elihu mentioned besides in the chapters that contain his speeches. But I am less interested in the possible stages of the book's composition than in the *function* of Elihu's speeches in their present position. Why were they put there?

One plausible suggestion is that the concluding section of Elihu's final speech, which contains a discourse on God's power in creation (36:24–37:24), may function as an overture to YHWH's speeches (which begin in chap. 38), especially since Elihu touches on some of the very meteorological themes found in YHWH's first speech (especially in 38:19–38).[62] Yet in contrast to

60. One interpreter who thinks that Elihu's speeches are crucial to the meaning of the book is E. W. Hengstenberg, "Interpreting the Book of Job," in *Classical Evangelical Essays in Old Testament Interpretation*, ed. Walter C. Kaiser Jr. (Grand Rapids: Baker, 1972; repr. Eugene, OR: Wipf & Stock, 2008), 104–12 (entire chapter 91–112). Hengstenberg views Elihu as God's "servant," "spokesman," "a speaker for God," who "uttered what God had given him" (104, 109, 112), whose distinctive contribution is that, out of love, God is chastising Job for his pride in his own righteousness (107).

61. William Brown objects to those who disparage Elihu's contribution to the book of Job, judging that some descriptions of Elihu in the commentaries "teeter on the edge of character assassination." He portrays Elihu as a "foil" or "literary nemesis" to Job's friends, in that he is depicted as significantly different from them and explicitly critiques their tradition of wisdom (Brown, *Wisdom's Wonder*, 104–5). I agree that Elihu is *presented* as different; but the paradox is that he brings no new perspective to bear on Job's sufferings or complaint.

62. William Brown is one of many who make this point. Brown suggests that "much of what Elihu says coheres with the divine speeches of YHWH that follow," so that his concluding words serve as "a fitting introduction to the theophany" of chaps. 38–41 (Brown, *Wisdom's Wonder*, 105). Robert V. McCabe likewise thinks that Elihu's concluding theocentric paean to God's greatness and power in creation prepares the reader for YHWH's speeches. McCabe, "Elihu's Contribution to the Thought of the Book of Job," *DBSJ* 2 (1997): 47–80.

Elihu's claim that God sends rain on humans so that they may know he cares for them (36:27–28, 31; 37:6–7), YHWH will later tell Job that he sends rain on a land where no one lives (38:26–27), and God will then parade before Job a cavalcade of wild animals that (with the exception of the warhorse) people do not know or care about (38:39–39:30); yet God seems to delight in these creatures.

So while the ending of Elihu's speeches may prime the pump thematically for YHWH's coming discourse, it does not quite match what God will say. And the extreme length of Elihu's speeches, with their rehearsing of prior themes under the guise of saying something new, may well be intended to frustrate the reader by prolonging the already interminable discussion (with no resolution) about Job's suffering. They thus heighten the tension that has been developing from the beginning of the book, pressing us to reflect on who has spoken what is right concerning God.[63]

We are now as ready as we will ever be for YHWH's response from the whirlwind. What will God say to Job? How will the One Job has been challenging to answer him evaluate his abrasive complaints? That is the focus of the next chapter.

63. Beyond thinking that Elihu prepares the way thematically for God's speeches, McCabe ("Elihu's Contribution") notes that since Elihu often quotes Job's arguments (often verbatim) and refutes him in much the same way the friends responded, Elihu's speeches are important for the flow of the book. They recapitulate the content of the dialogues between Job and his friends, thus providing a fitting transition from the dialogue section to what comes next. But I wonder why we need this transition. Elihu's repetition of the prior arguments reminds me of the oft-quoted saying about how to make a speech: "Tell 'em what you're going to say, say it, and then tell 'em what you said." Rather than being helpful, so much hammering home of a point is likely to give the audience a headache. This may be precisely the purpose of Elihu's speeches—their repetitious nature may be intended to frustrate the reader and thus heighten their desire for resolution. For an exploration of the origin of the oft-quoted saying about repetition in speechmaking, see "Tell 'Em What You're Going to Tell 'Em," Quote Investigator, August 15, 2017, https://quoteinvestigator.com/2017/08/15/tell-em.

4

Does God Come to Bury
Job or to Praise Him?

We now come to YHWH's response to Job from the whirlwind, with a very specific question: Does this response help us adjudicate between the various speech options proposed in the book? In particular: Does God approve of Job's abrasive complaint about his suffering? Put more generally: Is protest to God (or about God) concerning one's circumstances viewed in the book of Job as a form of speech that manifests wisdom?[1]

In the last chapter I suggested that Job can be fruitfully understood as a wisdom treatise that explores the question of appropriate speech vis-à-vis God in the face of extreme suffering. When tragedy befalls us, when the world does not seem just—when even God seems not to be acting in character—what should our response be? The book of Job gives us multiple options to ponder. The book presents at least seven possibilities for speech in the face of

1. A much shorter version of this chapter was presented as the Peter C. Craigie Memorial Lecture, sponsored by the Division of Humanities at the University of Calgary, Calgary, AB, November 1, 2005. A revised version was given at a Seminar in Biblical Theology at St. Mark's National Theological Centre, Canberra, Australia, October 7, 2016, and was published as "Does God Come to Bury Job or to Praise Him? The Significance of YHWH's Second Speech from the Whirlwind," *St. Mark's Review*, no. 239 (March 2017): 1–27. Used by permission.

suffering, two of which involve protest or complaint about suffering, spoken either about God (option 5) or directly to God (option 7).

The Extreme Nature of Job's Speech

Job models both forms of complaint (option 5 and option 7) throughout the dialogue section of the book. Indeed, Job's reputation for complaint is so well-known that it found its way into the TV show *Rizzoli & Isles*, when detective Jane Rizzoli (played by actress Angie Harmon) explained how impatient she was with a case she was working on by exclaiming, "Job was like a cranky toddler compared to me!"[2] While the quip worked nicely in the show, it downplays just how abrasive Job's speech actually is.

In lengthy cycles of dialogue, Job's friends try to explain to him why he is suffering, and why God's justice should not be questioned. The implication is that Job is sinful, or at least prideful, and should submit to God's discipline. But Job refuses to have any of it. He will accept no easy answers, especially answers that blame the victim. And he will not accept his friends' advice to calm down and not be upset—especially not upset with God. Indeed, he verbalizes his complaint about God's injustice in no uncertain terms, challenging God to either explain why he is suffering or to vindicate him of the charges made by his friends (that he is suffering justly for something he has done).

Although Job initially blessed God after suffering the first set of calamities, and then passively acquiesced in whatever God sent his way after the second set of calamities (yet without blessing God explicitly), later in the book he comes to quite audacious speech—even beyond cursing the day of his birth.

One extreme example is found in chapter 19, where Job tells his friends that God has wronged him (19:6) and says that though he cries aloud he gets no justice (19:7). He claims that God has uprooted his hope (19:10) and treated him as an enemy (19:11). Then in 27:4–6, Job swears adamantly that he is innocent and that he is telling the truth about his innocence. Indeed, he swears this in an unusual oath, which begins, "As God lives, who has taken away my right, / and the Almighty, who has made my soul bitter" (27:2).

Instead of swearing an oath based on some positive attribute of God, Job avers his innocence based on his experience of the deity's unjust treatment

---

2. *Rizzoli & Isles*, season 2, episode 5, "Don't Hate the Player," aired August 2011, on TNT, https://www.hulu.com/series/0ae1d076-5a13-477f-af52-b22e3cf518e4.

of him. His fundamental judgment about the nature and character of God is that God is *wrong*; God is *unjust*.

This is certainly speech made in extremity. It is not normal.

The Attraction and Problem of the Book of Job

Yet Job's speech, and his point of view, is attractive to many contemporary readers. We live in a world of massive suffering—with domestic violence, systemic racism, gang warfare, and oppressive political regimes; virulent diseases and toxic waste; terrorism, torture, and human trafficking; unpredictable tsunamis, earthquakes, and hurricanes that destroy life. And even if we have no personal experience of such extreme suffering, the media continually inundates us with terrible happenings around the globe.

And many of us have experienced suffering personally, in diverse and varied forms. So we are impatient with easy explanations, especially those that blame the victim. We're attracted to Job's honesty—audacious as it is—and intrigued by his boldness in speaking his mind, even to God (which he starts doing in chap. 7).

However, the book of Job is also deeply problematic and troubling.

An initial problem many readers have is the wager God makes with the Accuser in the prologue about whether Job will be faithful despite his suffering. Does God really play fast and loose with people (especially his faithful servants), subjecting them to terrible suffering just to prove a point?

But it is not clear that the prologue intends to teach theology. If (as I suggested in the last chapter) we take the book as a wisdom treatise presenting a hypothetical *what-if* scenario in order to stimulate reflection on right speech in the face of evident evil, we can read the Accuser as a literary figure used to get the story going. The fact that the Accuser disappears from the story after the prologue, along with the exaggerated (almost farcical) portrayal of Job's calamities, leads me to think that the scenario in the first two chapters is an imaginative setup for posing the question of appropriate speech vis-à-vis God. It does not intend to teach either history (that these events really happened) or theology (this is what God is really like).

But there is another, more significant problem in the book of Job, beyond the portrayal of God in the prologue. This is the blustery nature of God's response to Job's complaints. In the speeches from the whirlwind, YHWH seems to rebuke Job for his audacious speech, reprimanding him for daring to question the way God has ordered the world (and Job's life). An initial reading of the speeches from the whirlwind suggests that God tries to shut Job down, to make him feel inferior for his honesty and boldness. This would mean that protest to God about suffering is an inappropriate form of speech.

The interpretation of God's speeches to Job as a ringing rebuke or supreme put-down, intended to abase Job, has a long history and is in harmony with much traditional piety, which judges Job's abrasive speech as unseemly, even arrogant, in need of divine rebuke. I can testify that despite the initial attractiveness of Job's honesty to many in the church, it is very common for both clergy and laypeople to think that, in the end, God's speeches constitute a harsh reprimand of Job (and that it must have been deserved). That God is reprimanding Job is the dominant understanding found both throughout the history of interpretation and among those today of pious persuasion, who think that Job overstepped his bounds in complaining to God.[3]

A similar view of God's speeches is found among modern interpreters who side with Job for his honesty and object to God's response as bullying. Archibald MacLeish, for example, in his play *J.B.*, articulates a critique of God's speeches in the words of the Adversary: "What? That God knows more than he does. / That God's more powerful than he!— / Throwing the whole creation at him! / Throwing the Glory and the Power!"[4]

The Argument for God's Bullying of Job

Could both the pious affirmers and the contemporary critics be right about the thrust of God's response to Job? Is God verbally attacking Job in his speeches? At least five indicators from the text of Job itself suggest that God is, indeed, reprimanding Job for his arrogance. Let us feel the full force of the argument for God as a heavenly bully.

No Mention of Humans in the First Speech

First, as is often pointed out by commentators, there is no explicit mention of humans in the amazing catalog of creatures surveyed in God's first speech

---

3. This, for example, is the view classically articulated by John Calvin, *Sermons from Job*, trans. Leroy Nixon (Grand Rapids: Eerdmans, 1952), 220–23. See also Susan E. Schreiner, *Where Shall Wisdom Be Found? Calvin's Exegesis of Job from Medieval and Modern Perspectives* (Chicago: University of Chicago Press, 1994).

4. Archibald MacLeish, *J.B.* (Boston: Houghton Mifflin, 1958), scene 10, lines 57–60.

(chaps. 38–39).[5] Although YHWH essentially takes Job on a whirlwind tour of creation, from cosmology (surveying the stars, the weather, etc.) to zoology (educating Job on the habits of various animals), reference to humans is conspicuously missing.

The absence of any reference to the human role in the created order in God's first speech is often taken as a "decentering" of Job's anthropocentric point of view—humans are insignificant from God's perspective and Job has an overinflated sense of his own importance in the cosmic scheme of things, which has led to his insistent and arrogant questioning of God.[6]

The Display of God's Power in Both Speeches

The second indicator that the intent of God's speeches is to put Job in his place is the overwhelming display of God's raw power in creation found in the two speeches. The barrage of questions God throws at Job in the first speech (Who is this? Were you there? Do you know?), along with a vivid panorama of creatures (which God boasts that he both made and controls), seems like a rhetorical "shock and awe" campaign meant to abase Job and put him in his place.[7] In particular, the inclusion in the second speech of the two beasts, Behemoth and Leviathan—who seem to represent the chaos monsters of ancient Near Eastern mythology—suggests the vast extent of God's power. As Norman Habel puts it, "If Yahweh can control the terror of the ferocious Leviathan subduing Job will be a pushover."[8]

5. On the absence of humans in the first speech, see Kathryn Shifferdecker, *Out of the Whirlwind: Creation Theology in the Book of Job*, HTS 61 (Cambridge, MA: Harvard University Press, 2008), 66, 82–83.

6. For the first divine speech as a critique of anthropocentrism, see James Crenshaw, "When Form and Content Clash: The Theology of Job 38:1–40:5," in *Creation in the Biblical Traditions*, ed. Richard J. Clifford and John J. Collins, CBQMS 24 (Washington, DC: Catholic Biblical Association of America, 1992), 80 (entire chapter 70–84).

7. "Shock and awe" is the colloquial phrase used for the US military doctrine of Rapid Dominance developed by Harlan K. Ullman and James P. Wade in 1996 and used in the US attack on Iraq in 2003. "The key objective of Rapid Dominance is to impose this overwhelming level of Shock and Awe against an adversary on an immediate or sufficiently timely basis to paralyze its will to carry on. In crude terms, Rapid Dominance would seize control of the environment and paralyze or so overload an adversary's perceptions and understanding of events so that the enemy would be incapable of resistance at tactical and strategic levels." Ullman and Wade, *Shock and Awe: Achieving Rapid Dominance* (Washington, DC: National Defense University, 1996), xxv.

8. Norman C. Habel, *The Book of Job: A Commentary*, OTL (Philadelphia: Westminster, 1985), 572. John Day makes a similar point in *God's Conflict with the Dragon and the Sea: Echoes of a Canaanite Myth in the Old Testament*, UCOP 35 (Cambridge: Cambridge University Press, 1985), 83.

Whether it is the ancient Mesopotamian deity Ninurta subduing the fabled Anzu (a hybrid lion-bird) or the later Babylonian god Marduk subduing the sea monster Tiamat, this well-known ancient mythology of conquest extols the power of the creator over the forces of chaos. If God is able to subdue even the cosmic forces of chaos, how could Job be any match for God?

God's Challenge to Job to Exercise Power over the Cosmos in the Second Speech

Connected to this overwhelming display of divine power is the third indicator—namely, God's explicit challenge to Job at the start of the second speech to exercise power as Creator and govern the cosmos if he is able to (40:9–14). This would, of course, need to include mastering Leviathan the chaos beast—an impossible task, as YHWH indicates.

> Lay hands on it;
>> think of the battle; you will not do it again!
> Any hope will be disappointed;
>> one is overwhelmed at the sight of it. (41:8–9 [40:32–41:1 MT])[9]

This challenge to Job in 40:9–14 is often read as God's quite understandable response to Job's audacity at having questioned divine governance of the cosmos. Indeed, according to the introduction to the first speech, the Creator seems upset that Job has darkened "counsel" or "design" (*'ēṣâ*)—that is, *God's* design of the cosmos—without knowledge (38:2). This darkening of God's counsel or design may hark back to Job's desire to reverse creation and turn light back into darkness in his first speech (3:4–6, 9).

According to the introduction to the second speech, God clearly says that Job has tried to discredit his justice (*mišpāṭ*) and has condemned the Creator while justifying himself (40:8). Among the many places where Job has challenged God's *mišpāṭ*, while justifying himself, we may think of his words in 19:7 ("I call aloud, but there is no justice [*mišpāṭ*]") or in 27:2 ("As God lives, who has taken away my right [*mišpāṭ*]").

God thus lays down the gauntlet in 40:9–14. Job had better put up or shut up.

---

9. The translation of 41:9 is offered as an alternative in the notes to the NRSV. The Hebrew of 41:9 [41:1 MT] says "Behold, his hope is mistaken, / isn't it [or he] dashed [cast down] at the sight of it?"

> Have you an arm like God,
>   and can you thunder with a voice like his?
> Deck yourself with majesty and dignity;
>   clothe yourself with glory and splendor.
> Pour out the overflowings of your anger,
>   and look on all who are proud, and abase them.
> Look on all who are proud, and bring them low;
>   tread down the wicked where they stand.
> Hide them all in the dust together;
>   bind their faces in the world below.
> Then I will also acknowledge to you
>   that your own right hand can give you victory. (40:9–14)

The implication, of course, is that Job can do no such thing. And, in coming to realize this, he will change his attitude to one that is more appropriately submissive to the true Ruler of creation.

The Comparison of Job with the Beasts of the Second Speech

The fourth indicator that God wants to abase Job is found in an intriguing though implicit comparison between Job and the two beasts of the second speech. One possible reason for God's appeal to these monsters is that Job is like them in significant ways. Like these beasts, especially Leviathan, Job has become (by his speech) a monstrous, chaotic creature, in need of subduing.[10] If Job is, indeed, being compared to primordial chaos, would this not be the supreme denigration of Job on God's part?[11]

Job's "Repentance" after the Second Speech

But the clincher (the fifth indicator) that God's speeches are intended to reprimand and abase Job, is Job's response after the second speech. As almost all modern translations render it, Job replies to God's rhetorical "shock and awe" tactics by admitting: "I despise myself and repent in dust and ashes" (42:6).

---

10. Habel thinks that "the control of Behemoth implies the control and subjugation of Job." Habel, *Book of Job*, 566.

11. Kathryn Shifferdecker makes a slightly different point about the comparison of Job to the beasts, suggesting that Job comes off as seriously wanting (the beasts are much more powerful—and more important—than he is). This is another form of the idea that God is decentering Job's anthropocentrism. Shifferdecker, *Out of the Whirlwind*, 87–88, 92.

And Yet . . . a Reason for Questioning This Interpretation of God's Speeches

The initial problem for this overall interpretation of God's speeches (namely, that they are intended to rebuke Job for his audacity and to put him in his place) is that the two verses immediately following Job's "repentance" contain God's explicit *approval* of Job's speech. As God says twice to Eliphaz about him and his two friends in 42:7 and 8b: "You [plural] have not spoken of me what is right, as my servant Job has."

Nestled between these two identical statements is God's characterization of the speech of Eliphaz and his two friends as "folly" (*nəbālâ*)—at least, according to most translations. The Hebrew of 42:8a simply says that God will not deal with them according to folly ("your" is supplied by the translators). But the traditional translations are not far wrong, if God is saying that he will not respond in kind.[12]

Given that in the prologue Job called his wife's encouragement to curse God "foolish" (2:10), we seem to have two opposing forms of inappropriate speech identified in the book of Job—cursing God (option 3) and defending God, while explaining suffering (option 6). In contrast to these two options, the implication is that Job's speech has embodied wisdom.

Could this mean that Job's outrageous curse on the day of his birth, followed by his abrasive discourses with his friends and his seemingly impious and insistent demand that God answer him—that this could all be faithful speech, theological discourse characterized by wisdom?

It might be thought that God's approval of Job's speech in the epilogue applies only to Job's final words of submission and repentance in 42:1–6. But this unlikely, given that God is contrasting Job's speech with that of the friends. The poetic dialogues of the book are clearly in view here.[13]

Does this mean that there is unanimity between the epilogue and God's speeches from the whirlwind on the appropriateness of Job's complaint?[14] Although it goes against the grain of much traditional Joban scholarship, I

---

12. The CEB renders this as God promising not to make fools of the friends.

13. There is also the question of the import of Job's words to God in 42:1–6. It is not clear that Job is submitting or repenting in any traditional sense. I will come to this.

14. Carol Newsom is just one among many interpreters who thinks that there is a fundamental contradiction between the poetic dialogues and the prose epilogue (Newsom, *The Book of Job: A Contest of Moral Imaginations* [New York: Oxford University Press, 2003], 234). This assumed contradiction allows interpreters to downplay God's affirmation of Job's speech in 42:7–8, while taking the divine speeches as a critique of Job.

am impelled to explore the wild possibility that God's speeches might cohere with the explicit approval Job receives in the epilogue to the book. Could it be that God answers Job from the whirlwind not to bury him but to praise him?[15]

To explore this wild possibility, I will focus on YHWH's second speech from the whirlwind (chaps. 40–41), exploring the status of God's appeal to the primordial monsters, Behemoth (40:15–24) and Leviathan (chap. 41 [40:25–41:26 MT]). This exploration will take up most of the rest of this chapter. As a subsidiary to this, I will try to answer two other questions: Of what does Job "repent" in his response to God's second speech? And why is there a second speech at all? (Why didn't the first suffice?)

Why Does God Appeal to the Beasts in the Second Speech?

So, first of all, what is the status of God's appeal to the primordial monsters? Why does God introduce them? And what is the basic point (or points) that the second speech tries to make by reference to Behemoth and Leviathan?

The Beasts as Embodiments of Chaos

The conventional interpretation (that God is showing off his power to abase Job) usually involves assuming that these beasts represent the forces of chaos that God conquered or subdued at creation.[16] That is, they assume an ancient Near Eastern "combat myth" or *Chaoskampf* background here, in which God defeats the primordial waters (usually the sea) and/or various monsters associated with water (usually understood as serpents or dragons) in order to create the ordered world. In the Babylonian myth *Enuma Elish*, the god Marduk conquers the primordial ocean/monster Tiamat, while in Ugaritic mythology, Baal conquers Sea/River and also Litan, a seven-headed dragon. But are Behemoth and Leviathan in God's second speech intended to represent the primordial forces of chaos?

The assumption that the ancient Near Eastern combat myth is in the background of these two beasts is not entirely unwarranted. Although it is possible to see actually existing zoological species as the observational basis or model

15. This is, of course, a play on Mark Antony's words: "Friends, Romans, countrymen, lend me your ears; / I come to bury Caesar, not to praise him." William Shakespeare, *Julius Caesar*, act 3, scene 2, MIT Shakespeare, http://shakespeare.mit.edu/julius_caesar/full.html.

16. John Day draws extensively on the Ugaritic background of the combat myth for his view that Behemoth and Leviathan represent "demonic creatures" that God defeated at the time of creation. Day, *God's Conflict with the Dragon and the Sea*, 83.

for these beasts (Behemoth deriving from the hippopotamus or possibly the water buffalo and Leviathan from the crocodile), there is enough of a mythic overlay to suggest more than particular zoological species.[17]

Behemoth is the plural of majesty of *bəhēmâ*,[18] the typical Hebrew word for a large (usually domesticated) land animal (indeed, the singular is often used as a collective noun, often rendered "cattle" or "livestock"). So the plural here seems to designate a mega animal, a beast par excellence, though this beast is equally at home in the water and on land (and it certainly isn't domesticated). This, combined with the description of Behemoth in Job 40:19 as the "first of the great acts of God" (an expression almost identical to what is said about wisdom in Prov. 8:22), suggests something more than a mere hippopotamus or water buffalo.

In the case of Leviathan, we have the vivid description of its fire-breathing abilities (Job 41:18–21 [41:10–13 MT]) and the comment in 41:25 that even the gods tremble at its power; this certainly suggests something beyond an ordinary crocodile. Such descriptions evoke the chaos monster of Ugaritic mythology—the seven-headed dragon or serpent known as Litan (also vocalized as Lotan or Litanu), a word cognate to the Hebrew Leviathan.

In the Baal cycle, the goddess Anat claims to have defeated Baal's enemies, which include the twisting (or crooked) serpent with seven heads:

> What enemy has risen against Baal,
>> what foe against the Rider on the Clouds?
> Didn't I demolish El's Darling, Sea?
>> Didn't I finish off the divine River, the Mighty?
>> Didn't I snare the Dragon and destroy him?

17. The now common identification of Behemoth with a hippopotamus and Leviathan with a crocodile goes back to Samuel Bochart's *Hierozoïcon, sive, bipartitum opus de animalibus Sacrae Scripturae*, 2 vols. (London: n.p., 1663). My thanks for this reference to John J. Bimson, "Fierce Beasts and Free Processes: A Proposed Reading of God's Speeches in the Book of Job," in *Wisdom, Science and the Scriptures: Essays in Honour of Ernest Lucas*, ed. Stephen Finamore and John Weaver (Eugene, OR: Pickwick, 2014), 17 (entire chapter 16–33).

18. A plural of majesty (sometimes called a *pluralis intensivus*) is a plural used as a singular, connoting majesty, excellence, or greatness. The most common plural of majesty in the Hebrew Bible is the word translated as "God." Likewise, the word *'ădōnāy* ("Lord" [lit. "my Lords"]) is a plural of majesty used for God, as in Job 28:28). "Salvation" (in the expression "my salvation" or "my help") is a plural of majesty used as an epithet for God in Pss. 42:5 [6 MT], 11 [12 MT]; 43:5. The Hebrew for "mother-in-law" occurs ten times in the book of Ruth in the plural and may be a plural of majesty, intended to convey the greatness or excellence of Naomi.

I demolished the Twisting Serpent,
    the seven-headed monster.[19]

Elsewhere the god Mot gives Baal credit for the victory:

When you killed Litan, the Fleeing Serpent,
    finished off the Twisting Serpent,
    the seven-headed monster . . .[20]

This fleeing and twisting serpent shows up in the Bible, in a text that announces YHWH's eschatological victory over the forces of evil. "On that day the LORD with his cruel and great and strong sword will punish Leviathan the fleeing serpent, Leviathan the twisting serpent, and he will kill the dragon that is in the sea" (Isa. 27:1). Another biblical text, which pictures the battle in primordial time (at creation), mentions the heads of Leviathan, without specifying their number.

You divided the sea by your might;
    you broke the heads of the dragons in the waters.
You crushed the heads of Leviathan. (Ps. 74:13–14)

Furthermore, the book of Job itself contains at least one cosmology in which God clearly vanquishes primordial chaos in order to found the world (26:5–14). According to Job in 26:11–13:

The pillars of heaven tremble,
    and are astounded at his [God's] rebuke.
By his power he stilled the Sea;
    by his understanding he struck down Rahab.
By his wind the heavens were made fair;
    his hand pierced the fleeing serpent.

Even though this particular text does not mention Leviathan by name, the epithet "the fleeing serpent" is a dead giveaway. So this account of creation, which is placed in Job's mouth (though sometimes thought to be Bildad's

19. *Baal*, tablet 3, column 3, lines 38–42, in *Stories from Ancient Canaan*, ed. and trans. Michael D. Coogan and Mark S. Smith, 2nd ed. (Louisville: Westminster John Knox, 2015), 120.
20. *Baal*, tablet 5, column 1, lines 1–5, in *Stories from Ancient Canaan*, 139.

words displaced), shows that the book of Job is indeed acquainted with the *Chaoskampf* motif.

How the Beasts Differ from the Forces of Chaos

Yet the description of both Behemoth and Leviathan in God's second speech *differs* from the typical conception of the chaos monsters that God subdued to create the world, on at least three counts.

First, neither Behemoth nor Leviathan is presented as intrinsically aggressive or violent. Although they are, indeed, fierce and dangerous, a close reading of the second speech reveals that these beasts are to be feared only if someone tries to capture or subdue them. In that case, they will fight back.

Second, Behemoth is explicitly said to be created by God in Job 40:15. In ancient Near Eastern mythology the deity does not create the forces of chaos but conquers them in order to create (they are impediments to an ordered cosmos). Yet here, God presents this wild beast as part of the created order (as Leviathan is portrayed in Ps. 104:26).[21]

Third, there is absolutely no conflict portrayed between God and either Behemoth or Leviathan; although God is able to conquer them, the text suggests that God has no reason to do so.[22] On the contrary, God is clearly proud of these two wild beasts! In much the same way that God celebrates the irrepressible wildness of the cavalcade of animals in his first speech (Job 38:39–39:30), here God boasts to Job about the fierce, untamable strength of Behemoth and Leviathan. Sounding like the writer of Hebrews recounting the heroes of faith (Heb. 11:32), God says of Leviathan, "I will not keep silence concerning its limbs, / or its mighty strength, or its splendid frame" (Job 41:12).[23] God is here like a proud father showing photos of his children and telling of their accomplishments.[24]

21. Likewise, God is said to have created the great sea beasts or dragons (*tannînîm*) in Gen. 1:21.

22. C. L. Seow notes that "nothing is said of the subjugation of these entities that seem utterly dangerous to human existence." Seow, *Job 1–21: Interpretation and Commentary*, Illuminations (Grand Rapids: Eerdmans, 2013), 103.

23. "And what more should I say? For time would fail me to tell of Gideon, Barak, Samson, Jephthah, of David and Samuel and the prophets—" (Heb. 11:32).

24. Seow speaks of God's "tribute" to the monsters (*Job 1–21*, 104). And Robert Alter writes, "What is remarkable about this whole powerfully vivid evocation of Leviathan is that the monotheistic poet has taken a figure from mythology, traditionally seen as the cosmic enemy of the god of order, and transformed it into this daunting creature that is preeminent in, but also very much a part of, God's teeming creation." Alter, *The Wisdom Books: Job, Proverbs, and Ecclesiastes: A Translation with Commentary* (New York: Norton, 2010), 175.

So the point of God's appeal to Behemoth and Leviathan in the second speech is not that Job (unlike God) is unable to subdue the forces of chaos (and so he should shut up). Nor is it that Job (like these beasts) is himself in need of subduing.

The Similarity between Job and the Beasts

Yet, on one point the conventional reading of the second speech is probably right. Job is, indeed, being compared to these beasts. The first clue is the opening description of Behemoth in 40:15: "Look at Behemoth / which I made just as I made you" (NRSV) or "which I made along with you" (NIV). This is the only specific reference to the creation of humans in God's speeches, and it suggests a parallel of sorts between Job and this particular beast.

We should note that Job had earlier compared himself to the mythic forces of chaos in a manner that agrees with the assumptions of many contemporary interpreters. Thus in 7:12, he asks God, "Am I the Sea, or the Dragon, / that you set a guard over me?"[25] This question, coming right after Job's assertion in 7:11 that he will *not* restrain his mouth but that he will, indeed, give voice to his anguish and complain in his bitterness, suggests that he expects that God wants to subdue him, like the chaos monster, especially because of his untamed, wild speech.[26] That is certainly what Job's friends would like God to do.

But that is not the way God treats the Sea, according to 38:8–11. There, in God's first speech from the whirlwind, this traditional symbol of watery chaos is portrayed not as an enemy to be subdued but as a rambunctious infant that God wraps in swaddling clothes when it first burst energetically from the womb. And while it does need boundaries, as children do (and God prescribes them), the picture is less like a warlike conquest and more like a parent setting limits for a toddler who has hit the "terrible twos," or possibly like putting up a child gate to protect an overactive child. The picture is of energetic nurture, rather than anything adversarial.[27]

And this is true not only of God's relationship to the Sea but also of God's relationship to Behemoth and Leviathan (and thus, by implication, of God's

25. Note the echo of Anat's claim to have snared or bound the Dragon.

26. Job later makes a similar assumption about how God treats the Sea (trampling on it in 9:8) and the forces of chaos (causing them to cower before his anger in 9:13).

27. On God's parental care of the Sea, see J. Gerald Janzen, "On the Moral Nature of God's Power: Yahweh and the Sea in Job and Deutero-Isaiah," *CBQ* 56 (1994): 468 (entire article 458–78).

relationship to Job). Through a complex web of associations, Job's fearless and courageous strength, by which he stood up to the verbal and emotional assaults of his friends, is evoked in the description of Behemoth and Leviathan.[28] Like them, Job has been impervious to the assaults of his adversaries, and this is a good thing.

The core of the comparison is found in the description of the powerful mouth of each beast.[29] Whereas 40:23 pictures Behemoth standing fearlessly facing the turbulent Jordan, as its waters rush against its open mouth, Job had previously (in 6:15–21) compared his friends' attempts at consolation to a treacherous wadi or torrent bed that at first seemed full of rushing water but that quickly dried up and disappeared in the face of Job's sufferings and complaint. That Job was able to verbally stand against and outlast his companions (much as Behemoth is able to stand against the raging Jordan) belies his own sense of impotence just a few verses before (6:12–13). Indeed, Job's own self-description in 6:12 ("Is my strength the strength of stones? / or is my flesh bronze?") is echoed in God's description of Behemoth in 40:18 ("Its bones are tubes of bronze, / its limbs like bars of iron"). The implication is that Job, in standing up to his friends, is more powerful than he thinks.

But even Behemoth's strength is as nothing to Leviathan's, since he "counts iron as straw, and bronze as rotten wood" (41:27 [41:19 MT]). And Job is indeed like Leviathan, this most powerful of all beasts. Thus 41:1 portrays Leviathan as having an irrepressible tongue and 41:3–4 explains that this beast won't plead for mercy and speak soft words of acquiescence to its attackers (just like Job, we may add). On the contrary, we are told of Leviathan's fearful visage (his eyes, mouth, nostrils, breath) from which come heat, light, flames, and smoke:

> Its [Leviathan's] sneezes flash forth light,
>   and its eyes are like the eyelids of the dawn.

28. William Brown is particularly good at exhibiting these manifold associations. See Brown, *Wisdom's Wonder: Character, Creation, and Crisis in the Bible's Wisdom Literature* (Grand Rapids: Eerdmans, 2014), 123–24. Also John G. Gammie, "Behemoth and Leviathan: On the Didactic and Theological Significance of Job 40:15–41:26," in *Israelite Wisdom: Theological and Literary Essays in Honor of Samuel Terrien*, ed. John G. Gammie et al. (Missoula, MT: Scholars Press, 1978), 217–321; and Samuel E. Balentine, "'What Are Human Beings, That You Make So Much of Them?': Divine Disclosure from the Whirlwind," in *God in the Fray: A Tribute to Walter Brueggemann*, ed. Tod Linafelt and Timothy K. Beal (Minneapolis: Fortress, 1998), 271–74 (entire chapter 259–78).

29. Also noted by Balentine, "'What Are Human Beings,'" 273.

> From its mouth go flaming torches;
>> sparks of fire leap out.
> Out of its nostrils comes smoke,
>> as from a boiling pot and burning rushes.
> Its breath kindles coals,
>> and a flame comes out of its mouth. (41:18–21)

Leviathan is thus a living, breathing version of the Sinai theophany, mirroring in his wildness the manifestation of God's blazing glory at the mountain in Exodus 19.[30] And Job's friends had certainly experienced his incendiary speech and criticized his fiery, untamable talk as inappropriate. As William Brown puts it, "Job and Leviathan are linked together by their overpowering discourse."[31]

Different Estimates of the Human Condition

A particularly important critique of Job's speech by one of his friends is found in Job 4:17–21, where Eliphaz paints a particularly dreary portrait of the human condition. Using the word *'enôš* for mortal humanity (a term also found in Ps. 8), Eliphaz asks:

> Can mortals ['enôš] be righteous before God?
>> Can human beings [geber] be pure before their Maker?
> Even in his servants he [God] puts no trust,
>> and his angels he charges with error;
> how much more those who live in houses of clay,
>> whose foundation is in the dust,
>> who are crushed like a moth. (Job 4:17–21)

Eliphaz repeats his dreary estimate of the human condition in his second speech (15:14–16) and again in his third speech (22:1–3), followed by Bildad in his third speech (25:4–6). In each case, they begin with an almost identical rhetorical question about the human status in view of God, asking whether a human being can possibly be righteous or pure or of use to God. The answer is, of course, no. So Job, don't expect much from God. You're insignificant.

---

30. There is a parallel also in the danger of coming too close; anyone who touches the mountain will die (Exod. 19:12).
31. Brown, *Wisdom's Wonder*, 124.

This is dreary indeed, and it is quite different from the royal picture of humanity found in Psalm 8, which asks, "What is *'enôš* [this mortal creature] that you care about him / and the son of *'ādām* that you visit him?" (8:4 [8:5 MT]; my translation). And the psalm goes on to speak of the glory and honor with which mortals have been crowned and the rule over various creatures God has entrusted them with (8:5 [8:6 MT]). In all this, the text says, they are little less than God (or the gods), a very high status indeed.

It is important that Job himself echoes language from Psalm 8 in his answer to Eliphaz (in chap. 7). The trouble is that he seems to have internalized Eliphaz's negative evaluation of the human condition and thus Job's appeal to the psalm reads like a parody or satire.[32] What is *'enôš*? asks Job in 7:17–19.

> What are human beings [*'enôš*], that you make so much of them,
>> that you set your mind on them,
> visit them every morning,
>> test them every moment?
> Will you not look away from me for a while,
>> let me alone until I swallow my spittle? (7:17–19)

And he accuses God, the watcher of humanity, of targeting him (7:20).[33]

The intertextuality of Psalm 8 with Job 7 (and the similarity of Job's and Eliphaz's estimates of the human condition in chaps. 4 and 7) suggests that a significant part of the issue here is the question of the appropriate status and function of humanity vis-à-vis God.[34] Are humans in God's world merely

32. Although it is traditional to claim that Job is parodying the psalm, Raymond C. Van Leeuwen has argued that we might think of a movement in the opposite direction, since Ps. 8 deviates from a more common negative estimate of the human condition (in which Job's complaint participates) (Van Leeuwen, "Psalm 8.5 and Job 7.17–18: A Mistaken Scholarly Commonplace?," in *The World of the Arameans I: Biblical Studies in Honor of Paul-Eugene Dion*, ed. P. M. Michèle Daviau et al., JSOTSup 324 [Sheffield: Sheffield Academic Press, 2001], 205–15). Seow, perhaps wisely, recognizes the ambiguous directionality of the texts. Seow, *Job 1–21*, 41–44.

33. The second time Eliphaz articulates his negative estimate of the human condition (15:14), he echoes Job's phrasing from 7:17 ("What is *'enôš* . . . ?"). But before that, Job's response to Bildad in 9:2 ("How can a mortal [*'enôš*] be just before God?") had echoed Eliphaz's question from 4:17. Here also Job seems to have internalized Eliphaz's negative estimate of the human condition.

34. Kathryn Shifferdecker agrees that the question "What is humanity?" is important for understanding the book of Job, though she comes to quite different conclusions than I do about how the book answers this question. See Shifferdecker, *Out of the Whirlwind*, 82, where she suggests that God's initial question to Job (38:2) is "designed to put Job in his place."

insignificant, even degraded, beings (Eliphaz) or powerless victims (Job)? Or, on the contrary, do they have a God-ordained (and God-affirmed) royal dignity and status (Ps. 8)? And what are the implications of this dignity for human speech, even speech in relation to God?[35]

It is intriguing that there are royal overtones to the description of Leviathan in the book of Job. At the end of the second speech, God says of Leviathan, "On earth it has no equal, / a creature without fear. / It surveys everything that is lofty; / it is king over all that are proud" (41:33–34 [41:25–26 MT]). The first phrase "it has no equal" can also mean "it has no ruler" since *mošel* (derived from the verb *māšal*) can refer to either likeness or governance. Perhaps this is a double entendre. At any rate, this description of Leviathan as the most royal of God's creatures evokes the description of the human vocation—found not only in Psalm 8:3–5 but also in Genesis 1:26–28, where humans, in God's image and likeness, are granted dominion over the earth.

But the connection of Leviathan's royal status to his gaze over the lofty and his rule over the proud at the end of God's second speech (Job 41:33–34 [41:25–26 MT]) is important also for interpreting God's challenge to Job at the start of this same speech (40:6–14). If God positively values Leviathan's power over the proud, then perhaps we need to reevaluate God's challenge to Job to look at the proud and abase them (40:10–13).[36] Perhaps this is meant not as a put down of Job but as a challenge that Job might actually rise to.

The challenge to Job in 40:10 ("Deck yourself with majesty and dignity; / clothe yourself with glory and splendor") might well be alluding to the royal status of humans in Psalm 8, who are there said to be crowned with "glory and honor" (and one of the words in each case is the same). The very same word pair from Job 40:10, "glory and splendor" (*hôd wəhādār*), is used in

---

35. J. Gerald Janzen recognizes that the question of what it means to be human—in particular, the relationship of human mortality and human dignity—is central to understanding the book of Job: "What does it mean to affirm at one and the same time that to be human is to be dust and the royal image of God? Can these two metaphors be sustained together?" (Janzen, *Job*, Interpretation [Atlanta: John Knox, 1985], 13). A similar approach underlies Balentine's article, "'What Are Human Beings.'"

36. The term used for the "proud" whom Job is to bring low (40:11) is *gē'eh*, while the phrase in the Leviathan passage is *bənê-šāḥaṣ* (literally "sons of pride"; 41:34 [41:26 MT]), which occurs in only one other place in the Hebrew Bible (28:8), where context suggests it is a reference to wild beasts (thus JPS Tanakh translates the phrase as "proud beasts" in both places). Perhaps just as Leviathan rules the proud wild animals, Job is to exercise his rulership over proud humans (and, indeed, Job had been taking the pride and confidence of his friends down a notch in his replies to them; see, for example, 13:2–13).

Psalm 21:5 [21:6 MT] to describe what God endows the king with. And the fact that this same Hebrew word pair is used of *God* in other psalms (Pss. 96:6; 104:1; 111:3) suggests a clear *imago Dei* theme.[37] And, indeed, both Psalm 8 and Genesis 1 compare humans to God in their royal power and status. Consonant with both Psalm 8 and Genesis 1, the royal motif in God's second speech to Job is a matter of likeness to God. So when God asks Job in 40:9, "Have you an arm *like* God, / and can you thunder with a voice *like* his?" it is entirely possible that such bracing questions (much like the rhetorical questions addressed to the dispirited exiles in Isa. 40) are meant not as a put-down but to push Job beyond his passivity to take up his royal vocation.[38]

But what passivity is this? Hasn't Job been enacting his royal fearlessness, abasing the pride of his three friends in his fiery discourse, throughout the book? Indeed, he has. But after God's first speech, which was intended to correct his misjudgment of God's governance of the cosmos, Job is rendered mute.

The Lesson about Creation in the First Speech

Here it is important to clarify the difference between the two speeches, since this will help us to understand Job's response in 42:1–6, where he quotes from each speech and summarizes his response to them, sequentially. It will also help us understand Job's initial response to the first speech (at the start of chap. 40), which is quite different from his later response, after the second speech.

I wish there was space to fully explore the amazing and complex lesson about creation that God gives Job in chapters 38–39. We might reflect, for example, on Tom McLeish's insights on the wisdom embedded in creation and God's challenge to Job to involve himself in searching this out.[39] Or we

37. The NRSV translates the word pair *hôd wəhādār* in reference to the king as "splendor and majesty" (Ps. 21:5) and in reference to God as "honor and majesty" (96:6; 104:1; 111:3).

38. The terms for "counsel" (*'ēṣâ*) and "justice" (*mišpāṭ*), which God uses in his introductory questions to Job (38:2; 40:8), occur together in only one other text in the Bible—namely, in Isa. 40:12–14, where God questions the exiles about their understanding of his purposes. My thanks to J. Gerald Janzen for this insight. Janzen, "Job and the Lord of the East Wind," *HBT* 2, no. 1 (2004): 9–10 (entire article 2–47).

39. This is the theme of the brilliant chapter on Job in McLeish, "At the Summit: The Book of Job," in *Faith and Wisdom in Science* (Oxford: Oxford University Press, 2014), 102–48. McLeish, a Christian working in the field of biophysics, with a focus on "soft matter" (who had a role in discovering Brownian motion at the molecular level), draws on Job (and much else in the Bible in his other chapters) to develop a proposal about a thick theology of science that can help ground the actual practice of science today.

could follow J. Gerald Janzen's insight into the placement of God's speeches in the climatological cycle of the book, where the theophany from the storm signals the coming of the autumn rains to renew the land (and Job's arid life).[40] For my purposes it will be sufficient to focus on this speech as a response to Job's complaint, especially his protest concerning God's wisdom (or lack thereof) in ruling the world. The responsive nature of the speech is hinted at in God's opening challenge to Job: "Who is this that darkens counsel by words without knowledge?" (38:2). If we understand "counsel" (*'ēṣâ*) as a reference to God's design in constructing and administering the cosmos, which Job has been denigrating, then it is no wonder God wants to set Job right.[41]

However, God sets Job right not by telling him outright that he is wrong but by taking him on a tour of the wonders of the created order—all of which God had (and still has) a hand in—of which Job is ignorant. YHWH's opening question (38:2) suggests that in contrast to Job's attempt to "darken" or disparage God's design of the world (including his desire to reverse light back into darkness in chap. 3), the Creator plans to enlighten Job about what the world is really like.

40. Janzen explores the annual changes in the climate of Israel and environs in relation to the structure of the book of Job. Drawing on records of climate phenomena in the area, he notes that the rainy season typically lasts six months (mid-October to mid-April), with the hot, dry season in between (mid-June to mid-September). Taking his cue from the mention of storms in the prologue and the coming of YHWH in a storm at the end of the book, he correlates this with the two "interchange" periods between seasons (in mid-April and mid-September), where east and west winds alternate. Whereas the calamities of the prologue take place during the interchange period from rain to drought (note the mention of storms and lightning in the prologue), Job's unfruitful dialogues with his friends take place during the arid summer, which correlates with his acknowledgment that his soul or appetite (*nepeš*) has become bitter (3:20; 10:1; 21:25). The storm out of which YHWH speaks signals the beginning of the second interchange period, thus the beginning of the autumn rains, when both the land and Job's life will be restored. It took a biblical scholar like Janzen, who was raised in a Mennonite farming family, with a deep connection to the natural world, to attend to the climatological dimensions of the book of Job. For his full analysis, see Janzen, "Job and the Lord of the East Wind," 2–47.

41. Commentators have pointed out various ways in which both of YHWH's speeches respond to particular things Job has said—like the references to light and darkness in the first speech (38:12–13, 19–21), which may respond to Job's desire to curse the day and night of his birth (3:3–10). Or God's portrayal of Leviathan in the second speech (41:1–34 [40:25–41:26 MT]), including the comparison of this monster's eyes with "the eyelids of the dawn" (41:18). This clearly responds to Job's mention of Leviathan in 3:8 and his desire that the night of his birth not see "the eyelids of the morning" in 3:9 (the NRSV renders the identical Hebrew phrase differently in the two places, perhaps not recognizing the literary allusion). See Alex Breitkopf, "The Importance of Response in the Interpretation of Job," *Canadian Theological Review* 4, no. 1 (2015): 1–14.

What message is God trying to communicate to Job in the first speech? I propose that God is correcting Job's theology, his assumptions about what the world is like and the nature of God's relationship to that world.

Job had impugned God's administration of the cosmos based on the assumption of a strict act-consequence schema, in which God is expected to ensure (directly or indirectly) that the appropriate reward or punishment follows from righteous or sinful actions on the part of humans. This is the implicit basis of Job's complaint—God had been mismanaging the world, including Job's own life (since he had suffered the consequences for sins that he did not commit).

Contrary to the idea (often proposed) that God demonstrates to Job his power or control over creation, I submit that God shows Job his *delight* in creation. Of course, God is powerful; but that is not the point of either speech. Rather, in the first speech, the Creator opens up the vistas of creation—from the cosmic to the zoological—for Job to see. God does this in order to expand Job's perspective about the nature of created reality and God's role in it. God shows Job a world significantly different from what he had assumed.

How is the world that God exhibits different from the world of Job's assumptions? First of all, this world extends significantly beyond human knowledge and human concerns. God not only describes an intricately awe-inspiring cosmos but points out dimensions of creation (like the storehouses of the snow in 38:22 or the places of the constellations of the heavens in 38:31–33) that are simply inaccessible to humans.

The full range of the first speech moves from the founding of the earth (38:4–7) to the birth of the sea (38:8–11), the rising of the sun (38:12–15), the hidden depths of reality (including Sheol and the realms of light and darkness; 38:16–21), and the complexity of the rain cycle (38:22–30, 34–38), interrupted briefly by a reference to the constellations (38:31–33). God then describes various animals that exist beyond the borders of human habitation and that God is aware of and delights in (38:39–39:30).

To some extent, the view that God is decentering Job is valid, in that God opens up to Job vistas of reality that go beyond Job's anthropocentric concerns. However, as William Brown suggests, this new perspective also serves to comfort Job, who had earlier articulated his sense of alienation from human society (19:15).[42]

---

42. William P. Brown, "Job and the 'Comforting' Cosmos," in *Seeking Wisdom's Depths and Torah's Heights: Essays in Honor of Samuel E. Balentine*, ed. Barry R. Huff and Patricia Vesely (Macon, GA: Smyth & Helwys, 2020), 260 (entire chapter 249–68).

Not only had Job compared society's outcasts to wild asses (onagers) that scavenge in the wilderness for food and go naked in the cold and the rain, without shelter (24:5–8), but he described himself as "a brother of jackals, and a companion of ostriches" (30:29), animals that represent urban desolation, and even mourning, in the Bible.[43] Job had meant these comparisons disparagingly, as a way of expressing his low estate. But when God exhibits delight in wild animals (including the ostrich and the wild ass [38:13–18; 39:5–8]), this reframing invites Job to see that, even in his suffering and social ostracism, he is not beyond God's care.

The second characteristic of the world portrayed in the first speech is that God is intimately involved with creation. As Creator, God laid the earth's foundation (38:4), clothed the sea in clouds (38:8), commanded the dawn (38:12), stored up snow in vaults (38:22), cut a channel for the water (38:25), leads out the constellations (38:32), and calls to the lightnings so that they respond, "Here we are [*hinnēnû*]!" (38:35)—the plural form of Abraham's response when God calls him: "Here I am!" (Gen. 22:1, 11).

God also takes an interest in various wild and weird animals and is attentive to their strange habits—many of which are listed in Job 38:39–39:38. Indeed, God's active involvement with these animals includes providing food for the lion and raven (38:39–41), granting the wild ass its freedom and a home in the wilderness (39:5–6), giving strength to the horse (39:19) and wisdom for the flight of the hawk and eagle (39:26).[44] Contrary to Job's accusations, then, YHWH is no *Deus absconditus*, or even a distant Creator, who has set the world in motion and no longer attends to its needs.

Yet while God is involved in the world, this involvement does not match traditional notions of unilateral divine sovereignty. The third point communicated in the first speech is that God does not micromanage the cosmos; God's care for creatures does not entail his precise control of them. The Creator

43. Jackals especially are said to prowl in the ruins of cities (Isa. 13:22; Jer. 9:11 [9:10 MT]; 10:22; 49:33; 51:37). Jackals and ostriches are mentioned together roaming the ruins of Edom (Isa. 34:13); they are also mentioned together for their eerie cries, which are compared to human mourning (Mic. 1:8).

44. It is worth pointing out that God begins the list of animals with the lion, the wild and dangerous beast par excellence in Israel's world. But in contrast to the traditional ancient Near Eastern picture of the king as the master of animals—epitomized in numerous bas reliefs depicting the Neo-Assyrian king's lion hunt—YHWH asks Job not if he can *hunt* the lion but if he can hunt *prey for the lion* (38:39). For a detailed analysis of the widespread Assyrian evidence for the king as master of animals, see Michael Dick, "The Neo-Assyrian Royal Lion Hunt and Yahweh's Answer to Job," *JBL* 125, no. 2 (2006): 243–70.

is certainly involved with creatures but gives them significant freedom to be themselves (even to be their wild and quirky selves). This freedom God grants creatures includes their vulnerability, so that the strength, dignity, and beauty of various wild animals is intertwined with the realities of struggle and death—from which God does not automatically protect them. In this portrayal of the world, God is implicitly answering (and correcting) Job's assumptions of a tight act-consequence structure to the universe. As Terence Fretheim explains, "For all the world's order and coherence, it doesn't run like a machine; a certain randomness, ambiguity, unpredictability, and play characterize its complex life."[45]

Why Is There a Second Speech?

Although God intended to correct Job's theology in the first speech, it isn't clear that the speech accomplishes this goal. Rather, God's attempt at correction seems to have battered Job into submission and rendered him mute.

God begins the first speech by telling Job, "Gird up your loins like a man [like a *geber*—a word that often has connotations of vigor], / I will question you, and you shall declare to me" (38:3). But when God finishes his survey of the irrepressible wildness of the animal kingdom in 39:30 (ending admittedly on a somewhat distasteful and grisly note about birds of prey feeding on blood), there is only ringing silence.

This is why the narrator adds what I take to be a speech resumption formula in 40:1, followed by another challenge. "And the LORD [again] said to Job: / 'Shall a faultfinder contend with the Almighty? / Anyone who argues with God *must respond*.'" And Job finally does speak in 40:3–5 but only to admit his insignificance (Eliphaz's perspective has won out[46]); he lays his hand over his mouth, *refusing to answer*.

The irrepressible human speaker, who has poured out a torrent of honest, abrasive words to his friends, is here silenced by God, who actually wants a vigorous conversation partner—one who bracingly faces his Creator, in accordance with his royal calling. God, it seems, has unintentionally overpowered Job.[47]

45. Fretheim, *God and World in the Old Testament: A Relational Theology of Creation* (Nashville: Abingdon, 2005), 239.
46. Here we may remember Eliphaz's put-down: "Can human beings [*geber*] be pure before their Maker?" (4:17).
47. This has sometimes been my experience with students. Having challenged a student to clarify their ideas or having suggested an alternative way of thinking in response to a comment they made, I have waited for a response, only to find that the student is intimidated and

So God speaks again. And his opening challenge to Job in the second speech (40:7) repeats the words from the start of the first speech. "Gird up your loins like a *geber* / I will question you, and you *will* declare to me." By now it should be clear why there is a second speech. God was not satisfied with Job's abased silence. God desired a worthy dialogue partner.[48]

Why else would the Creator of the cosmos address Job personally, and at such length? God deems Job worthy of an answer (this subverts the notion that humans are insignificant in God's world, which a surface reading of the speeches might suggest).[49] Humans are so significant that God speaks at length to at least one of them in a personal theophany.[50] Indeed, God speaks twice to Job. And in his second speech, God encourages Job in his untamed (royal) wildness by praising (even glorying in) two powerful beasts who, like Job (at his best), will not be subdued.

And Job understands. The second speech has the intended effect. Job girds up his loins and rises to the challenge.[51] Whereas at the start of chapter 40 Job

---

unwilling to engage in dialogue (without some further prompting and assurance that I won't simply dismiss their reply).

48. Until recently I have thought that my proposal for why there is a second speech was unique to me. But since developing this interpretation, I have found anticipations of my proposal in the work of J. Gerald Janzen and Terence Fretheim, biblical interpreters with whom I have always sensed a deep kinship. Janzen suggests that Job's mature response to God in 42:1–6 "comes as a replacement of 40:3–5," since in his first response "Job had resolved on silence," but now he speaks (in agreement with YHWH), which is "remarkable" (Janzen, *Job*, 248). Fretheim comments: "God may also consider Job's initial response (40:3–5) much too self-effacing, and so God continues to speak until Job responds in more direct, less self-negating ways." Fretheim, *God and World in the Old Testament*, 238.

49. This point is also made by Janzen, *Job*, 229, and Balentine, "'What Are Human Beings,'" 265.

50. Janzen's insights about the link between YHWH's answer out of the storm and the coming of the autumn rains (in "Job and the Lord of the East Wind," 33–35) suggest, further, that before YHWH actually says anything, Job first would have smelled rain (which would have awakened and enlivened his previously bitter *nepeš* at a visceral level). As Janzen points out ("Job and the Lord of the East Wind," 7), Job himself "wistfully observed":

> For there is hope for a tree,
>   if it is cut down, that it will sprout again,
>   and that its shoots will not cease.
> Though its root grows old in the earth,
>   and its stump dies in the ground,
>   yet at the scent of water it will bud
>   and put forth branches like a young plant. (14:7–9)

51. Gerhard von Rad has suggested that what is important about the divine speeches is the mere fact that God answers Job (not the content of what God says). Job has demanded a direct encounter with God prior to this (13:22; 14:15; 23:5; 31:35), so he is finally getting his desire. Von Rad, *Wisdom in Israel* (Nashville: Abingdon, 1972), 221–26.

had refused to answer, at the start of chapter 42, we find his mature, measured response to *both* of God's speeches.

Job's Final Response to Both of God's Speeches

Job begins by addressing the upshot of YHWH's first speech, indicated by his (approximate) quotation of God's opening question at the start of that speech: "Who is this that darkens counsel by words without knowledge?" (38:2).

Job first admits: "I know that you can do all things, / and that no purpose of yours can be thwarted" (42:2).[52] Then comes the quotation (or paraphrase) from the first speech: "Who is this that hides counsel without knowledge?" (42:3a), which leads to Job's response: "Therefore I have uttered what I did not understand, / things too wonderful for me, which I did not know" (42:3b).

Job had questioned God's cosmic governance, assuming that God ruled unjustly, wreaking havoc in the world, with capricious power. But now he has come to understand the wonders (*niplā'ôt*) that he was previously unaware of—namely, that God celebrates the wildness of creation, giving untamable creatures great freedom to be themselves.[53] He acknowledges that God does not micromanage the cosmos. At least, that is my reading of the import of Job's response in 42:3, given the context of the two speeches.[54]

Then Job responds to the second speech also with a quote from the start of that speech. He says: "Hear, and I will speak; / I will question you, and you declare to me" (42:4). Both the NRSV and the NIV (following the opinion of many commentators) treat the entirety of verse 4 as a quotation of what God had previously said (by the insertion of quotation marks around the entire verse).[55] However, only the second line actually quotes God's words, reproducing verbatim God's demand that Job answer him—stated originally at the start of the first speech (38:3) and repeated at the beginning of the

---

52. The consonants of the MT (the *Ketiv*) indicate "You know," but the Masoretes corrected this with a marginal note (the *Qere*) indicating that it should be read as "I know." I am not sure that this change makes a great deal of difference to the interpretation of Job's response.

53. Although *niplā'ôt* is typically used of YHWH's astounding works of salvation or deliverance on behalf of Israel (Exod. 3:30; 15:11; 34:10; Josh. 3:5; Pss. 98:1; 106:22; Mic. 7:15), the term is also used of God's creative wonders (Job 5:9; 37:5, 14; Ps. 136:4; Prov. 30:18).

54. As Samuel Balentine puts it, "Through this review of creation, Job is invited to understand that God intends not to eliminate or banish forces of opposition and challenge but to preserve and direct them, because they are vital elements in the architecture of life." Balentine, "'What Are Human Beings,'" 267.

55. "Hear, and I will speak" is sometimes thought to replace God's opening words in 38:3 and 40:7, "Gird up your loins like a man."

second speech (40:7). In light of this demand that Job answer, it is significant that Job's opening words in verse 4 are: "Hear, and *I will speak.*"

Job has finally understood the point of God's challenge, that the Creator actually wanted a response from him. So Job replaces his prior silence after the first speech (implied in 40:1 and, paradoxically, *stated* in 40:3–5) with a clear response. But it took God's second speech (celebrating two untamable beasts with big mouths) to get Job to this point.

And what does Job actually say in response to YHWH's second speech? "I had heard of you by the hearing of the ear, / but now my eye sees you" (42:5). It took a personal theophany, a manifestation of YHWH (in which Job got an earful) to move him beyond his prior opinion of God (which was based on hearsay).[56] And then comes the fateful conclusion, in which (as the NRSV has it) Job confesses, "Therefore I despise myself, / and repent in dust and ashes" (42:6).

Of What Does Job "Repent"?

As for the meaning of 42:6, there are numerous proposed translations for this interpretive crux. Suffice it to say that few (if any) contemporary biblical scholars are satisfied with the rendering found in standard published translations of the Bible (from the KJV to the NIV to the NRSV) as it is unsupported from the Hebrew.[57]

My own proposed translation is: "Therefore I retract and am comforted about dust and ashes."

Here we need to examine three Hebrew words that underlie the traditional English rendering. But even beyond the translation per se, there is the question of the import of Job's words: What does he mean?

The verb *'em'as* (from the root *mā'as*), typically translated "I despise myself," has no object in 42:6 ("myself" is supplied by translators), and this root is never used elsewhere in the Hebrew Qal stem to mean "despising oneself."

56. William Brown makes the point that while Job mentions seeing God and God does appear to him in the whirlwind (a theophany), the focus of this appearance/theophany is what God *says* to Job (so Job's seeing comes through a new hearing). As Brown puts it, Job receives "a divine 'logophany,' for want of a better term." Even the powerful visualization of creation that is presented in these chapters is mediated "through the power of poetic discourse." Brown, "Job and the 'Comforting' Cosmos," 252–53.

57. For the variety of interpretations (and translations) possible for this verse, see Dale Patrick, "The Translation of Job XLII, 6," *VT* 26 (1976): 369–71; William Morrow, "Consolation, Rejection, and Repentance in Job 42:6," *JBL* 105 (1986): 211–25; and Ellen J. van Wolde, "Job 42,1–6: The Reversal of Job," in *The Book of Job*, ed. W. A. M. Beuken, BETL 114 (Leuven: Leuven University Press, 1994), 223–50.

Given the use of this verb elsewhere in the book of Job, where it means "to reject or refuse something" (5:17; 8:20; 9:21; 10:3; 19:18; 30:1; 31:13; 34:33; 36:5), I take it that Job here says something like, "I retract" or "I recant."[58] But what exactly is Job retracting or taking back?

I see two main possibilities. Job could be signaling that he is withdrawing his accusation of God's injustice (usually understood as a lawsuit), which was based on his mistaken assumptions of how God ran the universe.[59] But Job was already reduced to silence after God's first speech and refused to answer further; that refusal was equivalent to the retraction of his accusation/lawsuit. So in 42:6 he would be (re)stating the fact of this retraction.

Alternatively, Job could be retracting his inappropriate, passive response to God after the first speech, when he refused to answer (40:3–5). It is possible that both retractions could be in view (they are, after all, integrally connected); but only the second (the retraction of his silence) is new here.

The second verb in 42:6 is from the root *nāḥam* in the Niphal stem, which can refer either to regretting, being sorry, or changing one's mind (that is, "repentance") or to consoling oneself or being comforted.[60] The first option is typically found in published translations of the Bible, although the Common English Bible (CEB) bucks the trend and opts for the rendering of comfort: "Therefore, I relent and find comfort / on dust and ashes."

Given that the Niphal of the root *nāḥam* is consistently used in the book of Job for comfort and not for repentance (2:11; 7:13; 16:2; 21:34; 29:25; 42:11), comfort is the likely meaning here as well.[61] This still, of course,

---

58. There is another possibility for the meaning of the root *mā'as*—namely, "melt" or "dissolve," which is represented by the LXX. William Brown draws on this possibility in his earlier translation: "Therefore I waste away, / yet am comforted over dust and ashes" (Brown, *Wisdom's Wonder*, 126). But Brown later changed his mind about how to translate this (see below).

59. Job's last use of the verb *'em'as* prior to 42:6 fits this meaning. He stated that he never rejected or dismissed (*'em'as*) the cause (*mišpāṭ*) of one of his slaves if they ever brought a complaint against him (31:13). So here he could be saying that he is dismissing his own case against God. Legal language abounds in Job's speeches (9:2–35; 10:2, 6–7, 17; 13:6–12, 17–28; 14:3; 16:8, 19–21; 19:5, 7, 25; 23:6). See Michael Brennan Dick, "The Legal Metaphor in Job 31," *CBQ* 41 (1979): 37–50.

60. The first-person form used here is ambiguous and could theoretically be in the Piel stem, but most interpreters take the verb to be Niphal, since the meaning of the Piel ("to comfort, give comfort") does not make sense here.

61. I used to think that Job was repenting of (changing his position about) his previous "dust and ashes" stance of abasement. In that case, the line "I repent concerning dust and ashes" would basically repeat (and expand on) the first line, where he retracted his initial point of view (which was equivalent to "dust and ashes"). I proposed this interpretation in Middleton, "Why the 'Greater Good' Isn't a Defense: Classical Theodicy in Light of the Biblical Genre of Lament," *Koinonia* 9, nos. 1&2 (1997): 98 (entire article 81–113). But I now think that "comfort"

leaves open the point of the entire phrase (which ends with "dust and ashes").[62]

So we come to the preposition 'al, which does not mean "in" but rather "on" or "upon" (if taken spatially) or "concerning," "for," or "about" (signifying that for which Job is consoled or comforted). This second sense of 'al occurs with the verb nāḥam just a few verses later, when Job's family comes to *comfort* him *for* ('al) his troubles (42:11). That is most likely the meaning of 'al also in 42:6.

So I think that Job is saying that he is now "consoled" or "comforted" about the fact that he is simply "dust and ashes."[63] In other words, he has come to accept that the fragile nature of the human condition, with all its suffering (the human status as "dust and ashes," which he has experienced), is not incompatible with the royal dignity and importance of humanity in God's sight, evident in God's willingness both to hear Job's complaint and to answer him.[64]

This interpretation draws on the only other occurrences of the expression "dust and ashes" in the Hebrew Bible—Job 30:19 and Genesis 18:27.

Earlier in the book (during his final speech), Job complained that God had cast him into the mire and so he had become "dust and ashes" (30:19). Given that negative usage, it seems that in 42:6 Job moves beyond his despair and comes to accept that despite being but "dust and ashes" he has been heard— and taken seriously—by the Creator of the cosmos.

Beyond the two Joban references, the only other occurrence of the phrase is in Genesis 18:27, where Abraham describes himself as "dust and ashes," although this is combined with great boldness toward God, even audacity.

---

rather than "repentance" is much more likely to be the meaning in this context. Another factor in deciding on a translation is that when this verb means "repent" elsewhere in the Bible, it typically refers to *God* changing his mind.

62. Although Nicholas Ansell understands 42:6 as Job repenting of dust and ashes (with consolation or comfort being no more than a secondary meaning), his overall understanding of Job's transformation is in line with my own. Ansell, "Fantastic Beasts and Where to Find The(ir Wisdo)m," in *Playing with Leviathan: Interpretation and Reception of Monsters from the Biblical World*, ed. Koert van Bekkum, Jaap Dekker, Henk van de Kamp, and Eric Peels, TBN 21 (Leiden: Brill, 2017), 104 (entire article 90–114).

63. This is similar to William Brown's most recent translation proposal: "Therefore, I relent / and am comforted over dust and ashes." Brown, "Job and the 'Comforting' Cosmos," 252.

64. Job's comfort about "dust and ashes" may also be related to Leviathan's royal dignity. Although no one on earth (lit. "on dust") is Leviathan's ruler/master (41:33–34 [41:25–26 MT]), yet perhaps one on dust—namely, Job—may be his equal/likeness (playing on the dual meanings of *mošel*; see p. 115 above).

The context is Abraham's dispute with God over the justice of destroying Sodom if there are righteous people living there. In that context, Abraham tells God that he is going to be bold enough to speak—to try and change God's mind—even though he is just "dust and ashes." The paradox is that having been so bold as to upbraid God over the possible destruction of Sodom, he is silent when instructed to sacrifice his own son as a burnt offering (22:1–19).

This reversal of Abraham from bold speech to silence may well be addressed by Job's own move in the other direction—from silence to speech—a move that happens twice. Having sat for seven days with his friends, saying nothing, Job then takes up his lament (3:1). And having been (unintentionally) rendered silent by God's first speech, Job has now retracted this refusal to answer. He has come to a realization (similar to Abraham's in Gen. 18) that even "dust and ashes" may address the divine Ruler of the cosmos—and expect an answer.

Job's Restoration: Speech and Comfort in the Epilogue

Immediately after Job's response in 42:6, YHWH tells Eliphaz, "My wrath is kindled against you and against your two friends; for you have not spoken to ['el] me what is right [nəkônâ], as my servant Job has" (42:7; my translation). Most published translations of this verse take the preposition 'el ("to") as equivalent to 'al ("about"). And that would certainly get the basic point across—namely, that Job's honest voicing of his pain was appropriate, in contrast to that of the friends, who tried to defend God and explain Job's suffering: Job's complaint was upright or well-established (nəkônâ) speech.[65] But if we translate the preposition 'el more precisely, the point becomes even clearer—that while the friends spoke about God, Job actually spoke to God. And that is what God wants, even if God has to correct the content of what Job says.[66]

Having critiqued the speech of Job's friends, YHWH instructs them to go to Job (whom YHWH calls "my servant" four times in 42:7–8) and offer sacrifices, while Job prays for them: "I will accept his prayer not to deal with you according to folly; for you have not spoken to me what is right, as my servant Job has done" (42:8; my translation).

Here it is significant that Job not only follows the pattern of the psalmists who bring their complaints to God in honest prayer; he also functions like

---

65. From the verb kûn, "to establish" or "to make firm."
66. A point made by Seow, Job 1–21, 92; also Breitkopf, "Importance of Response," 10–13.

Moses, who intercedes for Israel, turning away God's wrath (after the golden calf episode at Sinai and again after the episode with the spies at the border of the Promised Land).[67]

And YHWH accepted Job's prayer on behalf of his friends (42:9) and "restored the fortunes of Job," giving him twice as much as he previously had (42:10), specified in the numbers of his livestock (42:12).[68] When it comes to interpersonal relationships, Job both receives and gives. He receives comfort (and gifts) from his brothers and sisters, and from others who knew him (42:11), and he also receives new children—seven sons and three daughters were born to him (42:13).[69]

Significantly, only the daughters are named—Jemimah, Keziah, and Keren-happuch (42:14), beautiful names that evoke the beauty of the daughters themselves, which the narrator tells us is beyond the ordinary (42:15a).[70] But more important than their names or beauty is the fact that Job gives his daughters an inheritance equal to his sons (42:15b), something highly unusual in the Hebrew Bible.

This goes beyond the case of the daughters of Zelophehad in Numbers 27:1–11. That text records an incident in which Zelophehad's five daughters (who are named [27:2], like Job's daughters) come to Moses after their father dies, requesting that his inheritance come to them, since there are no sons to carry on his name (27:1–4). Moses takes their request to YHWH, who not only agrees (27:5–7; also 36:2) but makes it a standing ordinance in Israel that the inheritance should go to daughters if there are no sons (27:8). But Job goes well beyond this, since he had sons, yet he gave his daughters an inheritance equal to theirs.

Why might this be important? Has Job's experience of being ostracized (at the bottom of the social ladder), along with his protest about the injustice he

---

67. See the discussion of Moses's intercession in the earlier chapter "God's Loyal Opposition." YHWH refers to Moses as "my servant" in Num. 12:7–8; Josh. 1:2; and 2 Kings 21:8; and Moses is called YHWH's "servant" many other times in the Bible.

68. The phrase "restored the fortunes" as well as the double restoration may be intended to hint that Job's suffering and restoration parallel Israel's exile and return. Not only is the distinctive phrase of the restoration of fortunes found in reference to the return from exile (Ps. 126:1; Jer. 30:3, 18; 33:7, 11; Ezek. 29:14; 39:25; Hos. 6:11; Joel 3:1; Amos 9:14), but Israel's double restoration after exile is mentioned in Isa. 40:12 and 61:7. For a discussion of this double restoration, see Middleton, *A New Heaven and a New Earth: Reclaiming Biblical Eschatology* (Grand Rapids: Baker Academic, 2014), 257–58.

69. Is it significant that while the Job of the prologue has many servants, no servants are mentioned in the epilogue? This shift is insightfully explored by Ansell, "Fantastic Beasts and Where to Find The(ir Wisdo)m," 94–95, 99–101.

70. The names most likely mean "Dove," "Cassia," and "Horn of Antinomy," respectively.

felt was being done to him and his recognition of YHWH's concern for him even in his suffering, profoundly impacted his ethical sensibilities and spilled over into advocacy on behalf of those suffering the injustice of patriarchy?[71]

The final two verses of Job summarize the end of his life. He lived another 140 years "and saw his children, and his children's children, four generations" (42:16), which suggests that Job experienced the precise opposite of the consequences of disloyalty to YHWH mentioned in Exodus 20:5 and 34:7. Instead of having his iniquity visited upon his children to the third and fourth generations, it was his blessing that was extended. "And Job died old and full of days" (42:17).[72]

However we evaluate the details of the epilogue, it is clear that Job's response to God at the end of the second speech involves a retraction of his earlier abased silence (along with his lawsuit against YHWH) because he has come to understand that God values this human dialogue partner, especially for his honest, abrasive, unsubdued speech. And Job is appropriately consoled or comforted over this. A careful reading of the book of Job thus suggests a fundamental coherence between God's intent in the speeches from the whirlwind, on the one hand, and God's explicit approval of Job in the prose epilogue, on the other.

The book of Job thus suggests that between the extremes of blessing God explicitly (which is, of course, appropriate speech and which Job does at the outset) and cursing God (which is clearly folly, and which Job therefore avoids), there is the viable option of honest, forthright challenge to God in prayer, which God (as Creator) both wants and expects of those made in the divine image—and this is right speech too.

While I do not expect this chapter to decisively settle the meaning of God's speeches, or of Job's response to the speeches—the text of Job remains fundamentally polyvalent and will undoubtedly continue to exercise interpreters for millennia to come—there is no good reason to maintain the traditional interpretation of God as an abusive tyrant attempting to silence Job (that would be to take the point of view of Job's friends, which is not "right"). On the contrary, it makes eminently better sense of the text to conclude that God comes not to bury Job but precisely to *praise* him.

---

71. I am indebted to my son Kevin for this profound suggestion.

72. As we shall see, this is similar to the notice of Abraham's death (just one of many parallels between the two patriarchs).

PART 3

UNBINDING THE AQEDAH FROM THE STRAITJACKET OF TRADITION

5

Is It Permissible to Criticize Abraham or God?

I never used to be troubled by the Aqedah. Like most Christians and Jews, and like many theologians and biblical scholars, I simply accepted Abraham's response to God's command to sacrifice his son as a model of faithful obedience (Christians tend to emphasize his faith, and Jews his obedience, but often they are combined).

I can still remember, as an eighteen-year-old, teaching a Sunday school class on Genesis 22 at my home church in Kingston, Jamaica. As we sat on benches under a tree behind the church building on a hot Sunday morning, I led the group in a discussion of Abraham's laudable devotion to God, a devotion that he put above every earthly value—including the life of his own son.

So it was only fitting that my first attempt at a critical reading of the Aqedah was presented just down the road from this church, at the Jamaica Theological Seminary (nearly forty years later).[1] Since then, I have been developing an interpretation of the Aqedah that is critical of Abraham, yet faithful to the text of Genesis. In developing this interpretation, I have sought also to be faithful to the God of Abraham.

1. Presented as the inaugural Zenas Gerig Memorial Lecture (in honor of the founding president of the seminary), titled "How Abraham Lost His Son: Faithful Interpretation of Genesis 22:1–19," Jamaica Theological Seminary, Kingston, Jamaica, September 16, 2012.

The Basis for My Questioning Abraham

My questioning of Abraham's response to God in Genesis 22 has developed out of three considerations.

The first and most basic consideration is that I simply do not believe the God I have come to know would ever want me to sacrifice the life of another as proof of faithfulness; nor do I believe that this God values blind, unquestioning compliance. So if I heard a voice—internal or even external—claiming to come from God, telling me to sacrifice my son, I would not automatically comply.

If (hypothetically) I heard such a voice, I would initially question its source; specifically, I would wonder if this really was from God. As one Jamaican theological student put it after hearing my presentation on the Aqedah, "If I heard a voice telling me to sacrifice my son, I would reply, *Get thee behind me, Satan!*" That might well be my initial response too.

And if (for the sake of argument), after probing and investigating, I somehow came to believe that this word genuinely came from God, I would vigorously object to the instruction and question why God would want such a thing. And I would certainly intercede for the life of my son.[2]

My second reason for reconsidering the traditional positive interpretation of Abraham in Genesis 22 is that there is significant biblical precedent *not* to acquiesce voicelessly in a situation that seems wrong or unjust. This precedent includes the lament prayers in the Psalter, the intercession of Moses after the golden calf episode, the prophetic tradition of intercession on behalf of Israel, and the vocal complaints of Job.

In the New Testament, we have Jesus's prayers as he anticipates his death, both in the garden before his betrayal (pleading with the Father, "Remove this cup from me"; Mark 14:36; Luke 22:42) and then again on the cross (praying a lament psalm, "My God, my God, why have you forsaken me?"; Matt. 27:46; Mark 15:34).

In all these ways, Scripture provides normative precedent for speaking one's mind directly to God, even challenging God over the injustice or wrongness of any situation in one's own life or in the wider world.

This biblical precedent of vigorous prayer raises the question of why Abraham didn't intercede for Isaac. Given this weighty precedent, we might wonder

---

2. I realize that biblical scholars rarely expose their personal biases in studying Scripture, and I certainly don't want to absolutize the perspective of the interpreter. Yet the fact is that subjectivity cannot be avoided when approaching a text as fraught with meaning as Gen. 22. It is simple honesty to admit this.

why he didn't cry out like the psalmist in Psalm 22, "My God, my God, why have you forsaken me?" Or he could have pleaded, as Jesus did in Gethsemane, "Remove this cup from me."

Indeed, just four chapters before the Aqedah, Abraham *does* challenge God, with great boldness. This is my third reason for questioning the traditional reading of the Aqedah.

In Genesis 18 we find an extended dialogue between Abraham and God, in which Abraham questions whether it is right for to God destroy Sodom. Abraham's concern, never actually voiced, is that his nephew Lot and his family are living in Sodom. Abraham's perception that God might bring judgment against the city for its sins leads him to upbraid God for being willing to destroy the righteous or innocent (ṣadîq) along with the wicked. Abraham's boldness in challenging God's supposed justice is striking: "Far be it from you to do such a thing, to slay the righteous with the wicked, so that the righteous fare as the wicked! Far be that from you! Shall not the Judge of all the earth do what is just?" (18:25).

Like Moses interceding on behalf of Israel after the golden calf episode, to avert divine judgment, Abraham laments the destruction of Sodom and intercedes on behalf of his nephew and family. In Genesis 18, Abraham joins the biblical pattern of vigorous prayer, and he is taken seriously by God. Just as with Moses, God accepts every request Abraham makes, even to save the city for the sake of ten innocent people. And when Abraham doesn't ask for anything more, God sends angels to rescue Lot and his family anyway (chap. 19).

But when it comes to his own son, who he is commanded *himself* to kill, Abraham is strangely silent. God says to Abraham, "Take, please, your son, your only one, whom you love—Isaac; and go to the land of Moriah; and offer him there as a burnt offering on one of the mountains that I will tell you" (22:2).[3] And Abraham has absolutely nothing to say in response; instead, he rises early the next morning to set out on the fateful journey.

In the entire story of the Aqedah (nineteen verses), Abraham is recorded as saying only two words to God; it is actually the same word, which he says twice—once prior to the request to sacrifice his son (22:1) and then later when the angel calls from heaven to prevent the sacrifice (22:11). That word is *hinnēnî*. "Behold, me," usually translated, "Here I am." But nowhere else in the narrative of the Aqedah does Abraham speak to God.

---

3. The translation of Gen. 22:1–19 used here and in following chapters is my own (the translation is given in full near the start of chap. 6 of this book).

The contrast with Genesis 18 is startling. Given Abraham's earlier boldness in prayer, we might have expected him to say something like, "Far be it from you to do such a thing, to slay the innocent [i.e., Isaac] with the wicked, so that the innocent fare as the wicked! Far be that from you! Shall not the Judge of all the earth do what is just?"

Why does Abraham shift from engaged protest and intercession on the one occasion (chap. 18) to silent compliance on the next (chap. 22)? Although this question is not explicitly raised in the text of Genesis, Terence Fretheim suggests that "the narrator may intend that the *reader*, having learned from Abraham in chapter 18 how to question God, is the one who is to ask questions here."[4]

However, just as my critical reading of Abraham in Genesis 22 would get off the ground, I am confronted by the positions of Jon Levenson and Walter Moberly, two contemporary biblical scholars who have written extensively on the Aqedah. Both Levenson and Moberly have issued stern warnings to anyone who would propose a critical interpretation of the Aqedah today.

Deeply rooted in their respective Jewish and Christian traditions, Levenson and Moberly each articulate a trusting, unabashedly positive reading of the Aqedah, including its relevance to the life of contemporary faith communities. Yet neither presents a simplistic, naive reading of the text. Rather, their readings of the Aqedah draw on the complex history of the text's interpretation and they each develop a nuanced view of Abraham as a model or paradigm for later generations. Their interpretations of the Aqedah also serve to ground their warnings against contemporary critical readings.

Here I will summarize the gist of Levenson's and Moberly's nuanced traditional readings of the Aqedah, which provide the basis for their warnings about critical readings of the text.

Levenson on the Historical Context of the Aqedah

Levenson's major work on the Aqedah is *The Death and Resurrection of the Beloved Son: The Transformation of Child Sacrifice in Judaism and Christianity* (1993). This book is a landmark study of Genesis 22, which articulates

---

4. Fretheim, "God, Abraham, and the Abuse of Isaac," WW 15, no. 1 (1995): 51 (emphasis original; entire article 49–57). Almost identical wording is found in Fretheim, *Abraham: Trials of Family and Faith*, SPOT (Columbia: University of South Carolina Press, 2007), 120.

Levenson's theory that the ritual of offering the firstborn son to God is the probable historical context of the Aqedah, along with his view that this ritual was transformed over time into a "sublime religious paradigm" relevant to both Judaism and Christianity.[5]

Levenson (following the lead of other biblical scholars) posits three stages in the development of the offering of the firstborn in Israelite religion. In the first stage, the literal offering of the firstborn to YHWH was understood as a requirement of Torah. Thus, according to Exodus 13:2, God tells Israel, "Consecrate to me all the firstborn; whatever is the first to open the womb among the Israelites, of human beings and animals, is mine." And in 22:29 we read, "The firstborn of your sons you shall give to me."[6] Levenson views the Aqedah as belonging to this stage of Israelite religion, so that God's command for Abraham to offer up his son as a burnt offering would be unproblematic from the ancient point of view.[7]

Later, the idea arose that the human firstborn son could be redeemed by substitution, a point noted in Exodus 13:13 ("Every firstborn male among your children you shall redeem"), Exodus 34:20 ("All the firstborn of your sons you shall redeem"), and Numbers 18:15 ("The firstborn of human beings you shall redeem"). The substitute might be an animal (a lamb), the payment

---

5. Jon D. Levenson, *The Death and Resurrection of the Beloved Son: The Transformation of Child Sacrifice in Judaism and Christianity* (New Haven: Yale University Press, 1993), x.

6. As evidence of this stage in the ritual, Levenson mentions Micah's question about whether God really wants the firstborn of his body as atonement for sin (Mic. 6:7), Jephthah's sacrifice of his daughter to fill a vow (Judg. 11:29–40), and the king of Moab's sacrifice of his son as a burnt offering to ensure victory in battle (2 Kings 3:26–27).

7. This is the basis for Levenson's distinguishing between the situation in Gen. 18 (where Abraham protests the destruction of Sodom) and Gen. 22 (where he submits to the command to kill his own son). Whereas the first is a forensic context (where ethical questions are relevant), the second is a sacrificial context (and so ethics isn't relevant). For this distinction between the forensic and sacrificial, see Levenson, "Abusing Abraham: Traditions, Religious Histories, and Modern Misinterpretations," *Judaism* 47, no. 3 (1998): 272 (entire article 259–77); see also his notes on the Aqedah in *The Jewish Study Bible*, ed. Adele Berlin and Marc Zvi Brettler (New York: Oxford University Press, 2004), 46. In *Death and Resurrection of the Beloved Son*, 129, Levenson articulates this contrast as one between "a guilty person administered capital punishment" (Gen. 18) and "a sacrificial victim" (Gen. 22); he goes on to claim that Gen. 18 and 22 represent different tests of Abraham, both of which he passes—the first by protesting, the second by unquestioning obedience. Although Levenson objects to Kierkegaard's notion of "the teleological suspension of the ethical" ("The Test," in *Inheriting Abraham: The Legacy of the Patriarch in Judaism, Christianity, and Islam*, LJI [Princeton: Princeton University Press, 2012], 223n58 [entire chapter 66–112]), his position has obvious analogies to Kierkegaard's; perhaps we might call it "the *sacrificial* suspension of the ethical."

of a monetary ransom, the service of the Levites, or the Nazarite vow.[8] The substitution of a ram for Isaac in Genesis 22 might represent (or even lead to) this stage in Israelite religion—namely, where the firstborn son could be redeemed by substitution.

Finally, Israelite religion came to reject outright the offering of the firstborn as ever having been legitimate. Thus YHWH castigates Israel for "building the high place of Topheth, which is in the valley of the son of Hinnom, to burn their sons and their daughters in the fire—which I did not command, nor did it come into my mind" (Jer. 7:31). A similar statement is found in Jeremiah 19:5 with reference to offering children to Baal.

Whereas Jeremiah's statements assume that child sacrifice was never God's will, Levenson notes that in Ezekiel 20:25–26 God takes responsibility for this ancient ritual: "Moreover I gave them statutes that were not good and ordinances by which they could not live. I defiled them through their very gifts, in their offering up all their firstborn, in order that I might horrify them, so that they might know that I am the LORD."

One of the points in tracing this historical background is to make it clear that while contemporary readers might balk at God's request for Abraham to offer up his son as a burnt offering, Levenson claims that this was part of a set of legitimate expectations in ancient Israelite religion. Given that the function of the burnt offering ('olâ) in Israel's sacrificial system was not for the expiation of sin but rather as a symbol of dedication and thanksgiving, Levenson reads God's request for Abraham's son to be offered as an 'olâ as a test of Abraham's dedication to God: Does Abraham love God more than his son?[9]

In *The Death and Resurrection of the Beloved Son*, Levenson goes on to explore the paradigmatic role of the Aqedah in both Judaism and Christianity. Here he focuses on Isaac's willing submission to the sacrifice (a point not mentioned in Gen. 22 but emphasized in later Jewish interpretation). This willing offering of the sacrificial victim grounds both the tradition of Jewish martyrdom and the Christian understanding of the sacrifice of Jesus as God's "beloved Son."[10]

---

8. The book of Numbers views the Levites as the God-ordained substitute for the firstborn sons of Israel (3:12–13, 41, 45, 48–50; 8:17–18).

9. Levenson, *Death and Resurrection of the Beloved Son*, 137.

10. Although Levenson follows a common stream of interpretation in claiming that the Aqedah grounds the New Testament's portrayal of the death of Jesus, it is also possible that the linkage of the Aqedah to Jesus's death is a later response to the Jewish use of the Aqedah to ground martyrdom. The evidence in the earliest Christian literature is ambiguous.

Levenson and Moberly on the Aqedah as Grounding Sacrifice and Prayer

Nearly twenty years after *The Death and Resurrection of the Beloved Son*, Levenson published a book called *Inheriting Abraham*, which contains his most recent essay (to this point) on the Aqedah, titled simply "The Test" (2012).[11] Although Moberly has written numerous articles and book chapters on the Aqedah, his most extensive (sixty-one pages) is "Abraham and God in Genesis 22," published in *The Bible, Theology, and Faith* (2000).[12] In these two works, these astute authors engage the text of Genesis 22 and explore various aspects of the history of Jewish interpretation, to arrive at remarkably similar understandings of the meaning of the Aqedah for today.[13]

In Levenson's case, after an exposition of Genesis 22, followed by a rehearsal of varied interpretations of the Aqedah through Jewish history (with some attention also to Christian, Islamic, and modern interpretations), he concludes that Abraham's obedience to God in Genesis 22 is a "paradigm" for Jews today, in that they can "reenact the profound message of the Aqedah in their self-surrender to the will of God in the form of observance of the mitsvot, the commandments of the Torah."[14] The Aqedah thus grounds and models the proper attitude of devotion in contemporary Jewish observance of Halakah (the commandments).

Levenson ultimately applies this point about Torah observance specifically to prayer. On the way to this application, he attends to the Chronicler's identification of the site of Solomon's temple as Moriah (2 Chron. 3:1). This late biblical text (fourth or third century BCE) is the beginning of a tradition that understands the Aqedah as "a foundation legend for the Jerusalem temple."[15] The result of this foundation legend is that Abraham's paradigmatic offering on Moriah becomes a model for later Israelite devotion when sacrifices are

---

11. Levenson, "The Test," 66–112 (nn. 219–23).

12. R. W. L. Moberly, "Abraham and God in Genesis 22," in *The Bible, Theology, and Faith: A Study of Abraham and Jesus* (Cambridge: Cambridge University Press, 2000), 71–131.

13. I am aware of at least nine essays or book chapters that Moberly has written on the Aqedah, as well as addressing its interpretation at various points in R. W. L Moberly, *The Old Testament of the Old Testament: Patriarchal Narratives and Mosaic Yahwism*, OBT (Minneapolis: Augsburg Fortress, 1992; repr., Eugene, OR: Wipf & Stock, 2001), 138–45, 188–90.

14. Levenson, "The Test," 112. Levenson presents a traditional exposition of Gen. 22 on pp. 67–89, then focuses on Jewish interpretation on pp. 89–99, followed by a brief survey of Christian, Islamic, and modern interpretations on pp. 99–112. His own conclusion (112) is based primarily on his analysis of the Aqedah, temple sacrifice, and prayer in later Judaism (89–91).

15. Levenson, "The Test," 89.

brought to the temple. Here Levenson notes that the Aramaic paraphrase of Genesis 22:14 in Targum Onqelos not only has Abraham establishing the site at Moriah as the basis for later Israelite service to God but depicts him praying there, "a point not to be underestimated."[16]

This is important because after the temple was destroyed, prayer becomes "one of the appropriate substitutes for sacrifice" in the time of the Talmud.[17] So the attitude of devotion modeled by Abraham was eventually transferred from the sacrificial system to prayer; or, as Levenson more forcefully puts it, prayer "re-presents and reactivates sacrifice, and the paradigmatic sacrifice, the one that lies at the foundation of Temple service and the service of the heart alike, is the Aqedah."[18] Given that Levenson concludes his essay with an application of the Aqedah to Torah obedience (something I noted earlier), it may be that he intends us to think of the halakic requirement for regular daily prayer, which reenacts Abraham's obedience in the Aqedah. Or perhaps such prayer is meant to be a prime example of Torah obedience.

This interpretation is similar to the main point that Walter Moberly derives from the Aqedah. Moberly's sophisticated version of the traditional interpretation is based on his exploration of four key terms in Genesis 22 (*fear* of God, divine *testing*, divine *seeing*, and divine *blessing*).[19] Two of these key terms show up in Exodus 20:20 (*test* and *fear* of God), a text that Moberly takes as crucial for understanding God's intentions for Israel.[20]

According to Exodus 20:20, "Moses said to the people, 'Do not be afraid; for God has come only to *test* you and to put the *fear of him* upon you so that you do not sin.'" Coming right after the theophany at Sinai and the Ten Commandments, these words suggest that the purpose of testing is to prove or exhibit Israel's allegiance and obedience to YHWH, arising out of the appropriate "fear" of God (which is distinguished in Exod. 20:20 from simply being afraid). In Moberly's view, the test of the Aqedah should be read in terms of this very purpose.[21]

---

16. Levenson, "The Test," 89.

17. Levenson, "The Test," 90.

18. Levenson, "The Test," 90–91.

19. After an introduction (71–80), Moberly structures his essay "Abraham and God in Genesis 22" by the four terms: fear of God (80–97), divine testing (97–107), divine seeing (107–18), and divine blessing (118–27).

20. Moberly notes, "Of these four terms, the primary narrative weight falls on the first two, 'test' and 'fear of God.'" Moberly, "Abraham and God in Genesis 22," 79.

21. Moberly, "Abraham and God in Genesis 22," 81–84.

Like Levenson, Moberly cites the later interpretation of 2 Chronicles 3:1 that Moriah is the site of the Jerusalem temple (which he admits was probably not the original intent of the story, though it is part of the story "as it now stands"[22]) and develops an interpretation of the Aqedah as articulating the right inner attitude that should accompany the offering of sacrifices. He especially notes that the burnt offering or ʿolâ (which is what God required of Abraham) is at the head of the list of sacrifices in the first chapter of Leviticus and that Israel is to offer the ʿolâ twice every day, according to Exodus 29:38–46 (the so-called Tamid sacrifice).[23] Even after the destruction of the temple and the cessation of sacrifices, Moberly explains, the Aqedah could continue to have significance for Jews—and also for Christians—by presenting a model of the right inner attitude of dedication to God.[24] This corresponds to what Jews would later call kavanah, or right intention, a concept that is today applied primarily to the attentiveness required in prayer, particularly when reciting from the Jewish prayer book (the siddur).[25]

Whereas Levenson and Moberly share an emphasis on the relevance of Abraham's inner attitude in Genesis 22 for contemporary devotion to God, the distinctive aspect of Levenson's interpretation is his typically Jewish focus on Torah observance.

In one of Moberly's more recent essays on the Aqedah (2009), he adds an emphasis on Isaac's submission to God's will as a model to be followed, something Levenson emphasized in The Death and Resurrection of the Beloved Son. At one point Moberly notes, "Traditionally, Jews and Christians have read this story as displaying costly right response to God on the part of Abraham and Isaac."[26] Then, citing an article by Clemens Thoma, Moberly suggests that "identifying with Isaac comes to mean, as Thoma puts it, being 'motivated to accept obediently and submissively in

---

22. Moberly, "A Specimen Text: Genesis 22," in Genesis 12–50, OTG (1992; repr., Sheffield: Sheffield Academic Press, 1995]), 47 (entire chapter 39–56).

23. Moberly, "Abraham and God in Genesis 22," 112, 117–18. Leviticus Rabbah 2:11 explicitly links the Tamid sacrifice with the Aqedah: "When our father Abraham bound Isaac his son, the Holy One (blessed be he) established the institution of the two lambs, one in the morning and one in the evening." Trans. Levenson, Death and Resurrection of the Beloved Son, 185.

24. Moberly, "Abraham and God in Genesis 22," 112–18.

25. I have not seen Moberly or Levenson explicitly connect the message of the Aqedah to the Jewish concept of kavanah, but it is implicit in their analyses.

26. Moberly, "Genesis 22: Abraham—Model or Monster?," in The Theology of the Book of Genesis (Cambridge: Cambridge University Press, 2009), 179 (emphasis added; entire chapter 179–99).

their lives what seemed incomprehensible, unendurable and contradictory and to reflect on it.'"[27] This emphasis coheres with the autobiographical comment from Moberly (which I quoted in the introduction to this book) about the value of the Aqedah for helping him accept difficult realities in his life that could not be changed.[28]

Warnings by Levenson and Moberly against Critical Readings of the Aqedah

Not only are Levenson and Moberly two of the most astute and respected interpreters of the Aqedah among contemporary scholars who take the text as normative, but they both have issued warnings to anyone who would propose a critical interpretation of the Aqedah. Both cite Immanuel Kant's famous critique in *The Conflict of the Faculties* (1798) as the starting point of the modern criticism of the Aqedah.[29]

In addressing the question of whether one should ever listen to a voice supposedly from God that contradicts the moral law, Kant writes,

> We can use as an example the myth of the sacrifice that Abraham was going to make by butchering and burning his only son at God's command (the poor child, without knowing it, even brought the wood for the fire). Abraham should have replied to this supposedly divine voice: "That I ought not to kill my good son is quite certain. But that you, this apparition, are God—of that I am not certain, and never can be, not even if this voice rings down to me from (visible) heaven."[30]

Kant questioned the ethics of someone who would sacrifice his son to his deity, and many modern readers also raise questions about the sort of God

---

27. Moberly, "Genesis 22: Abraham—Model or Monster?," 195–96, citing Clemens Thoma, "Observations on the Concept and Early Forms of Akedah-Spirituality," in *Standing before God: Studies on Prayer in Scriptures and in Tradition with Essays in Honor of John M. Oesterreicher*, ed. Asher Finkel and Lawrence Frizzel (New York: Ktav, 1981), 213 (entire chapter 213–22).

28. R. W. L. Moberly, "Learning to Be a Theologian," in *I (Still) Believe: Leading Bible Scholars Share Their Stories of Faith and Scholarship*, ed. John Byron and Joel N. Lohr (Grand Rapids: Zondervan, 2015), 205 (entire chapter 201–10).

29. Moberly, "Genesis 22: Abraham—Model or Monster?," 181–82; Levenson, "The Test," 106–8; and Kant, *The Conflict of the Faculties* (1798), trans. Mary J. Gregor and Robert Anchor, in *Religion and Rational Theology*, ed. and trans. Allen W. Wood and George Di Giovanni (Cambridge: Cambridge University Press, 1996), 233–327.

30. Kant, *Conflict of the Faculties*, 7:63 (p. 283).

who would require this sacrifice. These questions—indeed, critiques—have come fast and furious in contemporary times. As Moberly puts it, "What began as a trickle in the time of Kant has now become a torrent."[31]

Moberly has devoted no fewer than four essays explicitly to address (and counter) suspicious readings of the Aqedah, besides touching on the topic in other places.[32] Levenson, likewise, is highly critical of those who would disparage either God or Abraham in any way.[33] Moberly especially cites a variety of contemporary interpreters—both Jewish and Christian—who are suspicious of either Abraham or Abraham's God, as depicted in Genesis 22.[34] The attempt by Moberly and Levenson to deflect such criticisms seems to assume that there are only two possible stances toward the Aqedah—either one accepts some version of the traditional interpretation that Abraham is praiseworthy for his obedience or one rejects the authority of the biblical text by standing outside the text and the biblical tradition.[35]

Among the points that both Levenson and Moberly make in challenging suspicious readings of the Aqedah is that we should not judge either God or Abraham by the standards of contemporary morality. Not only would Abraham (in biblical times) have had the legitimate full power of life and death over his own progeny (who would have been valued for continuing the father's line), but God in ancient times was understood (even within Scripture) to require the life of the firstborn (of both humans and animals). This latter point is especially central to Levenson's argument in his monograph.

At one point Moberly addresses the criticism that "the instrumentalizing, or dehumanizing, of Isaac" (as a means to an end—namely, God's testing Abraham) could be the basis for child abuse.[36] Commending to the reader the significant precedent of the interpretation of the Aqedah in Jewish and Christian tradition, Moberly claims, "It is striking that within this literature,

---

31. Moberly, "Genesis 22: Abraham—Model or Monster?," 182.
32. Besides in "Genesis 22: Abraham—Model or Monster?" Moberly addresses suspicious readings of the Aqedah head-on in three other places: "Ancient and Modern Interpretations of Genesis 22," in *The Bible, Theology, and Faith*, 132–61; "Genesis 22 and the Hermeneutics of Suspicion," in *The Bible, Theology, and Faith*, 162–83; and "Living Dangerously: Genesis 22 and the Quest for Good Biblical Interpretation," in *The Art of Reading Scripture*, ed. Ellen F. Davis and Richard B. Hays (Grand Rapids: Eerdmans, 2003), 181–97. He also touches on this issue in "Abraham and God in Genesis 22," 76–78.
33. Levenson, "Abusing Abraham," 259–77; see also Levenson, "The Test," 108.
34. Moberly, "Abraham and God in Genesis 22," 76–77.
35. Moberly, "Abraham and God in Genesis 22," 76–78; Levenson, "The Test," 108.
36. Moberly, "Genesis 22: Abraham—Model or Monster?," 193.

one looks in vain for any account of believers considering the biblical text as a warrant for any kind of abuse, much less the killing, of their children."[37]

But perhaps Moberly has not looked deeply enough into this literature. While the Aqedah may not have been used to justify child abuse in any ordinary sense, the well-documented Jewish tradition of Kiddush HaShem, the sanctification of God's name through martyrdom, explicitly appeals to the Aqedah—both to Isaac's voluntary submission to death and to Abraham's willingness to sacrifice him. This use of the Aqedah as a paradigm in times of persecution suggests not only that one should be willing to give one's life for commitment to God (modeling oneself on Isaac) but that parents should be willing to offer up their children to death in God's name (taking Abraham as the paradigm). Indeed, by contrasting the vast numbers of martyrs with Abraham's single son, while also noting that Isaac was not actually killed, this literature sometimes suggests that later martyrs outperformed the Aqedah.

Perhaps the most famous example of this is the later rabbinic retelling of 2 Maccabees 7, the story of the mother who encourages her seven sons to endure martyrdom for their faith under Antiochus Epiphanes IV (she was killed after them). Unnamed in 2 Maccabees, but known in later tradition as Hannah, this mother is imagined (in Yalkut Shimoni) to have said to her martyred children, "Children, do not be distressed, for to this end were you created—to sanctify in the world the Name of the Holy One, blessed be He. Go. Tell Father Abraham: Let not your heart swell with pride! You built one altar, but I have built seven altars and on them have offered up my seven sons. What is more: Yours was a trial; mine was an accomplished fact."[38]

This midrash does not stand alone, since similar statements are found elsewhere, as in the Babylonian Talmud (where the story is placed in the time of the Bar Kochba revolt against the Roman Empire). There the mother says, "My son, go and say to your father Abraham, You bound one [son to the] altar, but I bound seven altars."[39] And in Lamentations Rabbah, the mother

---

37. Moberly, "Genesis 22: Abraham—Model or Monster?," 195.

38. From Yalkut Shimoni on Deut. 26, §938. Yalkut Shimoni is a collection of aggadic midrashim on each book of the Bible (this is from §§789–963, the section on Deuteronomy). Trans. Shalom Spiegel, *The Last Trial: On the Legends and Lore of the Command to Abraham to Offer Isaac as a Sacrifice; The Akedah* (Woodstock, VT: Jewish Lights, 1993 [Heb. orig. 1950; Eng. orig. 1967]), 15.

39. Babylonian Talmud, Gittin 57b. Trans. from Sefaria.org, https://www.sefaria.org/Gittin .57b.20?lang=bi&with=all&lang2=en.

(named Miriam bat Tanḥum) tells her children to convey a similar message to Abraham: "You built one altar and did not offer up your son; I built seven altars and offered up my sons on them."[40]

The paradigmatic nature of the Aqedah comes into its own in the Crusades and other massacres of Jews by Christians in the Middle Ages. In a liturgical synagogue prayer associated with Rosh Hashanah, there is a detailed remembrance of the massacre of Jews at Mainz by the Crusaders. We are told that after the victims recited the Shema with one accord, they called on anyone with a sharp knife to "come forth and cut our throats for the sanctification of Him who Alone lives Eternally; and finally let him cut his own throat."[41] After detailed recounting of multiple sacrificial killings of son by father, bride by bridegroom, infant by mother, "until there was one flood of blood," the text asks, "when were there ever a thousand and a hundred sacrifices in one day, *each and every one of them like the Akedah of Isaac son of Abraham?*"[42]

Rather than recount the multitudinous examples of Jewish martyrs appealing to the Aqedah as a model for their sacrifice (well documented by many authors), perhaps one final citation is sufficient.[43] Also from liturgical poetry for High Holy Day services, we find the narration of the ritual slaughter of a son by his father during a pogrom: "Now there was a certain saintly man there, an elder, well on in years, and his name was Rabbenu Samuel bar Yehiel. He had an only son, a splendid looking young man, who with his father fled into the water and there offered his throat for slaughter by his father. Whereupon the father recited the appropriate blessing for slaughter of cattle and fowl, and the son responded with 'Amen.' And all of those who were standing around responded in a loud voice, 'Hear O Israel, the Lord our God, the Lord is One.'"

Then the poem goes on to address the audience: "O citizens of the world, take a good look! How extraordinary was the stamina of the son who *unbound* let himself be slaughtered, and how extraordinary was the stamina

40. Lamentations Rabbah 1:50. Trans. Spiegel, *Last Trial*, 15n7. This is a commentary on the phrase in Lam. 1:16, "For these things I weep."

41. Trans. Spiegel, *Last Trial*, 18–19.

42. Trans. Spiegel, *Last Trial*, 19, 20 (emphasis original).

43. For documentation on Kiddush HaShem, see Spiegel, *Last Trial*, 17–27; and John H. Spitzer, "Judaism: Jewish Uses of the Akedah—Genesis 22:1–10," in *Interpreting Abraham: Journeys to Moriah*, ed. Bradley Beach and Matthew T. Powell (Minneapolis: Fortress, 2014), 13–21 (entire chapter 3–26).

of the father who could resist compassion for an *only son*, so splendid and handsome a young man."[44]

As Shalom Spiegel puts it, summarizing the attitude of many who suffered martyrdom, "The victims themselves constantly set before their own eyes the example of the Patriarchs' behavior on Mount Moriah, and yearned to act their own part in the image and likeness of the earlier dramatic personae."[45]

The paradigmatic nature of the Aqedah took on a contemporary (twentieth-century) twist when some Zionists appealed to Abraham's example for the sacrifices needed to found the State of Israel. Indeed, in the 1967 Six-Day War, the Aqedah functioned as a paradigm or founding myth, justifying fathers sending their sons to war over the land of Israel.[46] As part of a widespread backlash against this use of the Aqedah, Jewish singer-songwriter Leonard Cohen used the Aqedah as a template for his 1969 song "The Story of Isaac" to criticize American fathers sending their sons to the Vietnam War.[47]

These examples of the ancient tradition of Kiddush HaShem (and its modern permutation) are not meant to disparage Moberly's warnings against suspicious readings of the Aqedah; but they certainly complicate his warning.

Rare, Explicit, Premodern Questioning of the Aqedah

Levenson and Moberly seem to be on to something important in their claim that suspicion of God or Abraham in the Aqedah can be mounted only on the basis of an extrabiblical stance, since such suspicion is almost nonexistent prior to modern times.

It is almost, but not quite, nonexistent.

A rare example of criticism of Abraham in the early Christian tradition is found in a Latin text assigned to Pseudo-Hegesippus (late fourth century CE), who either adapted or loosely paraphrased (with his own interjected comments) Josephus's *Jewish War* (Hegesippus might be a corruption of

44. Quoted in Spitzer, "Judaism," 20 (emphasis original).
45. Spiegel, *Last Trial*, 24.
46. On this interpretation of the Aqedah, and the modern Jewish backlash against it, see the documentation in "Judaism: Akedah," Jewish Virtual Library, 2013, https://www.jewish virtuallibrary.org/akedah.
47. Leonard Cohen, vocalist, "The Story of Isaac," recorded October 1968, side 1, track 2 on *Songs from a Room*, Columbia Records, released 1969. Cohen wrote a more mature (and complex) song about the Aqedah, in the form of a prayer addressed to God, titled "You Want It Darker," recorded April 2015–July 2016, track 1 on *You Want It Darker*, Columbia Records, released 2016. The song incorporates language from the Kaddish and includes a synagogue choir with the cantor singing *hinnēnî*. The album was released only nineteen days before Cohen died.

Iosippus, which is Latin for Josephus).[48] At one point the writer comments on Josephus's portrayal of Abraham as a devoted priest of God in Genesis 22: "I do not condemn his devotion but I question his piety. . . . Of what kind is that people, who consider the killing of a human being a religious act, and what sort is the priest, who is able to do this?"[49]

One critical Jewish voice is the philosopher and exegete Joseph Ibn Kaspi. A prolific writer (twenty-one treatises are extant), Ibn Kaspi was born in Provence (southeastern France) in the late thirteenth century and lived into the fourteenth century CE (1279/80–1340).[50] Concerning the Aqedah, Ibn Kaspi raises a number of points that suggest he was not fully on board with a positive reading of the text.

To begin with, he suggests a fundamental distinction between Abraham's obedience to God's original command to sacrifice his son and his obedience to the command from the angel to desist (the latter being morally superior); he traces this distinction in the text to the phrases "because you have done this thing" (22:16) and "because you have listened to my voice" (22:18).[51] He also notes that God never specifically tells Abraham that the offering of his son was meant to be dedicated to YHWH (a significant omission, which disassociates child sacrifice from legitimate worship).[52] And he suggests that during the three days of journeying, "Abraham earnestly wondered how the Lord could command him to perform such an abomination . . . , and he silently struggled to understand the Lord's intention."[53]

In the end, Ibn Kaspi thought that the Aqedah was a great warning against child sacrifice, which was an abomination to God. And he thought that the greatness of Abraham was not his silent obedience to the command to sacrifice his son but rather his obedience to the word from the angel to desist.[54]

---

48. The work goes by various names, including "On the Ruin of the City of Jerusalem," and is usually dated 370–375 CE. Besides drawing primarily on *Jewish War*, there are insertions from Josephus's *Jewish Antiquities*, as well as insertions from some other authors.

49. Translation from Isaac Kalimi, "'Go, I Beg You, Take Your Beloved Son and Slay Him!': The Binding of Isaac in Rabbinic Literature and Thought," *Review of Rabbinic Judaism* 13, no. 1 (2010): 16n49 (entire article 1–29). Josephus's portrayal of Abraham as a priest offering up his son to God is found in *Antiquities* 1.223–24.

50. Albert van der Heide, *"Now I Know": Five Centuries of Aqedah Exegesis*, ASJP 17 (Cham, Switzerland: Springer, 2017), 231. Van der Heide's section on Ibn Kaspi is found on pp. 231–57.

51. Ibn Kaspi, *Gevia' Kesef* 14.35. See van der Heide, *"Now I Know,"* 240.

52. Ibn Kaspi, *Gevia' Kesef* 14.25. See van der Heide, *"Now I Know,"* 238–39, 253.

53. Ibn Kaspi, *Gevia' Kesef* 14.19. Translation from van der Heide, *"Now I Know,"* 238, 252.

54. The case of Ibn Kaspi is also discussed in Kalimi, "'Go, I Beg You,'" 5, also n. 14.

There are also early Jewish poems from the Byzantine era (around 500 CE), written in the land of Israel, that criticize Abraham's response to God in Genesis 22.[55] One such poem is a *piyyut* or liturgical poem for Shavuot (the Feast of Booths), which celebrates the giving of the Torah. In the poem, ascribed to El'azar be-Rabbi Qillir, God and the Torah have a discussion about why the Torah (which predates creation, according to Genesis Rabbah 8:2) was only revealed to Moses and not before. God reviews history, mentioning various people who might have been worthy of the revelation, but the Torah rejects each one for some flaw. When they get to Abraham, the Torah admits that his offering of Isaac was accepted (and so approved) by God. "But he forgot how a father is supposed to have mercy on his children. / A prayer or plea he should have offered." Perhaps Abraham had no choice but to obey, but he did not live up to Psalm 103, which the poem alludes to: "As a father has compassion for his children, / so the LORD has compassion for those who fear him." Because he did not intercede for Isaac, Abraham is not worthy of receiving the Torah.[56]

There is also an Aramaic poem discovered in the Cairo Geniza, dating from around the same time as Qillir's *piyyut*, which characterizes the Aqedah this way: "This is the day that they will say, / A father had no pity, and a son did not delay." Later in the poem, Isaac addresses his father, encouraging him to overcome his hesitancy: "Be like a man who has no mercy on his son. / Like a cruel man, take your knife / And slaughter me, do not defile me. / Do not cry, that I should not delay you, / And I will not take myself away from you." Although the poem valorizes Isaac for his commitment to martyrdom (which was becoming a common trope in Jewish tradition), the characterization of Abraham as "a cruel man," a father with "no pity" and "no mercy" for his son, suggests an implicit critique. Aaron Koller notes that this looks like an over-the-top, satirical affirmation of the tradition of valorizing Abraham.[57]

---

55. Kalimi also notes that there were "some silky criticisms" concerning Abraham's readiness to offer up his son that can be found in seventh-century and later *piyyutim*, though he doesn't give any details. Kalimi, "'Go, I Beg You,'" 13.

56. Quoted in Aaron Koller, *The Significance of the Akedah for Modern Jewish Thought* (Philadelphia: Jewish Publication Society, 2020), 17 (for the Hebrew sources Koller cites, see 161n57, 196). Also addressed in Koller, "Abraham Passes the Test of the Akedah but Fails as a Father," TheTorah.com, 2019, https://www.thetorah.com/article/abraham-passes-the-test-of-the-akedah-but-fails-as-a-father.

57. Koller, *Significance of the Akedah*, 16 (for the Hebrew sources Koller cites, see 161n53, 215). His comments about the poem being satirical are found in "Abraham Passes the Test."

A Yiddish poem from around 1500 CE is more clearly critical. After admitting the pain the Aqedah will inflict on both Abraham and Sarah, the poem goes on to note that many people nevertheless affirm that merit accrues to later generations by the Aqedah (a theme addressed later in this chapter). But the author of the poem articulates a contrary position. "If you want to know the truth, / I do not think much of [such] people. / I swear to you as a true Jew: / they are only so pious that they indeed need another Binding just about every day. / Now, be that as it may, I cannot change it. / I will ask His name, blessed be He, that He hasten and end it / and soon send us the Redeemer. / And with that I will conclude and make an end."[58]

So it is not quite true that there are no premodern critiques of the Aqedah. Yet these critiques are anomalies. The tendency in both Christian and Jewish traditions was to valorize Abraham's devotion to God in Genesis 22. It is not typical in the history of ancient or medieval interpretation to raise explicit criticisms of either Abraham or God in the Aqedah.

The relevant question, however, is why premodern critiques of the Aqedah are so rare. It could be, of course, because premodern interpreters placed themselves under the authority of Scripture, standing within the world of the text, rather than making judgments from an extrinsic stance.

But there could be another explanation.

The Jewish Tradition of Protest to God as Sin

During the first three centuries of the Common Era, a tradition began to develop in Jewish literature that explicitly *prohibited* protest or questioning of God (and if God should not be questioned, certainly Abraham couldn't be faulted for not protesting the command to sacrifice his son). This tradition, which stands in significant contradiction to the more ancient model of lament psalms and prophet intercession, has been explored in some depth by Dov Weiss.[59]

Examples of this anti-protest tradition are found in texts from the third century CE, such as Sifre Devarim (a midrash on Deuteronomy). This text

---

58. Koller, "Abraham Passes the Test." The full poem (in translation) is found in Jerrod C. Frakes, *Early Yiddish Epic* (Syracuse: Syracuse University Press, 2014), 149–55.

59. Dov Weiss, "The Sin of Protesting God in Rabbinic and Patristic Literature," *ASJR* 39, no. 2 (2015): 367–92; Weiss, *Pious Irreverence: Confronting God in Rabbinic Judaism*, Divinations: Rereading Late Ancient Religion (Philadelphia: University of Pennsylvania Press, 2017), esp. chap. 1: "Confrontation as Sin." Weiss's research on the topic comes from his dissertation, "Confrontations with God in Late Rabbinic Literature" (PhD diss., University of Chicago, 2011).

uses Deuteronomy 32:4 ("The Rock, his work is perfect, / and all his ways are just") to make the point that no one should criticize God's deeds since they are exemplary.[60]

Likewise, the Mekhilta de-Rabbi Ishmael has Rabbi Akiva cite Job's words about God: "But he stands alone and who can dissuade him? / What he desires, that he does" (Job 23:13). Although, in context, Job meant this as a critique of God's intransigence in response to his complaint, Akiva takes this verse to mean the opposite—that since God always rules with justice, there is no moral basis to ever protest what God does.[61]

In a similar vein, Midrash Tannaim (a commentary on Deuteronomy) links the admission of humility in Psalm 131:1 ("O LORD, my heart is not lifted up, / my eyes are not raised too high; / I do not occupy myself with things / too great and too marvelous for me") with Deuteronomy 18:13 ("You must remain completely loyal to the LORD your God") in order to argue that it is never appropriate to criticize God.[62]

These examples of texts prohibiting criticism of God or Scripture are all from the third century CE, toward the end of the period of the Tannaim, the earliest rabbinic sages who taught in the land of Israel during the first two centuries and into the early third century CE. The views of these Tannaitic sages are recorded in the Mishnah.

Weiss notes that the prohibition of protest in the Jewish tradition largely matches the rise of a similar tradition among the Christian church fathers, whether Greek or Latin. In both cases this anti-protest tradition seems to have been generated by learned pagan and gnostic critiques of the God of the Old Testament / Hebrew Bible in the first centuries of the Common Era. However, while the typical early Christian response to such critiques was to shift from literal to allegorical readings of Scripture in order to protect God's righteous character (since a literal reading seemed unable to do this), the Jewish response was to defend God's actions in the objectionable texts as above

---

60. Sifre Devarim 307 on Deut. 32:4. See *Sifre Devarim*, ed. Louis Finkelstein (New York: Jewish Theological Seminary, 2001), 344, cited in Weiss, "Sin of Protesting God," 370. For an English translation see Reuven Hammer, *Sifre: A Tannaitic Commentary on the Book of Deuteronomy*, YJS 24 (New Haven: Yale University Press, 1987). In fact, Deut. 32:4 becomes something of a proof text that various rabbis use to explain why it is inappropriate to question God's ways.

61. Mekhilta de-Rabbi Ishmael to Exod. 15:19. See *Mekhilta de-Rabbi Ishmael*, ed. Haim Shaul Horovitz and Israel Rabin (Jerusalem: Bamberger and Wahrman, 1960), 112, cited by Weiss, "Sin of Protesting God," 370.

62. Midrash Tannaim on Deut. 18:13. See *Midrash Tannaim*, ed. David Tzvi Hoffmann (Berlin: Itzkowski, 1908), 110–11, cited by Weiss, "Sin of Protesting God," 375.

reproach, sometimes creatively rereading these very texts in such a way that rendered illegitimate any critique of God's ways.[63]

Weiss goes on to show that later, in the post-Tannaitic period, during the time of the sages of the fourth and fifth centuries known as the Amoraim (whose views are found in the Gemara, the section of the Talmud that is a commentary on the Mishnah), and even in the post-Amoraic period of the sixth through eight centuries, there are examples of taking what are on the surface morally problematic biblical texts and using them actively to prohibit critique of God's justice.[64] Indeed, this anti-protest tradition developed beyond merely prohibiting protest to describing punishments for those who dare to critique God's ways. Weiss suggests that this radicalization was a response to the vigorous Jewish protest tradition that was developing precisely during this time among the Amoraim.[65] So there were two competing Jewish traditions developing in tandem about the validity of protest or challenge to God.

Validating Protest to God in Jewish Texts after the Bible

The tradition that validated protest, which is already found in Scripture, can be seen in various post-biblical Jewish writings, beginning in the Second Temple period, even prior to rabbinic times. Some writings from this period affirm the validity of protest on the part of the faithful concerning what seems to be God's injustice.[66] Thus, Philo of Alexandria (20 BCE–40 CE) applauds both Moses and Abraham for their bold challenges to God in Exodus 32 and Genesis 18, respectively.[67] And in the pseudepigraphal texts 2 Baruch and 4 Ezra (= 2 Esdras), we find the biblical figures of Baruch and Ezra complaining to God over the destruction of Jerusalem, with no divine reprimand ensuing. In 2 Baruch 10, Baruch laments the destruction of Jerusalem, and chapters 11–19 recount his dialogue with God, as he raises various questions, to which God responds without reprimand. Likewise, 4 Ezra 3 has Ezra in Babylon,

---

63. See Weiss, "Sin of Protesting God," 372–75, on various motivations for the anti-protest prohibition. Weiss goes on to give illuminating examples of how the anti-protest rabbinic and patristic traditions diverged in their method of dealing with the biblical protests of Job, Moses, and Habakkuk (384–90).

64. Weiss, "Sin of Protesting God," 377–79.

65. Weiss, "Sin of Protesting God," 379–84.

66. Beyond this, the rabbinic tradition in general had no problem criticizing various biblical characters (whether patriarchs or prophets) for their failings.

67. See Philo, *Quis rerum divinarum heres sit* 5–28; see Weiss, "Sin of Protesting God," 372, nn. 15–16.

thirteen years after the destruction of Jerusalem, lamenting the destruction. And while he is answered by the angel Uriel, who corrects his understanding, he is not reprimanded for his lament.

Later, we have rabbinic voices, from the fifth through seventh centuries CE, that retell biblical stories, with words of protest to God coming from various biblical heroes—even when there were no such protests mentioned in the original biblical texts.

A classic example is in the midrashic text Numbers Rabbah, where Moses is portrayed as disputing God's word three times. In each case God responds, "You have taught me." The second case refers to the statement (found in Exod. 20 and other places) that God will bring judgment on the third and fourth generations, to which Moses responds that this is not right since evil people can have righteous children (he gives the example of Terah and Abraham, along with some others). God responds that Moses is right and changes his mind about this: "Behold, you have taught Me! I will nullify my words and preserve your words."[68]

These competing ancient Jewish traditions of prohibiting and legitimating protest to God complicate the question of how one should read the Aqedah, since there is precedent for both submission and critique among the faithful. Yet even in the tradition that legitimates protest, we do not find any significant questioning of either God's command to Abraham or of Abraham's response to God in Genesis 22.

Traces of Unease in Ancient Jewish Interpretation

What is fascinating, however, is that there are many classic Jewish readings of the Aqedah that, on the surface, valorize Abraham for his exemplary response to God's command, yet leave distinct traces of the sages' unease with the text. These readings are classic in that they are well known in the history of Jewish interpretation (though they may be new to many Christians).

While they do not explicitly critique either Abraham or God in Genesis 22, a closer look suggests that some ancient Jewish interpreters were seeking to mitigate the terror of the Aqedah in subtle ways. They did this by what is known as *midrash*, derived from the Hebrew verb *dāraš*, meaning to "seek" or "inquire." Midrashic readings are not strictly speaking "exegesis" (the Jewish

---

68. Numbers Rabbah 19:33. Trans. from Sefaria.org, https://www.sefaria.org/Bamidbar
_Rabbah.19.33?lang=bi&with=all&lang2=en.

equivalent of exegesis is known as *peshat*); rather, midrashim probe beneath the surface of a text to uncover meanings that are not immediately obvious (and that might not occur to anyone doing what we would call exegesis).

Midrashic readings tend to be found in collections or anthologies of such texts, which explicitly go by the name *Midrash* (such as Midrash Rabbah, which names a series of anthologies of midrashic readings on various books of the Bible, including Genesis Rabbah, which I will cite in what follows). Such collections consist in stories, parables, legends, and homilies on biblical texts, and they are known as Aggadah or aggadic midrash (from the Hebrew *nāgad*, meaning to "tell" or "recount").[69] But not all aggadic midrashim are found in collections of Midrash; they could be interspersed among various types of Jewish literature. As a point of clarification, I will be citing midrashic interpretations of the Aqedah whether or not they are found in formal collections of Aggadah, since midrashic readings cannot be limited to collections of texts explicitly called *Midrash*.[70]

I take with utmost seriousness the point made by many scholars of the Aggadah that the variety of creative readings we find there, while certainly not exegesis (that is, an attempt to uncover the original intent of the biblical text), do not constitute simply fanciful interpretation. Rather, these midrashim are attempts by Jewish writers to contemporize the biblical text, making it relevant to the issues of their times. Alan Avery-Peck is typical in his explanation that "midrashic literature is not so much exegetical as polemical. It has at its heart the comprehension that Scripture speaks to an age other than the one in which it was written."[71] Or as Abraham Heschel puts it, "To find the true meaning of Aggadah, search deeply into each interpretation. You will find there struggles, worries, and yearnings, eternal problems and contemporary

---

69. Aggadic midrash (which is my focus here) is in contrast to halakic midrash. Halakah refers to legal or ethical teaching, from the Hebrew *hālak*, meaning to "walk," a metaphor for "live," which is often found in the Old Testament / Hebrew Bible and is central to Paul's ethical injunctions in Eph. 4–5 (though many modern translations obscure this by rendering phrases like "walk in love" and "walk in the light" as "live in love" and "live in the light").

70. This means that there are two different (though related) meanings of midrash (plural midrashim). The term can refer to a particular *mode* of biblical interpretation or to a *collection* of such interpretations. When it refers to the latter, the term is usually capitalized, as in Midrash Rabbah or Midrash Tanḥuma.

71. Alan J. Avery-Peck, "Midrash and Exegesis: Insights from Genesis Rabbah on the Binding of Isaac," in *Method Matters: Essays on the Interpretation of the Hebrew Bible in Honor of David L. Petersen*, ed. Joel M. LeMon and Kent Harold Richards, SBLRBS 56 (Atlanta: Society of Biblical Literature, 2009), 443 (entire chapter 441–57).

questions, the travails of community and individual that vexed both the Sages and the nation as a whole."[72]

Specifically in the case of Genesis 22, Karen Winslow speaks of the function of this text as "apologia"—an argument on behalf of the Jewish faith—in which the sages attempt to demonstrate to their pagan neighbors during the Persian period both that the founder of the Jewish religion was willing to give up everything for his God and that this God did not, in the end, require child sacrifice.[73]

Marvin A. Sweeney suggests that the Aqedah is relevant to many different historical periods.

> The critical examination of YHWH's fidelity would be particularly appropriate in the context of the early Persian period as well given the recent experience of the Babylonian exile and questions concerning divine commitment to the restoration. It would also be pertinent in relation to other experience of exile and challenge, for example, the destruction of the Second Temple by Rome in 70 CE, the failure of the Bar Kochba revolt in 135 CE, the massacres of Jews along the Rhine by the Crusader armies in the late eleventh century, the expulsion of Jews from Spain in 1492, the Chmielnitzki massacres of Jews in the mid-seventeenth century, and others.[74]

Without questioning this entirely correct judgment about the nature of midrashic interpretation as addressing the particular context of the interpreters, I want to suggest that many readings of the Aqedah can be understood as attempts to come to grips with two fundamental religious and ethical questions generated by Genesis 22 (perhaps these fit Heschel's "eternal problems," in that they present as problems for interpreters of every age)—namely, Why would God ask this terrible thing of his faithful servant? and Why didn't Abraham protest or intercede for his son?

72. Abraham Joshua Heschel, *Heavenly Torah: As Refracted through the Generations*, ed. and trans. Gordon Tucker and Leonard Levin (New York: Continuum, 2007), 7.

73. Karen Strand Winslow, "*Akedah* as Apologia: The Function of Genesis 22 for Second Temple Jews," in *Orthodoxy and Orthopraxis: Essays in Tribute to Paul Livermore*, ed. Douglas R. Cullum and J. Richard Middleton (Eugene, OR: Pickwick, 2020), 11–26. Winslow attributes this apologetic function to Gen. 22 itself. This depends on a particular dating of Gen. 22, of which I am not convinced. But Winslow's analysis of the uses to which the Aqedah is later put is convincing.

74. Marvin A. Sweeney, *Tanak: A Theological and Critical Introduction to the Jewish Bible* (Minneapolis: Fortress, 2012), 68.

John Spitzer explains that although the orthodox Jewish tradition affirms the validity of God's demand for Abraham to sacrifice his son (and views Abraham's obedient response as normative), "the rabbis, both ancient and modern, cannot allow this understanding of the text to stand. The very core of our being rebels at the very thought that God, who creates and loves and guides and teaches, would demand such a thing."[75]

Whereas a surface reading of many midrashim may seem to justify God or exalt Abraham, such readings leave behind what I take to be traces of the sages' implicit discomfort with the Aqedah.[76] By filling in perceived gaps in the narrative, these ancient interpreters attempt to provide a justification for the excruciating test God put Abraham through, or they suggest a rationale for Abraham's silent obedience (both of which seem, on the surface, irrational, if not unethical).[77]

Approaches That Attempt to Explain Away the Terror of the Aqedah

To begin with, some explanations of the Aqedah simply sidestep the problem of the terrible test.[78] One approach is to link the Aqedah to statements in Jeremiah where YHWH denies that child sacrifice (which Israel was evidently tempted to engage in at the time) was something he ever intended (Jer. 7:31; 19:5; 32:35). The Babylonian Talmud (Ta'anit 4a) quotes lines from Jeremiah 19:5 about child sacrifice ("which I did not command or decree, nor did it enter my mind") and applies the last phrase ("nor did it enter my mind") specifically

---

75. Spitzer, "Judaism," 8.

76. I am grateful to Isaac Kalimi for his wide-ranging essay on the interpretation of the Aqedah ("'Go, I Beg You'"), which first opened my eyes to many of the midrashim that I cite from here on.

77. Spitzer notes that "midrash helps to fill in the silences in [the] text, and to address what seem like obvious questions: Why indeed would God test Abraham?" (Spitzer, "Judaism," 10). A similar point is made by Harold Schulweis: "Rabbinic midrashim of dissent . . . fill in the moral lacunae of biblical narratives, unburdening the believer from a submissive reading of scriptures and a subservient stance toward the Sovereign Commander." Schulweis, *Consciences: The Duty to Obey and the Duty to Disobey* (Woodstock, VT: Jewish Lights, 2008), 12, quoted in Spitzer, "Judaism," 8–9.

78. I presented a preliminary version of the material that follows (combined with a summary of Moses's intercession from chap. 2), titled "What Christians Can Learn from Jewish Interpretation of the Aqedah: Reading Genesis 22 with Moses and the Rabbis," in the Jewish Interpretation of the Bible program unit, at the Society of Biblical Literature annual meeting, Denver, CO, November 18, 2018. Since I utilized the work of Isaac Kalimi as an initial guide to the rabbinic literature, I was delighted to meet him in person in the Denver airport on the way home from the conference. My thanks to Isaac Kalimi for his willingness to chat about my research and for his encouragement.

to "Isaac, son of Abraham."[79] Given God's clear statement in Jeremiah 19:5, the rabbis seem to be claiming that God could never have wanted Abraham to sacrifice Isaac. Nevertheless, we have God's unequivocal instruction to do so in Genesis 22:2.[80]

But linking the Aqedah to Jeremiah 19:5 might not be a tactic to deny that God ever asked Abraham to sacrifice his son. It could be used to emphasize that the Aqedah was intended *only* as a test; God never meant for Abraham to actually go through with the sacrifice.[81]

One way to make this point is to emphasize that God did not coerce Abraham to offer his son, but simply made a request of him. Thus the Babylonian Talmud, Sanhedrin 89b has Rabbi Simeon ben Abba emphasize God's use of the Hebrew particle *nā'* (equivalent to "please") in Genesis 22:2, which softens what would have been a command, making it only a request ("an expression of entreaty"), which Abraham was therefore free to refuse.[82] This may be thought to let God off the hook.[83]

79. The Hebrew with an English translation of Ta'anit 4a can be found on Sefaria.org (https://www.sefaria.org/Taanit.4a?lang=bi). While the third phrase is applied to Isaac, the first phrase ("which I did not command") is applied to Mesha, the Moabite king, who sacrificed his son as a burnt offering (2 Kings 3:27) and the second phrase ("which I did not decree/speak") is applied to Jephthah's sacrifice of his daughter (Judg. 11). Ta'anit 4a is cited by Isaac Kalimi (though with reference to Jer. 7:31, not 19:5) in "'Go, I Beg You,'" 5.

80. Furthermore, there is the famous statement (noted earlier) in Ezek. 20:25 that God gave Israel "statutes that were not good and ordinances by which they could not live," which seems to be a reference to child sacrifice in the next verse (20:26): "I defiled them through their very gifts, in their offering up all their firstborn, in order that I might horrify them, so that they might know that I am the LORD."

81. This is the interpretation given for the cryptic phrase "Isaac, son of Abraham" on the Sefaria website in the expansive English translation (it is typical to have explanatory expansions in translations of the Talmud, meant to clarify the often compressed statements in the original).

82. Babylonian Talmud, Sanhedrin 89b. For the Hebrew with English translation, see: https://www.sefaria.org/Sanhedrin.89b?lang=bi. For another translation, see Kalimi, "'Go, I Beg You,'" 5–6.

83. Although this is supposed to soften the command to a mere request, the way that Rabbi Simeon frames the request ends up sounding like the abuse of power by a superior. He explains the request by using a parable or analogy of a king encouraging a warrior to do one more battle so that all the previous battles wouldn't be viewed by the king's enemies as having no substance. "Likewise, **the Holy One, Blessed be He, also said to Abraham: I have tried you with several ordeals, and you have withstood them all. Now, stand** firm **in this ordeal for Me, so that** others **will not say: There is no substance in the first** ordeals." (Sefaria uses bold for the Babylonian Talmud translation, while the other words are added for clarity). This encouragement for Abraham to "man up" (as we might say), which would show the world that the previous trials that Abraham went through on behalf of God actually meant something, sounds to my ears quite abusive.

Taking a different tack, Midrash Tanḥuma (Buber edition) 17:2 explains that "Abraham's ram was created at twilight" on the first Sabbath eve at the end of God's six days of creation. That the ram Abraham sacrificed in the place of Isaac was prepared from the beginning of the world means that God never intended for Abraham to sacrifice his son.[84] There are also examples of ancient Jewish synagogue art that portray the ram tied to a tree nearby (instead of caught by its horns in a thicket, as Gen. 22:13 says), while Abraham lifts the knife.[85] Although there is no known Jewish *literary* tradition about the tethered ram, this synagogue art testifies to the idea that the ram was not present by accident, but was intended by God to be the replacement of Isaac. So the visual representations suggest that the Aqedah was only a test; God always knew that Isaac would not be sacrificed.[86]

But perhaps the simplest way of exonerating God for the Aqedah is found in Genesis Rabbah 56:8 (an idea attributed to Rabbi Aḥa). When Abraham asks why the change of instruction from "Offer him up" (Gen. 22:2) to "Don't touch the boy" (22:12), God explains that he didn't change his mind. "Did I ever tell you to kill him? No, I told you, 'Bring him up.'"[87] So God tells Abraham:

84. The standard print edition of *Midrash Tanḥuma* is based on a sixteenth-century manuscript from Constantinople, but there is an alternative edition based on manuscripts from the Oxford Library, published by Solomon Buber (the grandfather of Martin Buber) in the late nineteenth century. The interpretation cited here is found in the Buber edition. The translation is taken from Kalimi, "'Go, I Beg You,'" 5nn16–17. The claim that the ram was prepared at dusk on the sixth day of creation is found also in Pirqe Avot 5:6; in Sifre Devarim 355; and in Pirqe de-Rabbi Eliezer 19. For various lists of the ten things created at dusk/twilight on the sixth day, see van der Heide, *"Now I Know,"* 463–65 ("Appendix II: The Ten Things Created at Dusk").

85. The image of the tethered ram is found in a fresco in the Dura-Europos synagogue (mid-third century CE) and in floor mosaics of both the Sepphoris synagogue (early fifth century CE) and the Beit Alpha synagogue (early sixth century CE). A Christian representation of the tethered lamb in an Aqedah scene can be found in the Chapel of Peace (mid-fourth century CE) in the El Bagawat necropolis (an ancient burial site in Egypt that was at some point taken over by Christians). For a discussion of these (and other) artistic representations of the Aqedah, see Edward Kessler, "The Sacrifice of Isaac (the *Akedah*) in Christian and Jewish Tradition: Artistic Representations," in *Borders, Boundaries and the Bible*, ed. Martin O'Kane, JSOTSup 313 (Sheffield: Sheffield Academic Press, 2002), 74–98. A version of this book chapter is published online as Kessler, "A Response to Marc Bregman," *JTR* 2, no. 1 (June 2003), http://jtr.shanti.virginia.edu/volume-2-number-1/response-to-marc-bregman/ (there is significant overlap between the chapter and the online article, but they are not identical).

86. Although there is no known Jewish literary tradition for the tethered ram, there seems to be an early Christian tradition for this idea. Kessler cites a fourth-century Coptic Bible that mentions the ram tied to a tree. Kessler, "Response to Marc Bregman" (not cited in Kessler, "Sacrifice of Isaac").

87. Given that this midrash has God quote Ps. 89:34 (ET 89:35) to Abraham ("I will not alter what has gone out of my lips"), it is possible that part of the issue being addressed is divine mutability.

"Well and good! You did indeed bring him up. Now take him down" (Genesis Rabbah 56:8).[88] This reading suggests that Abraham misunderstood when God used the Hiphil of '*ālâ* (22:2). Since the verb '*ālâ* means to "go up," and the Hiphil stem gives it a causative meaning, God meant only for Abraham to *bring Isaac up* on the mountain (possibly to worship), but Abraham mistakenly thought it meant to *offer him up* as a sacrifice.[89] This softening of the troubling command is another way to address the scandal of the Aqedah and to clear God of wrongdoing.[90]

"After These Words": Attempts to Explain Why God Tested Abraham

In order to explain why God would put Abraham through this test, some midrashim appeal to the opening phrase of Genesis 22:1, '*aḥar haddəbārîm hā'ēlleh*, which means (in context) "after these things"—that is, "sometime later" (as it does in 15:1; 39:7; and 48:1). But since *dābār* can also mean "word," some later interpreters read this phrase as "after these words." The assumption was that some conversation must have taken place that would explain why God subjected his servant to this severe test. So the question became, What "words" (*dəbārîm*) are being referred to?

After the Words of Satan (Babylonian Talmud, Sanhedrin 89b)

One suggestion is that words spoken by Satan led to the test. Rabbi Yoḥanan (in the name of Rabbi Yose ben Zimra) suggests that in response to the great feast that Abraham gave the day that Isaac was weaned (mentioned in Gen.

88. *Genesis Rabbah: The Judaic Commentary to the Book of Genesis—a New American Translation*, vol. 2, *Parashiyyot Thirty-Four through Sixty-Seven on Genesis 8:15–28:9*, trans. Jacob Neusner, BJS 105 (Atlanta: Scholars Press, 1985), 284. This interpretation was followed by medieval Jewish writers such as Rashi (1040–1105) in his commentary on Gen. 22:2, Ibn Ezra (1089–1164 or 1093–1167 [dating varies]) on Gen. 22:1 and Abarbanel (1437–1508) on Gen. 22:2 and 12, cited in Lippman Bodoff, "The Real Test of the *Akedah*: Blind Obedience versus Moral Choice," *Judaism* 42, no. 1 (1993): 71–92; reprinted under the same title in *The Binding of Isaac, Religious Murders, and Kabbalah: Seeds of Jewish Extremism and Alienation?* (Jerusalem: Devora, 2005), 32, 51n16 (entire chapter 29–58).

89. However, this is quite far-fetched, since the Hiphil of '*ālâ* is, indeed, the usual way to describe offering a burnt offering (that is, *to cause it to go up* in smoke), and Gen. 22:2 has not only the verb but also the *noun* for "burnt offering": "Take . . . your son . . . and offer him [Hiphil of '*ālâ*] . . . as a burnt offering ['*olâ*] on one of the mountains that I will tell you."

90. As Lisa Brush puts it in a D'var Torah (sermon) for Rosh Ha-Shana Day 2, this "emphasis on 'bring him up,' instead of 'slaughter him'" is an example of "the rabbinic tradition's clutching at straws to resolve a clumsy problem in the text"—namely, that the test "seems so likely to brutalize the spirit of both Abraham and Isaac." Brush, "The Akedah/The Binding of Isaac = Genesis 22:1–24."

21:8), "Satan said before the Holy One, Blessed be He, 'This old man whom you graced with fruit of the womb at one-hundred years, did he not have one turtledove or one pigeon to offer before you from the entire feast that he made!?'" God then rose to Abraham's defense. He acknowledges that Abraham was honoring his son at the banquet, but goes on to say: "If I say to him 'Sacrifice your son before me' he would sacrifice him immediately.'" Which leads to the test in Genesis 22.[91]

After the Words of Prince Mastema (Jubilees 17-18)

The idea that the test was prompted by Satan goes back to the earliest post-biblical Jewish commentary on the Aqedah—namely, the book of Jubilees.[92] Drawing on the role of the Accuser in the first chapters of Job (and also 1 Chron. 21:1), Jubilees 17–18 (specifically 17:15–18:19) has Prince Mastema incite God to test Abraham to see if he loves God as much as he loves Isaac.

We are told that "words came in heaven concerning Abraham that he was faithful in everything which was told him and he loved the Lord and was faithful in all afflictions. And Prince Mastema came and he said before God, 'Behold, Abraham loves Isaac, his son. And he is more pleased with him than everything. Tell him to offer him (as) a burnt offering upon the altar. And you will see whether he will do this thing. And you will know whether he is faithful in everything in which you test him'" (Jub. 17:15–16). However, God does not doubt Abraham's ability to pass the test; and when Abraham *does* pass, we are told that "Prince Mastema was shamed" (18:11–12).[93]

After the Words of the Angels (Biblical Antiquities 32:1-4)

A different interpretation is given in Pseudo-Philo (*Biblical Antiquities* 32:1–4), which implicitly addresses the question of which words preceded the Aqedah. There we are told that "all the angels were jealous of him and the

91. Babylonian Talmud, Sanhedrin 89b. Trans. Levenson, *Death and Resurrection of the Beloved Son*, 177. For another rendering, see Sefaria.org, https://www.sefaria.org/Sanhedrin .89b?lang=bi.
92. Walter Moberly suggests that the second angel speech (Gen. 22:15–18) is actually the first commentary on the Aqedah (which originally consisted of 22:1–14, 19). Moberly, "The Earliest Commentary on the Akedah," *VT* 38, no. 3 (1988): 302–23.
93. O. S. Wintermute, trans., "Jubilees: A New Translation and Introduction," in J. H. Charlesworth, *The Old Testament Pseudepigrapha*, vol. 2, *Expansions of the Old Testament and Legends, Wisdom and Philosophical Literature, Prayers, Psalms, and Odes, Fragments of Lost Judeo-Hellenistic Works*, ABRL (Garden City, NY: Doubleday, 1985), 90–91 (entire work 35–142).

worshiping hosts envied him," though no words are actually quoted at this point.[94] This jealousy leads God to test Abraham.[95] And when Abraham willingly goes to offer his son, God stops him and notes that this would shut the mouths of those who speak evil against him (which suggests that the angels had, indeed, been trash-talking).[96]

After the Words of Isaac (Babylonian Talmud, Sanhedrin 89b; Targum Pseudo-Jonathan)

In another interpretation, Isaac's boast to Ishmael prods God to act. One version is found in the Babylonian Talmud, Sanhedrin 89b, where Rabbi Levi says, "Ishmael said to Isaac: I am greater than you in the fulfillment of mitzvot, as you were circumcised at the age of eight days . . . and I at the age of thirteen years." In other words, Ishmael willingly submitted to circumcision, whereas Isaac had no choice. Isaac replies, "And do you provoke me with one organ? If the Holy One, Blessed be He, were to say to me: Sacrifice yourself before Me, I would sacrifice myself." So God takes him up on it, which leads to the command in Genesis 22:2.[97]

In another version (Targum Pseudo-Jonathan on Gen. 22:1), the dispute between Isaac and Ishmael is about who is the rightful heir of Abraham, with Ishmael arguing that he should inherit since he is the firstborn and Isaac arguing that he should inherit since he is the son of Sarah. When Ishmael makes the point about the different ages at which they were circumcised, to show who is more worthy of being the heir, Isaac replies, "Behold now, today I am thirty and six years old; and if the Holy One, blessed be He, were to require all my members, I would not delay. These words were heard before the Lord

94. The "him" is ambiguous. In context, it most likely refers to Abraham, though some interpreters (e.g., Kalimi, "'Go, I Beg You,'" 9) think it is Isaac (since this line comes right after God's gift of a son to Abraham and Sarah).

95. Pseudo-Philo, *Biblical Antiquities* 32:1–2. Trans. D. J. Harrington, "Pseudo-Philo (First Century A.D.): A New Translation and Introduction," in Charlesworth, *Old Testament Pseudepigrapha* 2:345 (entire work 297–377). On the angels' jealousy, see also Genesis Rabbah 55:4.

96. Pseudo-Philo, *Biblical Antiquities* 32:4. Trans. Harrington, "Pseudo-Philo," 346.

97. Trans. from Sefaria.org, https://www.sefaria.org/Sanhedrin.89b?lang=bi. The English text on the Sefaria website gives the translation in bold, with ordinary font filling in the gaps: "**Ishmael said to Isaac: I am greater than you in** the fulfillment of **mitzvot, as you were circumcised** at the **age of eight days,** without your knowledge and without your consent, **and** I was circumcised at the **age of thirteen years,** with both my knowledge and my consent. Isaac **said to Ishmael: And do you provoke me with one organ? If the Holy One, Blessed be He,** were to **say to me: Sacrifice yourself before Me, I** would **sacrifice** myself. **Immediately, God tried Abraham,** to confirm that Isaac was sincere in his offer to give his life."

of the world" and, as Pseudo-Jonathan puts it, the word (*mêmrā'*) of the LORD tested Abraham.[98]

The above are some examples of speculation about what possible "words" could have prompted the otherwise inexplicable test.

"After These Things": Further Attempts to Explain Why God Tested Abraham

But it is possible to take '*aḥar haddəbārîm hā'ēlleh* as "after these things," or "after these deeds." What "things" or "deeds" (events) could have led to the test?

After God's Many Blessings Showered on Abraham

The earliest example of this approach comes from pre-rabbinic times. In his *Jewish Antiquities*, Josephus suggests that the deeds were God's benevolent acts on behalf of Abraham. He suggests that God enumerated all the blessings and benefits he had bestowed on Abraham throughout his life, including military and political advantages, as in Genesis 14 (Josephus being a historian of political history). Then God tested Abraham's "piety" (*thrēskeia*), to see if he was genuinely grateful, evident in his devoted response to these benefits.[99]

After Abraham's Pride in Isaac, Which Led to His Covenant with the Philistines

Another possibility, suggested by Rashbam (Rabbi Samuel ben Meir, 1080–1160 CE), is that the test was prompted by Abraham's inappropriate pride in Isaac, which led him to make a covenant with the Philistines (in Gen. 21:32). Although nothing in Genesis suggests that this covenant was problematic, much less that it was prompted by pride in Isaac, Rashbam pictures God as upset by this covenant and especially by Abraham's underlying pride. So God tells Abraham, "You became proud of your son that I gave you and made a covenant with them; now go and make him a burnt offering, and we shall see what will happen with the covenant."[100] In this account, the test came on account of a failing of Abraham.

98. Trans. from Sefaria.org, https://www.sefaria.org/Targum_Jonathan_on_Genesis.22 .1?lang=bi.

99. Josephus, *Jewish Antiquities* 1.223–24. See Kalimi, "'Go, I Beg You,'" 9–10.

100. Rashbam's commentary on Gen. 22:1. Trans. Kalimi, "'Go, I Beg You,'" 10. For a fuller discussion, see Martin I. Lockshin, *Rabbi Samuel Ben Meir's Commentary on Genesis: An Annotated Translation*, Jewish Studies (Lewiston, NY: Edwin Mellen, 1989), 96.

After Abraham's Unworthy Thoughts about God

But *Midrash Tanḥuma* goes even further. In order to explain why God would command this thing of Abraham, the midrash (seventh century CE) interprets the Aqedah not as God testing Abraham but as God essentially punishing Abraham for harboring thoughts in his heart about God's mal-treatment of him. Or, if not exactly punishing him, then requiring atone-ment from him for this sin. This text is an example of the Jewish anti-protest tradition mentioned earlier, which disallows any questioning of God.

According to the text (citing the words of Rabbi Levi), "Abraham once pondered over the matter of divine justice" by wondering whether God had treated him too kindly in this world, with the result that he might have no reward in the world to come (this is based on the developing idea in Juda-ism at the time that the righteous are punished for small sins in this world, which protects them from more serious punishment in the world to come; but Abraham had received only God's blessing).

To this implicit criticism of God in Abraham's thoughts, God responded, "Since you dare to reflect upon My actions, you must bring a burnt offering to Me. Therefore, He said: *Take now thy son, thine only son, whom thou lovest, even Isaac, and get thee into the land of Moriah; and offer him there for a burnt offering upon one of the mountains which I will tell thee of.*"[101]

Yet this is clearly an unusual text. By far, the dominant approach to the Aqedah in the Jewish interpretive tradition is to valorize Abraham as God's faithful servant.

The Attempt to Provide a Motivation for Abraham's Silent Obedience

This valorization is particularly emphasized in the next midrash, which ad-dresses the terror of the Aqedah by attempting to supply a plausible reason or motivation for Abraham's seemingly silent obedience (since, on the surface, this seems inexplicable). Surely Abraham should have protested this terrible command (or request, given that God did say *nā'*). Couldn't he have at least interceded for Isaac, as he did for Sodom (or for Lot)?

Pseudo-Philo noted that "Abraham did not argue, but set out immediately."[102] The question is, *Why* this immediate and silent obedience?

101. *Midrash Tanḥuma*, Lekh lekha 10:2. Trans. from Sefaria.org, https://www.sefaria.org /Midrash_Tanchuma%2C_Lech_Lecha.10 (emphasis original). Weiss addresses this episode in "Sin of Protesting God," 384.

102. Pseudo-Philo, *Biblical Antiquities* 32:2. Trans. Harrington, "Pseudo-Philo," 345.

Abraham Withholds Fatherly Compassion for the Sake of Later Generations (Genesis Rabbah 56:10)

An important explanation in the Jewish tradition is to treat Abraham's silent obedience as his strenuous overcoming of natural father-love, in order to intentionally sacrifice his own son; the reason he does this is so that later generations might benefit. In Genesis Rabbah 56:10, Rabbi Yoḥanan explains that after the test, Abraham told God, "I conquered my mercy to do Your will. May it be your will, Ad-nai our God, that in the hour when the sons of Itzchak come to do transgressions and bad deeds, that this very Binding [*Akeidah*] be remembered for them, and may You be filled with Mercy on them!"[103]

Of course, this motivation makes sense only after Isaac is spared; it couldn't actually be the motivation in advance, since if Abraham actually expected to go through with the sacrifice, Isaac wouldn't exist to have any descendents. Nevertheless, this midrash turns what might be viewed as a liability into an asset. God now owes Abraham, big time. On this view Abraham's silent obedience accrues merit to later generations.[104]

How Abraham's Obedience Brought Merit to Later Generations

Other texts accept the above motivation and attempt to explain how and why Abraham's act of obedience brought merit to later generations (the mechanism, if you will, of the transaction).[105]

Some interpretations focus on the repetition of God *seeing* in the Aqedah (the verb *rā'â* for "see" or "see to"/"provide" is mentioned in Gen. 22:8 and 14). Thus the Mekhilta de-Rabbi Ishmael (a halakic midrash on Exodus) links the theme of God seeing in the Aqedah to the Passover in Exodus 12:13 (where God says that when he *sees the blood* on the lintels he will spare the

---

103. Trans. from Sefaria.org, https://www.sefaria.org/Bereishit_Rabbah.56.10?lang=bi&with=all&lang2=en.

104. This is the famous doctrine of the merit of the ancestors (*zaḥut avot*). Moses's appeal to God's covenant with the ancestors in Exod. 32:13 as the basis for mercy toward Israel after the golden calf episode is quite different. Moses's appeal was not based on any merit that accrued from the ancestors' actions, but was grounded in God's own pledge that the descendants of Abraham, Isaac, and Jacob would inherit the land.

105. Genesis Rabbah 56:8 connects the merit to Abraham's willing obedience as if he were sacrificing himself. God explains to Abraham, "I ascribe merit to you as though I had told to you to sacrifice yourself and you did not refuse." Trans. from Sefaria.org, https://www.sefaria.org/Bereishit_Rabbah.56.8?lang=bi&with=all&lang2=en.

household), and also to the outcome of David's census in 1 Chronicles 21:15, when the angel is about to destroy Jerusalem and God relents of the evil he was about to do because of what he sees. According to this interpretation, God relented (in Exodus and in Chronicles) because he saw "the blood of the binding of Isaac."[106] So Isaac's spilt blood on Moriah leads to God's later leniency toward Israel (and Chronicles understands Moriah as the very place where the angel relented).

This interpretation assumes that Isaac's blood (at least some of it) was actually spilled, which certainly goes beyond Genesis 22. This led to a great deal of debate, with one text suggesting that a quarter of a measure of Isaac's blood was spilt (Mekhilta de-Rabbi Shimon bar Yoḥai, Sanya 6.2),[107] and another that Abraham had *intended* to shed a quarter of a measure of Isaac's blood, though he was prevented (*Midrash Tanḥuma*, Vayera 23),[108] and yet another suggesting that Isaac's blood was not actually spilt, but that God saw the blood of the ram that Abraham offered *as if* it were Isaac's blood (Genesis Rabbah 56:9).[109]

Other texts (like Babylonian Talmud, Berakhot 62b; Targum Chronicles on 1 Chron. 21:15) claim that the angel of the LORD in 1 Chronicles 21:15 saw the *ashes*, not the blood, of Isaac—which assumes that Abraham went through with the 'olâ, which clearly goes beyond the text of Genesis 22.[110] There is so much speculation about the ashes of Isaac that it would be impossible to list

106. Trans. Levenson, *Death and Resurrection of the Beloved Son*, 180. For another translation, see, Jacob Z. Lauterbach, *Mekhilta de-Rabbi Ishmael*, 2nd ed. (Philadelphia: Jewish Publication Society, 2004), 40. This interpretation is found in Pisha 7 (on Exod. 12:11–14).

107. The commentary on Exodus known as the Mekhilta de-Rabbi Shimon bar Yoḥai has God telling Moses, "I am trustworthy to pay the reward [for the devoted action of] Isaac son of Abraham, from whom departed a fourth [of a log] of blood on top of the altar." God then says that he will bring about the redemption from Egypt because of Abraham's "great strength." Trans. W. David Nelson, *Mekhilta de-Rabbi Shimon bar Yoḥai* (Philadelphia: Jewish Publication Society, 2006), 9 (Sanya 6.2).

108. According to *Midrash Tanḥuma*, Vayera 23, "after they had constructed the altar, Abraham bound Isaac upon it and took the knife in hand to slaughter him until a fourth of a measure of blood would flow from his body," but he was prevented from doing so. Trans. Samuel A. Berman, Sefaria.org, https://www.sefaria.org/Midrash_Tanchuma%2C_Vayera.23.4?lang=bi&with=all&lang2=en.

109. In Genesis Rabbah 56:9, Abraham prays to God, "Sovereign of the Universe! Look upon the blood of this ram as though it were the blood of my son Itzchak." Trans. from Sefaria.org, https://www.sefaria.org/Bereishit_Rabbah.56.9?lang=bi&with=all&lang2=en.

110. A translation of Babylonian Talmud, Berakhot 62b can be found on Sefaria.org, https://www.sefaria.org/Berakhot.62b.15?lang=bi&with=all&lang2=en. For Targum Chronicles, see J. Staley McIvor, *The Targums of Ruth and Chronicles*, ArBib 19 (Wilmington, DE: Michael Glazier, 1994).

all the references here. But a fascinating one is the Talmudic reference to the returning exiles knowing where to rebuild the temple because they were able to locate the ashes of Isaac.[111] However, not all the sages agreed that Isaac was actually sacrificed; one interpretation is that the ram's name was "Isaac" (Midrash Hagadol on Gen. 22:13), while another reading suggested that God saw the ashes of Isaac *as if* they were gathered from the altar (Jerusalem Talmud, Hagigah 2:1, 8a; Midrash Hagadol on Gen. 22:19).[112]

These explanations about God seeing the blood or ashes of Isaac are all attempts to make the Aqedah relevant to later times, initially by having the Aqedah ground the efficacy of sacrifice at the Jerusalem temple and later providing the basis for God's deliverance of his people from persecution in Selucid, Roman, or Christian eras. Whether it is Isaac's blood or his ashes, a seemingly inexplicable incident is given a rationale, such that merit accrues from the Aqedah to later generations of Abraham's children.

There are other examples of midrashic attempts to propose a rationale for the Aqedah. But perhaps these are sufficient to make the point. Whereas a surface reading of these texts may seem to justify God, or exalt Abraham, the very need to propose such readings is testimony to the sages' implicit discomfort with the Aqedah.

But the sages' discomfort is surely tame when compared with the abrasive prayers of the lament psalms, with Moses's challenge to God over perceived injustice in God's action toward Israel, or with Job's vocal protests about his suffering. Indeed, the sages' discomfort is tame when compared with Abraham's own challenge to God over the possible destruction of Sodom in Genesis 18.

Given that Abraham himself voiced honest protest in Genesis 18, the question remains why Abraham attempts to obey the divine instruction to sacrifice his son without so much as a word of demurral in Genesis 22. In the chapters that follow, I will propose my own interpretation of the Aqedah.

---

111. Found in the Zevahim 62a. For a translation of this text, see Sefaria.org, https://www.sefaria.org/Zevachim.62a.5?lang=bi&with=all&lang2=en.

112. These sources are given in Kalimi, "'Go, I Beg You,'" 25; see also Speigel, *Last Trial*, 40–43.

6

Reading Rhetorical Signals in the Aqedah and Job

So far we have taken a look at some of the ways in which ancient Jewish interpretation attempted to fill in the gaps in the Aqedah, ways that suggest unease with the story as it stands in Genesis 22. It is now time to begin laying out my own interpretation of Abraham's test.

As a step toward this interpretation, this chapter notes evidence internal to the story of the Aqedah for signs that things are not as they should be, especially that all is not right with Abraham—or with Isaac, for that matter. My approach to Genesis 22 here is similar to what William P. Brown describes as "reading with wonder": "It is a way of abiding in the text while also bumping around within it, feeling the text's jagged contours, peering into its dark crevices, looking for anomalies and subtleties that raise eyebrows as well as, on occasion, the hair on the back of the neck."[1] Although this will involve probing beneath a surface reading of the text, I will nevertheless attempt to stay close to the text itself—that is, I am attempting not a midrashic reading (with a creative filling in of the gaps) but rather a nuanced literary or rhetorical reading of textual details (closer to the Jewish notion of peshat).

1. William P. Brown, *Sacred Sense: Discovering the Wonder of God's Word and World* (Grand Rapids: Eerdmans, 2015), 11.

The Question of a Responsible Approach to Reading the Aqedah

This, however, raises the thorny issue of whether it is responsible to infer significance from textual clues left by the narrator, if their point is not explicitly stated. And what about probing beneath the surface to try to sympathetically read the attitude or point of view of the characters? This is an especially pointed question for a narrative like the Aqedah, which is particularly reticent about such details. As Erich Auerbach famously put it in his classic study, whereas the Homeric epics are characterized by "fully externalized description," Hebrew narrative (and especially Gen. 22) is "fraught with background."[2] But very little is in the foreground. A lot is left to the imagination of the reader.

In keeping with Auerbach's description, Jon Levenson reminds us that "the narrator's technique . . . keeps us in the dark on the issue of Abraham's subjectivity."[3] Robert Alter likewise notes that Hebrew narrative produces "a certain indeterminacy of meaning, especially in regard to motive, moral character, and psychology."[4]

But just because we are not explicitly told about a character's mental or emotional state does not mean that we are prohibited from making reasonable inferences from clues the narrator gives us. As Shai Held notes, this would be "an extremely odd way to read the Bible—or any other literature, for that matter. Textual positivism of this sort can blind us to the subtle emotional richness of the text."[5]

Of course, we cannot claim to know definitively what any character is thinking or feeling, if the text does not tell us in so many words. Yet Held's comments on Genesis 22 are surely on the mark:

> Part of the power of the text lies precisely in the fact that the narrator does
> not tell us what Abraham is feeling. But the implication of that silence is

2. Erich Auerbach, *Mimesis: The Representation of Reality in Western Literature*, trans. Willard R. Trask (Princeton: Princeton University Press, 1953), 22, 12. Auerbach addresses this characteristic of Hebrew narrative in chap. 1, "Odysseus' Scar," 3–23. His discussion of the Aqedah is found on pp. 7–12.

3. Jon D. Levenson, *The Death and Resurrection of the Beloved Son: The Transformation of Child Sacrifice in Judaism and Christianity* (New Haven: Yale University Press, 1993), 131.

4. Robert Alter, *The Art of Biblical Narrative* (New York: Basic Books, 1981), 12.

5. Shai Held, "A Response to My Respondents," *Canadian-American Theological Review* 9, no. 1 (2020): 53 (entire article 43–54). This is Held's response to a critique of how he read the Joseph story in his two-volume work, *The Heart of Torah* (Philadelphia: Jewish Publication Society, 2017). From a symposium on November 24, 2019, at the Society of Biblical Literature annual meeting in San Diego, CA.

not that Abraham isn't feeling anything, or that the reader should remain completely agnostic about the patriarch's inner life. On the contrary, the narrator's silence invites us in, opens the door for us to imagine the thoughts and feelings that were undoubtedly swirling inside Abraham on that fateful climb.[6]

Although uncovering the possible thoughts and feelings of the characters is not my primary purpose, this will enter the exposition at various points. My focus in what follows will be on a range of rhetorical signals left by the narrator that complicate a simple reading of the Aqedah—only some of which suggest Abraham's interior state. I will explore the significance of these signals as a preliminary gesture toward my alternative interpretation of the Aqedah.

At the end of this chapter, as a transition to my full-fledged interpretation of the Aqedah, I will turn to clues in the book of Job that link the characters of Job and Abraham; these thematic and intertextual links are what initially led me to wonder about the relationship (especially the contrast) between Abraham's response in the Aqedah and Job's response to his test. Could it be that the book of Job is an intentional response to (and critique of) the Aqedah? And how might that impact our interpretation of the latter?

But first, let us attend to rhetorical signals in Genesis 22. My observations from here on will follow the approximate sequence of the narrative, beginning with the first verse. For that we need to have before us a relatively literal translation of the text.

Translation of Genesis 22:1-19

[1]After these things God tested Abraham.

He said to him, "Abraham!" And he said, "Here I am." [2]He said, "Take, please, your son, your only one, whom you love—Isaac; and go to the land of Moriah, and offer him there as a burnt offering on one of the mountains that I will tell you."

6. Held, "Response to My Respondents," 53. Held comments further, "Genesis 22, for example, tells us nothing explicit about what Abraham feels as he climbs Mount Moriah to sacrifice his son. Is it anachronistic to imagine that Abraham may have been bewildered by God's command, wondering how God could demand that a father slay his son; confused about how God had finally fulfilled God's promises to Abraham and now threatened to undo them; terrified that perhaps he would not be able to sacrifice his son, and no less terrified that perhaps he would? Guilt-ridden, about what Sarah would say? And so on" (53).

³So Abraham rose early in the morning, and saddled his donkey; then he took two of his young men with him, and Isaac his son; and he cut the wood for a burnt offering. Then he arose and went to the place that God had told him.

⁴On the third day Abraham lifted his eyes and saw the place from afar. ⁵Then Abraham said to his young men, "Stay here with the donkey; I and the young man will go over there; we will worship, and we will return to you."

⁶Abraham took the wood of the burnt offering and placed it on Isaac his son, and he took in his hand the fire and the knife.

So the two of them went together.

⁷Isaac said to Abraham his father and he said, "My father!" And he said, "Here I am, my son." He said, "Here are the fire and the wood, but where is the sheep for a burnt offering?" ⁸Abraham said, "God himself will see to/provide the sheep for a burnt offering, my son."

So the two of them went together.

⁹When they came to the place that God had told him, Abraham built an altar there and laid out the wood. He bound Isaac his son, and placed him on the altar, on top of the wood. ¹⁰Then Abraham stretched out his hand and took the knife to slaughter his son.

¹¹But the angel of YHWH called to him from heaven, and said, "Abraham, Abraham!" And he said, "Here I am." ¹²He said, "Do not stretch out your hand to the young man or do anything to him; for now I know that you are a God-fearer, since you have not withheld your son, your only one, from me."

¹³And Abraham lifted his eyes and saw—there—a ram behind, caught in a thicket by its horns. Abraham went and took the ram and offered it up as a burnt offering instead of his son. ¹⁴So Abraham called that place "YHWH sees/provides"; as it is said to this day, "On the mount of YHWH it shall be seen/provided."

¹⁵The angel of YHWH called to Abraham a second time from heaven, ¹⁶and said, "By myself I have sworn, declares YHWH: Because you have done this thing, and have not withheld your son, your only one, ¹⁷I will certainly bless you, and I will greatly multiply your offspring like the stars of the heaven and like the sand that is on the seashore, and your offspring shall possess the gate of their enemies. ¹⁸And by your offspring shall all the nations of the earth bless themselves, because you have listened to my voice."

¹⁹So Abraham returned to his young men, and they arose and went together to Beersheba; and Abraham lived at Beersheba.

The Shift from YHWH to *hā'ĕlōhîm* (Gen. 22:1)

The first clue that something unusual is going on in Genesis 22 is that it is *hā'ĕlōhîm* and not YHWH who speaks to Abraham. Every *other* time God speaks to Abraham in Genesis, the narrator uses the covenant name YHWH to introduce God's speech (12:1, 7; 13:14; 15:1, 4, 7; 17:1; 18:13, 17, 20, 26, 33).[7] So the introduction in 22:1 is unique.

Besides the narrator's own introduction, on one prior occasion, God as speaker self-identifies to Abram as YHWH (15:7) and another time as El Shaddai (17:1). In Genesis 17, the narrator first uses YHWH to introduce God's speech (17:1), then goes on to use *'ĕlōhîm* in the rest of the chapter for introducing God's speech resumptions (17:3, 9, 15, 19, 22) and at one place notes that Abraham spoke to *hā'ĕlōhîm* (17:18).[8] But 22:1 is the only place in the book of Genesis that the narrator himself uses *'ĕlōhîm* to introduce a speech from God to Abraham. The attentive reader will note this deviation from the pattern.[9] While we don't know for certain what the purpose of this deviation is, the effect is striking—and, I might add, ominous.

One possible parallel to this shift from YHWH to the generic term for God is found in the garden story in Genesis 3. There the snake and the woman refer to the Creator merely as "God" (*'ĕlōhîm*) in their dialogue, rather than as YHWH *'ĕlōhîm*. They avoid the unique covenant name that the narrator consistently uses throughout Genesis 2–3, perhaps as a distancing tactic, which contributes to the woman's false discernment of the tree.[10]

And yet the name used in Genesis 22:1 is not simply *'ĕlōhîm* but includes the definite article (*hā'ĕlōhîm*). It is possible that this is not a significant variation. However, it could be taken to mean "the gods," since *'ĕlōhîm* can

---

7. These references represent six separate occasions on which God speaks to Abraham (twice in chap. 12, once each in chaps. 13, 15, 17, and 18). Genesis 22 represents the seventh and final occasion.

8. Genesis 17 is typically thought to be from the Priestly source, which tends to avoid the name YHWH in reference to God prior to the revelation of the name to Moses. Apart from the narrator's use of YHWH in the introduction and God's initial self-identification as El Shaddai (17:1), the chapter is characterized by the predominant use of *'ĕlōhîm*.

9. Of course, this could be a source-critical matter, since the bulk of the Aqedah (apart from the angel speeches) has historically been assigned to the putative Elohistic source. Whether or not this is correct (and contemporary scholars tend to doubt the existence of an Elohistic source), it doesn't change the fact that the editor who put the Abraham story together elected to leave *hā'ĕlōhîm* here and not change it to YHWH. Thomas Römer explores possible reasons why there is a preponderance of *'ĕlōhîm* in Gen. 20–22 if there is no Elohistic source. See Römer, "Abraham's Righteousness and Sacrifice: How to Understand (and Translate) Genesis 15 and 22," CV 54 (2012): 7–9 (entire article 3–15).

10. For this rhetorical shift (along with others) in the dialogue between the snake and the woman, see J. Richard Middleton, "Reading Genesis 3 Attentive to Human Evolution: Beyond Concordism and Non-overlapping Magisteria," in *Evolution and the Fall*, ed. William T. Cavanaugh and James K. A. Smith (Grand Rapids: Eerdmans, 2017), 67–97.

have a plural meaning; but given the narrator's use of singular verbs with *hā'ĕlōhîm* (22:1, 3, 9), the fact that God speaks in the first person singular (22:2), and that Abraham uses a singular verb with *'ĕlōhîm* (22:8), it seems to be intended as singular. Thomas Römer suggests that *hā'ĕlōhîm*, which is common in Ecclesiastes and other late biblical texts, "is used to denote a god that dwells far away from humans and appears to be incomprehensible. The same may hold true for Genesis 22."[11] Römer, therefore, suggests that we translate *hā'ĕlōhîm* as "the deity" to convey the sense of distance; so 22:1 could be rendered, "After these things *the deity* tested Abraham."[12]

Although we cannot be sure of the reason for the narrator's switch from YHWH to *hā'ĕlōhîm* in 22:1, 3, and 9, my hunch is that we are thereby put on notice that the issue at stake is whether Abraham's God is just a generic deity, like the gods of the nations (*hā'ĕlōhîm*), or the one known as YHWH, whose distinctive character Abraham needs to come to understand.[13] Indeed, while it is *hā'ĕlōhîm* who commands the sacrifice of Isaac, this sacrifice is stopped by a messenger or angel of YHWH (22:11), who speaks in YHWH's name; and the name YHWH becomes connected to the place of Isaac's rescue (22:14)—in both a place name ("YHWH sees/provides") and a saying ("On the mount of YHWH it shall be seen/provided"). Perhaps this switch from *hā'ĕlōhîm* to YHWH in the narrative is a signal to the reader that the instruction to sacrifice Abraham's son could not be something that the deity known as YHWH really wants (or expects) Abraham to do.[14]

11. Römer, "Abraham's Righteousness and Sacrifice," 9.

12. Römer, "Abraham's Righteousness and Sacrifice," 9–10.

13. As we saw in an earlier chapter, after his series of intercessions with God in Exod. 33–34, Moses came to an understanding of the distinctive character of God; thus the golden calf narrative climaxes with a revelation of the meaning of the name YHWH (34:5–7). I believe that the issue of Abraham's coming to know the character of YHWH is crucial to the Aqedah; I will address this in the next chapter.

14. A search for *hā'ĕlōhîm* in the ancestral narratives shows that it is used three other times in the Abraham story—all by the narrator—to describe occasions when Abraham speaks to God (17:18), when God speaks to Abimelech (20:6), and when Abraham prays to God (20:17); that is, it is used in situations narrating human interaction with God. It is possible that this usage communicates the perspective of the person doing the interacting.

This may be an example of what Robert Polzin, in a different context, calls "concealed reported speech"—that is, where the narrator voices the perspective of a character, rather than his own point of view. See Polzin, *Samuel and the Deuteronomist: A Literary Study of the Deuteronomistic History*, part 2, *1 Samuel* (Bloomington: Indiana University Press, 1993), 20–21. The use of *hā'ĕlōhîm* in the three situations listed above might be intended to convey the understanding of God (as somewhat distant, according to Römer's analysis) from the point of view of the person in the narrative.

But that still leaves the nagging question: *Why* does God (under any name) ask Abraham to do this thing? I will return to this question explicitly in the next chapter.

The Initial Description of Isaac (Gen. 22:2)

For now, let us notice how Isaac is described in verse 2. For anyone who knows the earlier Abraham story, it is quite strange that Isaac is described as "your son, your only one [*yǝḥîdǝkā*]." After all, didn't Abraham have *two* sons— Ishmael and Isaac?

Some translations (like NJPS) render *yǝḥîdǝkā* as "your favored one," in an attempt to make sense of the term.[15] But there is a famous midrash in Genesis Rabbah 55:7 that assumes the word (no matter how translated) would be confusing to Abraham, and so imagines a conversation between Abraham and God, where Abraham tries to clarify which son is intended.

> Said God to him: "Take, I beg you—please—Your son." "Which son? I have two sons" he said. "Your only son," replied He. "This one is the only one of his mother, and this one is the only one of his mother." "The one you love"—"Is there a limit to the affections?" "Itzchak" said He.[16]

The relevance of Polzin's suggestion to Gen. 22 can be explored by noting that in the rest of the ancestral story (after Abraham), *hā'ĕlōhîm* occurs (with one exception) in human speech—in words spoken by Isaac (27:28), Jacob/Israel (31:11; 48:15), Joseph (42:18; 45:8), and Judah (44:16). It is possible that this distinctive way of referring to God signals a particular understanding of deity bequeathed by Abraham to his descendants. The exception to the use of *hā'ĕlōhîm* in direct speech is the narrator's note that God had revealed himself to Jacob at Bethel (35:7). Like the three cases of *hā'ĕlōhîm* in the earlier Abraham story, this might well signal the point of view of the person interacting with God. I admit that this is speculative.

15. This translation is found Levenson, *Death and Resurrection of the Beloved Son*, 12, 127, 138, 222, 225. E. A. Speiser renders it "your beloved one," while later admitting that it means "the unique one, one and only." Speiser, *Genesis: Introduction, Translation, and Notes*, AB 1 (New York: Doubleday, 1964), 161, 163. Likewise, the Septuagint has *ton agapēton* ("the beloved one") in place of *yǝḥîdǝkā* ("your only one"), which makes the next phrase, *hon ēgapēsas* ("whom you have loved"), sound redundant. However, none of the twelve occurrences of the adjective *yāḥîd* (with or without a pronominal suffix) in the Hebrew Bible clearly means "favored" or "beloved" (Gen. 22:2, 12, 16; Judg. 11:34; Pss. 22:20 [22:21 MT]; 25:16; 35:17; 68:6 [68:7 MT]; Prov. 4:3; Jer. 6:26; Amos 8:10; Zech. 12:10). Although two of the uses in the Psalms (concerning the psalmist's soul/life) are sometimes translated this way (my "precious" life), context suggests the meaning of my "lonely," "deserted," or "solitary" life.

16. Although this conversation is often quoted from Rashi, it goes back to Genesis Rabbah 55:7. Trans. from Sefaria.org, https://www.sefaria.org/Bereishit_Rabbah.55.7?lang=bi &with=all&lang2=en.

Although this midrash is a bit fanciful, it is helpful in revealing how strange the use of *yəḥîdəkā* (your only one) is in this context. Terence Fretheim reads *yəḥîdəkā* as meaning "the 'only son' he has left," since Ishmael was sent away back in chapter 21.[17] So, when God refers to Isaac as "your son, your only one," this may mean (in context) your only *remaining* son.

However, the full phrase indicating Isaac in 22:2 is "your son, your only one, *whom you love*—Isaac." Here we should note that the verb for love ('*āḥēb*) tends to signal trouble whenever it occurs later in Genesis—a point fruitfully explored by Jonathan Sacks.[18] With the exception of 24:67, it signals some sort of favoritism.

In the story of Isaac, Rebekah, Esau, and Jacob, '*āḥēb* is used to designate Isaac's love for Rebekah (24:67), the favoritism of Isaac for Esau and of Rebekah for Jacob (25:28), and Isaac's love for the savory food that Rebekah prepares in order to deceive him (27:4, 9, 14). In the story of Jacob and his two wives, Leah and Rachel, '*āḥēb* is used to signify Jacob's love for Rachel (29:18)—that he loved her more than Leah (29:30)—and Jacob's missing love for Leah that she desperately wanted to gain (29:32). The verb '*āḥēb* is also used to introduce the tragic rape of Dinah (and slaughter of Shechem's family), by noting that Shechem loved Dinah (34:3). Finally, '*āḥēb* signals Jacob's favoritism for Joseph (37:3–4) and for Benjamin (44:20) among the other brothers, as bookends of a highly dysfunctional family narrative.

Given that 22:2 is the first use of '*āḥēb* in Genesis, perhaps we should be put on notice that something is not quite right here; and this may well have to do with Abraham's relationship to his two sons (one of whom is no longer with him). However, the relationship of this initial use of '*āḥēb* to later (troubling) uses would not be immediately evident. It would require reading through the Aqedah story and the rest of Genesis. As Ehud Ben Zvi has persuasively argued, biblical texts were not meant to be read only once, but re-read (again and again).[19]

Further, we should note that this reference to Abraham's love for Isaac is not actually stated as a fact by the narrator (as is typically assumed by

17. Fretheim, "God, Abraham, and the Abuse of Isaac," *WW* 15, no. 1 (1995): 51 (entire article 49–57).

18. Jonathan Sacks traces the use of love ('*āḥēb*) throughout Genesis in connection with sibling rivalry in *Not in God's Name: Confronting Religious Violence* (New York: Schocken Books, 2015), passim.

19. Ehud Ben Zvi, *The Signs of Jonah: Reading and Rereading in Ancient Yehud*, LHBOTS 367 (New York: Sheffield Academic, 2003), 1–14.

commentators) but occurs as what is effectively a parenthetical description of Isaac in God's instructions to Abraham. We could take the phrase "whom you love" to have the rhetorical force of, "You love him, don't you?" So prove it by your response to the test. Could it be that Abraham's actions are meant to reveal *whether or not* he loves Isaac?[20]

With that in mind, let us note how Abraham relates to his (remaining) son within the story at various points. This will require us to enter imaginatively into the narrative, to try to discern the textual clues to the complex relationship between Abraham and Isaac.

Abraham's Methodical Activity Surrounding Isaac's Passivity (Gen. 22:3)

First of all, there is Abraham's ominous silence and almost methodical preparation for obeying God's command to sacrifice Isaac, which portrays the initial mood of the story and suggests Abraham's complicated interior state. According to verse 3, "Abraham rose early in the morning, and saddled his donkey; then he took two of his young men with him, and Isaac his son; and he cut the wood for a burnt offering. Then he arose and went to the place that God had told him."

Abraham *rose early*, *saddled* his donkey, *took* two of his servants—and his son Isaac. That's three verbs, three actions of Abraham, then Isaac. Then come three more verbs: Abraham *cut* the wood for the offering, he *arose*, and he *went*. These last two verbs tend to be conflated in many English translations, but the Hebrew has a nice symmetry. Isaac is surrounded on either side by three silent actions of his father. No word is spoken, no explanation given, not to the servants or to Isaac. And while Abraham is active, busily making preparations, Isaac is passive, the subject of no verbs.[21]

20. The midrash in Genesis Rabbah 55:7, where God reveals step-by-step the identity of the one to be sacrificed, goes on to interpret this as God attempting to make Isaac "even more beloved in his [Abraham's] eyes and reward him for each and every word spoken" (trans. from Sefaria.org, https://www.sefaria.org/Bereishit_Rabbah.55.7?lang=bi&with=all&lang2=en). While I agree that this may serve to stir up Abraham's love for Isaac, the purpose might be different from what the midrash suggests (namely, that Abraham's reward for sacrificing him will be even greater). Perhaps the point is to get Abraham to show his love for Isaac by interceding for him. I will return to this possibility.

21. On this rhetorical structure, see Phyllis Trible, "Genesis 22: The Sacrifice of Sarah," in *"Not In Heaven": Coherence and Complexity in Biblical Narrative*, ed. Jason P. Rosenblatt and Joseph C. Sitterson Jr., ISBL (Bloomington: Indiana University Press, 1991), 174–75, 177 (entire chapter 170–91; nn. 249–53).

Why Did He Arise Early? (Gen. 22:3)

Beyond the portrayal of Abraham's busy agency in contrast to Isaac's passivity, it is noteworthy that he rose early. Did this signify enthusiasm on Abraham's part? Or did he intentionally not want to have to deal with Sarah? *Where are you going?* she might ask. *Oh, to sacrifice our son. What? Are you crazy?* Maybe he didn't want to have to explain himself to anyone, especially not her—a possibility suggested in Midrash Tanḥuma.[22]

Or maybe he never really decided anything. Perhaps he just couldn't sleep. And once awake, it may be that he acted by rote, in a shell-shocked state, putting one foot before the other, going through the actions, with a sense of inevitability.

Why Did Abraham Saddle the Donkey Himself? (Gen. 22:3)

Beyond rising early, we are told that Abraham saddled the donkey and cut the wood himself, instead of leaving these tasks to his servants. Midrash Tanḥuma comments on this anomaly in relation to the saddling: "How many servants and maids that righteous man possessed! Yet he saddled the ass himself. This reveals his eagerness to fulfill God's command."[23]

Given that there are only two biblical characters who rise early and saddle their own donkeys (Abraham and Balaam), a task which would have normally been left to their servants, Genesis Rabbah 55:8 comments on the difference between the two saddling events, both of which testify to an unusual state of mind. Since Baalam was on his way to curse Israel, this shows that "hate upsets the natural order." However, since Abraham was on his way to obey God, this shows that "love upsets the natural order."[24]

The explanations given by Genesis Rabbah and Midrash Tanḥuma, however, make assumptions about the normative character of Abraham's action and so read too much into his motivations. The narrative is quite reticent about *why* he does what he does.

22. *Midrash Tanḥuma*, Vayera 22:7 assumes he had previously spoken to Sarah about it: "He said to himself: Perhaps Sara will change her mind and not permit me to go; I will arise before she does." Trans. from Sefaria.org, https://www.sefaria.org/Midrash_Tanchuma%2C_Vayera .22.7?lang=bi&with=all&lang2=en.

23. *Midrash Tanḥuma*, Vayera 22:4. Trans. from Sefaria.org, https://www.sefaria.org/Midrash_Tanchuma%2C_Vayera.22.4?lang=bi&with=all&lang2=en.

24. Genesis Rabbah 55:8. This interpretation is attributed to Rashbi (Rabbi Simeon ben Yohai). Trans. from Sefaria.org, https://www.sefaria.org/Bereishit_Rabbah.55.8?lang=bi &with=all&lang2=en. Abraham and Balaam also have in common the fact that both are from Mesopotamia.

Why Did Abraham Cut Wood Himself before the Journey?

Then there is the question of why Abraham cut wood for the offering himself, rather than have his servants do this. That he saddled the donkey and cut the wood himself might be evidence of Abraham's confused state of mind. Or could he have been so hyperfocused on the goal (performing the sacrifice) that he was not thinking clearly about the process? Beyond this, there is the question of why he cut the wood *in advance*. Couldn't they have just collected dried branches on the journey or at the site of the sacrifice? Might the cutting of the wood be a delaying tactic on Abraham's part?[25]

The Strange Order of Abraham's Actions (Gen. 22:3)

Abraham's state of mind when he saddled the donkey and cut the wood might also be inferred from the relative placement of these two actions in the narrative. Although on the surface Abraham's preparation for the sacrifice seems methodical, this is belied by the strange sequence of the second and fourth verbs: Abraham saddled the donkey *before* he cut the wood; it is more logical to do it the other way around. It is somewhat counterintuitive to have the beast saddled and waiting while the wood is being cut. Donkeys are not patient animals. One would normally have saddled the donkey last. Indeed, the CEV changes the order and puts the saddling of the donkey immediately before the departure. But that is not the order of the actions in the Hebrew text. Perhaps Abraham is under such stress and emotional turmoil that he is not thinking clearly; but then who would be, in such a situation?[26]

Abraham's Silence and the Mood on the Journey (Gen. 22:4)

Then the narrative jumps ahead three days to when Abraham sees the mountain (22:4). Nothing is mentioned as happening during those three days. Presumably they are traveling toward Moriah, the place God told Abraham to go. Did anybody speak? Judging by Abraham's silent preparations in verse 3, we may surmise that talk was limited to what was necessary to stop, eat, and break camp. Certainly, there would have been no extended explanations of

---

25. This is the suggestion of Jonathan Jacobs, "Willing Obedience with Doubts: Abraham at the Binding of Isaac," *VT* 60 (2010): 554 (entire article 546–59).

26. Jonathan Jacobs notes that Abraham taking his son comes late in the list of his actions (after he saddles the donkey and takes his servants), when we might expect this to be his first action. Could it be that Abraham was delaying taking Isaac, hoping against hope that the sacrifice request would be rescinded? Jacobs, "Willing Obedience with Doubts," 553.

what was happening. What was Abraham thinking during those three days? What was Isaac thinking? We are not told.

Lippman Bodoff suggests that Abraham took his time traveling three days toward Moriah on what should have been a single day's journey of forty-six miles by donkey (assuming that Moriah is the site of the later temple; see 2 Chron. 3:1) in order to give God time to rescind the test. In other words, Abraham was testing God, to see if his God was just and moral.[27] However, even if Moriah is to be identified with the Temple Mount, there was only one donkey, so they would need to have traveled at a walking pace to accommodate Isaac and the servants.

Indeed, we should note that it was *God* who told Abraham to go to a spot three days distant for the sacrifice. Why couldn't Abraham perform the sacrifice right where he lived (or somewhere nearby)? Could it be that *God* was intentionally giving Abraham time to think about the command, to allow his feelings for Isaac to grow, that he might come to a decision to question the command or to intercede for Isaac?[28]

Abraham's Instructions to the Servants (Gen. 22:5)

Once he spots the mountain, Abraham breaks the silence to give his servants (lit. his "young men") instructions to stay with the donkey, explaining that he and "the young man" (the same term used for the servants) will go over there, worship, and return (22:5). What does Abraham mean by telling them this?

Jon Levenson cites interpretations found in rabbinic tradition that Abraham keeps the truth from Isaac and the servants in order to prevent them from protesting his decision (which might lead to his loss of resolve to go through with the sacrifice) or to prevent Isaac fleeing (Ibn Ezra's suggestion). Another rabbinic opinion is that Abraham uses the euphemism "worship" to prevent himself from having to explicitly face his own decision, which might also lead to a weakening of resolve.[29]

---

27. Bodoff, "The Real Test of the *Akedah*: Blind Obedience versus Moral Choice," *Judaism* 42, no. 1 (1993): 71–92; reprinted under the same title in Bodoff, *The Binding of Isaac, Religious Murders, and Kabbalah: Seeds of Jewish Extremism and Alienation?* (Jerusalem: Devora, 2005), 29–58.

28. This suggestion was sparked by comments made by Arlyn Drew in her dissertation on the Aqedah. See Arlyn Sunshine Drew, "A Hermeneutic for the Aqedah Test: A Way beyond Jon Levenson's and Terence Fretheim's Models" (PhD diss., Andrews University, 2020), 235–36, 340.

29. Levenson, *Death and Resurrection of the Beloved Son*, 131; and Levenson, "The Test," in *Inheriting Abraham: The Legacy of the Patriarch in Judaism, Christianity, and Islam*, LJI (Princeton: Princeton University Press, 2012), 74–75 (entire chapter 66–112; nn. 219–23).

Levenson also cites Bachya ben Asher's fourteenth-century commentary on Genesis 22:5, which suggests that when Abraham says "We will return to you," this signals his intent to bring Isaac's bones back with him after the sacrifice.[30]

Another rabbinic tradition understands the verb for "worship" (the Hishtaphel of *ḥāwâ*, which literally means "to prostrate oneself" or "to do obeisance") as a reference to Abraham's intention to pray on the mountain, in order to ask God to rescind the command.[31] Yet Levenson himself admits, "If Abraham did harbor such a plan, . . . he seems to have given it up by the time he and Isaac finally ascend the mountain, for there is no indication that they engaged in any prostration or petition there."[32] Indeed, when they arrive at the mountain, Abraham immediately builds an altar and prepares to sacrifice his son (22:9).

Abraham's Activity and Power vis-à-vis a Passive Isaac (Gen. 22:6, 9–10)

Although Abraham speaks to his servants, instructing them to wait for his return, he is not recorded as saying anything to Isaac at this point. Instead, there is a flurry of Abraham's activity in verse 6—still without speaking to Isaac. "Abraham took the wood of the burnt offering and placed it on Isaac his son, and he took in his hand the fire and the knife" (22:6). The literary structure is similar to that of verse 3, where a passive Isaac is surrounded by Abraham's actions. One difference is that here Isaac is surrounded not by two triplets of Abraham's actions, but on one side by two actions of Abraham with one direct object (Abraham *took the wood* and *placed* it on Isaac) and on the other side by one action of Abraham with two direct objects (Abraham *took* in his hand *the fire* and *the knife*). Once again Abraham's agency is contrasted with Isaac's passivity; and once more there is no speech recorded between.

A similar literary structure is found again later in the story, at the pivotal point in verses 9–10. "When they came to the place that God had told him, Abraham built an altar there and laid out the wood. He bound Isaac his son, and placed him on the altar, on top of the wood. Then Abraham stretched out his hand and took the knife to slaughter his son."

---

30. Cited in Levenson, *Death and Resurrection of the Beloved Son*, 131.

31. Cited in Levenson, *Death and Resurrection of the Beloved Son*, 131; see also Levenson, "The Test," 73. Although the verb for "worship" in 22:5 is used in connection with sacrifice (1 Sam. 1:3), it can signify the prostration of a supplicant (Gen. 23:7–9; 2 Chron. 20:18; Isa. 44:17).

32. Levenson, "The Test," 73.

In these verses we are told that Abraham *built* the altar, *laid out* the wood, *bound* Isaac; then he *placed* Isaac on the altar, *stretched out* his hand, and *took* the knife. Just as in verse 3, Isaac is here surrounded by three of Abraham's silent actions. This reinforces the previous rhetorical effect of portraying Abraham's agency in contrast to Isaac's passivity, with no speech passing between father and son.[33]

A further point of note is that both verses 6 and 10 contain a reference to Abraham's "hand" (*yād*). In verse 6, as they head for the mountain, Abraham took in his *hand* the fire and the knife; in verse 10 he stretched out his *hand* and took the knife to kill his son. Although "hand" can certainly have a literal meaning, the Hebrew *yād* often has the symbolic sense of "power" (and the literal and symbolic meanings are not always separate). In these verses, we certainly see Abraham's power over Isaac—indeed, the power of life and death.

The Touching Conversation between Father and Son (Gen. 22:7-8)

Significantly, between these two episodes of Abraham's silent activity vis-à-vis his son (vv. 6, 9–10), Isaac breaks the silence after they leave the servants (22:7).

According to the end of verse 6, the two of them "went" or "walked" (*wayyēlǝkû*) "together" (*yaḥdāw*). As they walk, there is a touching conversation between father and son.[34] It is a poignant moment worth lingering over. "My father," says Isaac. "*Hinnennî*, my son," says Abraham. This is the same response he made when God called him in verse 1, and the same response he will make when the angel calls out from heaven in verse 11. It signifies readiness: Here I am, ready to listen, ready to act.[35]

Having got Abraham's attention, Isaac then notes that they have the *fire* (the fire stone or the fire pot, which Abraham is carrying) and the *wood* (which Isaac is carrying); he omits mention of the *knife*, which the narrator says Abraham had in his hand (verse 6). But then Isaac asks, somewhat tentatively, I imagine: "Where is the *sheep* for a burnt offering?" (22:7). The tentativeness

---

33. This is in contrast to the later rabbinic tradition of seeing Isaac as a willing victim (and so as a paradigm for Jewish martyrdom).

34. The poignant nature of the Aqedah narrative is enhanced by the constant reminder that Isaac is Abraham's son. God or the angel refers to Isaac as "your son" three times (22:2, 12, 16). Abraham refers to Isaac twice as "my son: (22:7, 8). And the narrator refers to Isaac as "his son" five times (22:3, 6, 9, 10, 13).

35. There is a slight difference in spelling between the forms of the word when Abraham addresses God and when he addresses his son—*hinnēnî* in the first case, *hinnennî* in the second. These are two of the three variant spellings of this word found in the MT (the other is *hinēnî*).

of Isaac's question (which is prefaced by his comments about the fire and the wood) is conveyed in the Hebrew by the strange repetition of "he said" (*wayyō'mer*), although this is obscured by most English translations. The text reads, "And Isaac said to his father and he said" (22:7).[36] It is as though he began to speak and hesitated, perhaps initially stumbling over his words; then the difficult words came out.[37]

Abraham's Freudian Slip or the Narrator's Intentional Ambiguity (Gen. 22:8)

Abraham's answer to Isaac's question about the sheep, often taken as expressing his faith, is actually ambiguous: "God will see to the sheep for a burnt offering, my son" (22:8).

Does Abraham's answer mean that he has faith that God will provide a sheep, so that he won't have to go through with the command to sacrifice Isaac? Is he uncertain, but hoping against hope that a sheep will be provided?[38] Or is he trying to deceive Isaac, so that the intended victim won't bolt?

But there is an even more intriguing ambiguity in Abraham's answer to Isaac. If "my son" (in "God will see to the sheep for a burnt offering, *my son*") was meant to be a vocative (that is, direct address to Isaac), it might better have come at the start of the sentence. This is where the CEV puts it: "'My son,' Abraham answered, 'God will provide the lamb.'" But this rearrangement obscures the ambiguity of the Hebrew.

In its present position, at the end of the sentence, "my son" could be a vocative of address or it could be in *apposition* to "the sheep for a burnt offering."[39] Earlier, in Genesis 22:2, God listed a series of descriptions in apposition, culminating in *Isaac* (take "your son, your only one, whom you

---

36. If the text had said, "And Isaac *spoke* [yǝdabbēr] to his father and said [*wayyō'mer*]" (with a variation of verbs, *dābar* and *'āmar*), this would be unremarkable as a speech introduction. This very formula is found in 19:14 and 42:7, though it is more common for the second verb to be *lē'mōr* (the infinitive of *'āmar*), which is typically translated in the KJV as "he spoke . . . saying." But the repetition of *'āmar* is unusual.

37. This is Arlyn Drew's suggestion, in "Hermeneutic for the Aqedah Test," 89.

38. In the next chapter, I will address these possibilities. The evidence is against Abraham actually believing there would be an animal substitute.

39. Many scholars have noted these two possibilities: Trible, "Genesis 22," 176; Victor P. Hamilton, *The Book of Genesis: Chapters 18–50*, NICOT (Grand Rapids: Eerdmans, 1995), 110; James L. Crenshaw, *A Whirlpool of Torment: Israelite Traditions of God as an Oppressive Presence*, OBT (Philadelphia: Fortress, 1984), 23; Meir Sternberg, *The Poetics of Biblical Narrative: Ideological Literature and the Drama of Reading*, Biblical Literature (Bloomington: University of Indiana Press, 1985), 192.

love—Isaac"). If this applies also to verse 8, it would, in effect, identify "my son" as equivalent to the sheep for the sacrifice.

There is a cartoon by Man Martin making its way around the internet that depicts the ambiguity in verse 8, though not specifically with reference to the Hebrew.[40] In the cartoon, Isaac asks his father, "Where's the sacrifice?" Abraham responds, "God will provide Isaac." Isaac then queries, "Wait! Did you say, 'God will provide, Isaac," or 'God will provide Isaac'?" Abraham says, "Come here, son," to which Isaac responds, "I ain't budgin' til you put in a comma!" This is an excellent example of the sort of ambiguity found in Abraham's answer in verse 8.

Figure 6.1. God will provide Isaac. Cartoon by Man Martin, *Man Overboard*, http://manmartin .blogspot.com/.

Given that the syntax of this sentence ("my son" directly following "the sheep for a burnt offering") admits of two possible meanings, we are left to wonder whether this ambiguity is intentional. If so, it might be a signal from the narrator about the complexity of Abraham's response. It might even communicate what we could call a Freudian slip on Abraham's part. But, of

40. My thanks to the author for permission to reproduce the cartoon here. It can be viewed online at "Religious Humor Goes Overboard with Comic Strip," interview by John Longhurst, March 16, 2019, *On Faith Canada* (blog), http://onfaithcanada.blogspot.com/2019/03/religious -humour-goes-overboard-with.html.

course, we don't have access to Abraham's actual intent; we only have his verbal response.

A classic rabbinic midrash seizes on the ambiguity of Abraham's statement. According to Genesis Rabbah 56:4, Abraham imagines both alternatives and explains them to Isaac: "'God will provide himself the lamb, my son'; and if not, you are 'the lamb for the burnt-offering my son.' So 'they went both of them together'—one to slaughter and the other to be slaughtered."[41] Midrash Tanḥuma is more direct. After Isaac asks his father about the lamb for the burnt offering, Abraham responds, "Since you ask, the Holy One, blessed be He, has selected you." And Isaac accepts this, only noting that he is worried about his mother. Then the two of them went together "of one mind: convinced that one was to slaughter and the other to be slaughtered."[42]

While the narrator has left Abraham's answer ambiguous, these midrashim actively fill in the gaps in the narrative (as midrash is wont to do). But perhaps we should respect the ambiguity of the text and refrain from making judgments about Abraham's intentions or state of mind underlying his response to Isaac (except that he was likely under great stress and possibly ambivalent about the commandment). We also don't know what Isaac thought of this response. Just as at the end of verse 6, so at the end of verse 8—all we are told is that the two of them "went" (*wayyēləkû*) "together" (*yaḥdāw*). This inclusio brackets the touching, tender—though ambiguous—conversation between father and son, the only conversation between them recorded in Genesis 22 (in fact, the only conversation between them in Genesis). Both before and after the conversation, the two of them "went" (*wayyēləkû*) "together" (*yaḥdāw*).[43]

Throughout the first ten verses of the Aqedah the narrator has skillfully conveyed a series of rhetorical signals that suggest tension, stress, and perhaps internal confusion on Abraham's part, while portraying a significant power differential between an active father and a passive son. He has done this by giving very few details, while leaving a lot to the reader's imagination. Although we should be reluctant to definitively fill in the gaps in this narrative, such as claiming to know the mental state of either Abraham or Isaac, the attentive

41. Genesis Rabbah 56:4. Trans. from Sefaria.org, https://www.sefaria.org/Bereishit_Rabbah .56.4?lang=bi&with=all&lang2=en.

42. *Midrash Tanḥuma*, Vayera 23. Trans. from Sefaria.org, https://www.sefaria.org/Midrash _Tanchuma%2C_Vayera.23.3?lang=bi&with=all&lang2=en. That Isaac willingly goes to the sacrifice becomes a major theme in the rabbinic tradition.

43. The full phrase for "the two of them went together" in verses 6 and 8 is *wayyēləkû šənêhem yaḥdāw*.

reader is nevertheless left to wonder about the validity of Abraham's response to God. The rhetorical signals of this artfully crafted story, together with the pervasive biblical background of vigorous prayer in situations of difficulty, combine to raise questions about whether Abraham's silent obedience to God's command should be viewed as exemplary.

The Shift in Abraham's Traveling Companions (Gen. 22:19)

But perhaps the most important datum within Genesis 22 that supports a critical reading of Abraham's response is that Isaac is missing at the end of the story.[44] In verse 5 Abraham tells his servants that he and the boy will go up the mountain to worship and "*we* will return to you." Yet the narrator tells us in verse 19 that "*Abraham* returned to his servants." Isaac is conspicuously absent. Abraham's son is not recorded as returning with him down the mountain. And this is a very well-crafted narrative, in which every detail matters.[45]

Back in Genesis 11:31, at the start of the Abraham story, we are told that Terah (Abram's father) took Abram and Lot and Sarai, and they set out together from the land of the Chaldeans to go to Haran. The story begins with the family traveling together.[46]

Then in 22:6 and 8 Abraham and Isaac "went" (*wayyēləkû*) "together" (*yaḥdāw*) up the mountain.

But then we come to the last verse of the Aqedah (22:19). After noting that Abraham returned to his servants (and omitting mention of Isaac), the narrator says that *they* (Abraham and the servants) arose and "went together" (*wayyēləkû yaḥdāw*) to Beersheba. Abraham went, together with others, but no longer with his family, no longer with his son.[47]

Abraham's life is marked by a series of separations. In differing circumstances, he sends away Lot, Hagar, and Ishmael. Then he travels up the mountain without Sarah, with his only (remaining) son. Then he returns (without Isaac) to his servants, and they travel together to Beersheba. Having noted

---

44. This has been noted by numerous interpreters, both ancient and modern, though there has been no unanimity as to its significance.

45. Jon Levenson has an important objection to the interpretation that Isaac does not return with Abraham, which will be addressed in the next chapter.

46. Genesis 11:31 says they set out "to go" (*lāleket*) to Haran, using the infinitive of the same verb for "went" in 22:6, 8, and 19.

47. Apart from the occurrences of "together" (*yaḥdāw*) in 22:6, 8, and 19, there are only two other places in Genesis where this word is found; in both cases the text mentions people who could *not* live/dwell (*yāšab*) together (Abram and Lot in 13:6; Esau and Jacob in 36:7). My thanks to Matthew Anstey for pointing this out to me.

Abraham's return (without mention of Isaac), the Aqedah narrative concludes with the simple (even tragic) comment that Abraham lived (*yāšab*) at Beersheba (22:19)—with no mention of Isaac (or Sarah, for that matter).

The loss of Abraham's son by the end of the Aqedah narrative raises the question of the significance of this datum and whether it might be connected to Abraham's test—something I will address more explicitly in the following chapter.

Thematic and Intertextual Connections between Abraham and Job

So far in this chapter I have noted various rhetorical signals in the narrative of the Aqedah that may be read as putting the reader on notice about the tense, ambiguous relationship between Abraham and God—and between Abraham and Isaac. In the next chapter I will examine more fully the evidence for an interpretation of the Aqedah that does not valorize Abraham's response to God.

But I am not the only one who seems to have noticed a problem with Abraham's response to God in Genesis 22. It is fascinating that the book of Job contains numerous thematic and intertextual links with the Aqedah and the wider Abraham story, which suggest that the author of Job was gesturing toward the Abraham story, inviting a comparison (and especially a contrast) between the two patriarchs—one gentile, the other the father of the Jewish nation.

Both Abraham and Job Are Tested by God

To start with the most obvious connection, God is explicitly said to test Abraham (22:1), while the entire book of Job is framed as a test. This is what led the ancient author of Jubilees to draw a parallel between the two stories. According to Jubilees 17–18, Prince Mastema—like the Accuser in Job—prods the Lord to test Abraham for his faithfulness. In my introduction to this book, I noted that Abraham and Job have so often been linked in the midrashic tradition that one author coined the term *Jobraham* to highlight this point.[48]

Both Abraham and Job (and Only They) Use the Expression "Dust and Ashes"

Beyond the idea of Abraham and Job being tested, the phrase "dust and ashes" occurs in the Hebrew Bible nowhere else but on the lips of Abraham

48. Nicholas J. Ellis, "The Reception of the Jobraham Narratives in Jewish Thought," in *Authoritative Texts and Reception History: Aspects and Approaches*, ed. Dan Batovici and Kristin de Troyer, BibInt 151 (Leiden: Brill, 2016), 124–40.

(Gen. 18:27) and Job (Job 30:19; 42:6). In Abraham's case, it occurs in the context of his bold intercession for Sodom (prior to the Aqedah). And it occurs twice in Job—first in the midst of Job's complaints, describing his sense of powerlessness (30:19), then linked to his sense of comfort, after YHWH's second speech (42:6). This was the original intertextual link that prodded me to wonder about the relationship of Job to the Aqedah.

Both Abraham and Job Are God-Fearers

Furthermore, the term "God-fearer" is applied to both figures. Significantly, it is applied to Abraham after his test in the Aqedah (Gen. 22:12) and to Job at the beginning of his test (Job 1:1, 8; 2:3). While the idea of fearing God/ YHWH is common in the Hebrew Bible (especially in the Wisdom Literature), the particular phrase "God-fearer" (yərē' 'ĕlōhîm) is rarer. Besides its occurrences in Genesis and Job, it is found only in Ecclesiastes 7:18.[49]

It therefore makes sense that Walter Moberly would turn to Job in an attempt to clarify the meaning of Abraham's fear of God (affirmed by the angel after the test). In the previous chapter I noted that Moberly took Exodus 20:20 as a key text in clarifying the meaning of Abraham's fear of God in the Aqedah. But Moberly also views the prologue of Job (specifically Job 1:1–2:10) as a second important parallel to the Aqedah, primarily because it is there that Job, like Abraham, is called a God-fearer.[50]

In his discussion of Job, Moberly zeroes in on Job's "integrity" (tummâ), which he suggests is a "closely related notion" to the fear of God, and he interprets this in terms of the Accuser's question of whether Job served God out of self-interest (2:3).[51] Noting that Job's integrity (his commitment to God independent of the blessings that accompany such commitment) withstood the calamities that befell Job in the prologue, Moberly emphasizes that the figure of Job is "clearly paradigmatic, a model to be considered and emulated" as one whose allegiance to God is constant, even in suffering, without need for reward.[52]

49. The term "YHWH-fearer" is likewise rare, used in only five places (Pss. 25:12; 128:1, 4; Prov. 14:2; Isa. 50:10). In these nine cases ("God-fearer" and "YHWH-fearer"), yr' is pointed in the MT not as a verb but as a verbal adjective (in the construct). But even if the particular phrasing "God-fearer" is not sustainable (after all, the vowel pointing of the MT is not original), the fact is that both Abraham and Job are said to fear God.

50. Moberly translates yərē' 'ĕlōhîm as "one who fears God." R. W. L. Moberly, "Abraham and God in Genesis 22," in The Bible, Theology, and Faith: A Study of Abraham and Jesus (Cambridge: Cambridge University Press, 2000), 84 (entire chapter 71–131).

51. Moberly, "Abraham and God in Genesis 22," 84.

52. Moberly, "Abraham and God in Genesis 22," 86–87.

However, what Moberly takes as paradigmatic is limited to Job's response to his troubles in the first two chapters of the book, which come *prior* to Job's vigorous articulation of lament.[53] Moberly's sole concession to the poetic dialogues (which dominate the book of Job) is his admission that the prologue "is qualified by its position within the book of Job as a whole, where Job subsequently speaks differently"; but instead of exploring the quite significant difference Job's move to lament would make for understanding the opening chapters, Moberly simply affirms the ongoing validity of the prologue, concluding, "There is nothing within the story itself to diminish its demanding implications."[54]

Where Moberly sees a parallel between the God-oriented integrity of Abraham in the Aqedah and Job in the prologue (both being willing to submit to God, without complaint or hope of reward), I wonder about the *contrast* between Abraham and Job. After all, Job moves beyond his initial praise of God (chap. 1), followed by his passive acceptance of whatever God sends him (chap. 2), to voice abrasive protest about his sufferings (from chap. 3 onward). Might this indicate that the book of Job intends to contrast *two different ways of fearing God*—one that is manifest in silent submission (Abraham), the other that is compatible with vocal protest (Job)?

But there is another possibility. Given that Job started out (Job 1:1, 8; 2:3) where Abraham ended (Gen. 22:12)—with the fear of God—could the point of the comparison be that Job progressed beyond that? Although the fear of God/YHWH is a positive attribute, highly praised in the Wisdom Literature, and is identified with wisdom in Job 28:28 ("Truly, the fear of the Lord, that is wisdom; / and to depart from evil is understanding"), what are we to make of the prominent thematic statement that the fear of YHWH is the *beginning* of wisdom or knowledge (Ps. 111:10; Prov. 1:7; 9:10; also Sir. 1:14), rather than its culmination?[55] Even Moberly admits that "'fear of God' . . . is a comprehensive and open-ended term, whose meaning can be

53. "Job 1:1–2:10" is the heading of Moberly's section on Job ("Abraham and God in Genesis 22," 84–88).

54. Moberly, "Abraham and God in Genesis 22," 87.

55. Job 28:28 (at the end of the interlude on the difficulty of finding wisdom) serves to remind the reader that Job started out with a form of wisdom (he was described in the prologue as a God-fearer, who turned from evil). But the implicit question raised by the interlude is whether Job's vocal protests could also be characterized by wisdom (perhaps a different kind of wisdom—a mature, tempered wisdom). Of course, the word for "beginning" (*rēʾšît*) in Ps. 111:10 and Prov. 1:7 can signify first in time (beginning) or first in priority (chief), like the Greek *archē* in Sir. 1:14. But Prov. 9:10 has *təḥillâ*, which does in fact mean "beginning."

extended and deepened according to context."[56] Might this suggest that in order to achieve mature wisdom, both Abraham and Job needed to move from their initial, somewhat immature fear of God to a position where godly fear is not antithetical to, but undergirds, vigorous interaction with the divine covenant partner?[57]

Both Abraham and Job Intercede for Others (at God's Behest)

Abraham and Job are also connected in that they both engage in intercession at God's behest—Abraham for Abimelech (Gen. 20:7, 17) and Job for his friends (Job 42:8–9). Indeed, even the way in which this intercession is introduced is similar; in both cases God tells the person in need of prayer that Abraham ("a prophet") or Job ("my servant") will pray for them and that he will accept their prayer (Gen. 20:7; Job 42:8).

It may also be significant where these episodes are located in the larger stories of Abraham and Job, respectively. Abraham is asked to intercede for Abimelech because he has proved himself a "prophet" by his prior intercession on behalf of Sodom, whereas Job is asked to intercede for his friends after his vocal complaints to God have demonstrated that he is as much a "servant" of God as Moses was.

But we should also note that the accounts of Abraham's intercession (on behalf of Sodom and Abimelech) come *before* the Aqedah, at which time Abraham becomes strangely silent in the face of God's command to sacrifice his son (he does not intercede for Isaac). As I suggested in my earlier discussion of Job (in chap 4), the reversal of Abraham from passionate speech (Gen. 18) to later silence (Gen. 22) may be addressed by Job's own move in the other direction—from initial silence at the end of the prologue (implied in Job 2:13) to bold speech (starting in 3:1), and then again from his refusal

---

56. Moberly, "Abraham and God in Genesis 22," 80.

57. Of course, Job is not an Israelite and so is not in explicit covenantal relationship with God. Nevertheless, the book of Job is an Israelite wisdom text permeated by covenantal expectations, which underlie the very possibility of Job's complaints. See Jamie A. Grant, "'When the Friendship of God Was upon My Tent': Covenant as Essential Background to Lament in the Wisdom Literature," in *Covenant in the Persian Period: From Genesis to Chronicles*, ed. Richard J. Bautch and Gary N. Knoppers (Winona Lake, IN: Eisenbrauns, 2015), 339–55. Beyond that, J. Gerald Janzen has addressed the essentially similar relationship with God assumed in the ancestor narratives (Gen. 12–50) and the book of Job, which explains the preponderance of the divine name Shaddai in these texts. See Janzen, "Israel's Default Position before God," in *At the Scent of Water: The Ground of Hope in the Book of Job* (Grand Rapids: Eerdmans, 2009), 15–36.

to answer after God's first speech (40:3–5) to his articulation of comfort after the second speech (42:6).

God Reveals His Counsel to both Abraham and Job

Another thematic connection between Abraham and Job is that God reveals his counsel or plan to both of them. Indeed, one of the possible reasons for referring to Abraham as a prophet, besides his intercession on behalf of Sodom, is that God tells him of his plans concerning the city (Gen. 18:17–21), which is what prompts Abraham's intercession. Jeremiah 23:18 specifically contrasts false and true prophets, noting that only the latter have "stood in the council [sôd] of the LORD / so as to see and to hear his word." And according to Amos 3:7, "Surely the Lord GOD does nothing, / without revealing his secret [sôd] / to his servants the prophets."

In Job's case, God first challenges Job for "darkening" (questioning) his counsel or design for the cosmos (38:2), and then proceeds to enlighten him, with a tour of the workings of the heavens and earth, along with the kingdom of wild animals (chaps. 38–39). Indeed, the phrase "his servants the prophets" from Amos 3:7 (repeated in many other texts) serves to link Abraham (called a "prophet" in Gen. 20:7) with Job (called "my servant" in Job 42:7).

The Children of Abraham and Job

There are also significant thematic links between Abraham and Job in terms of their children. While Job's first calamity includes the loss of his children (Job 1:18–19), Abraham is threatened with the loss of his son. Whereas Job presents burnt offerings to God on behalf of his children (1:5), Abraham prepares to offer his own son as a burnt offering.

But beyond these (perhaps superficial) similarities, there is an important contrast. Job "saw his children, and his children's children, four generations" (42:16) and ended his life "old and full of days" (42:17). Not only did Job receive new children (seven sons and three daughters) from God, he was blessed by being surrounded by them, including his grandchildren and great-grandchildren.

Although the description of Abraham's end is similar, in that he died (literally) "old and full" (Gen. 25:8; almost identical to Job 42:17), his children are nowhere to be seen. After the death of Sarah, we are told that Abraham married Keturah (Gen. 25:1), and he also seems to have had concubines (25:6), all of whom are recorded as bearing him children (25:2–4, 6). However, Abraham "sent them away from his son Isaac" (25:6), presumably so there would be no competition for the inheritance.[58]

Earlier Abraham had sent Ishmael away with Hagar (21:14), and Ishmael lived in the wilderness of Paran (21:21). Then Abraham descended the mountain without Isaac (22:19), and Isaac lived in Beer-lahai-roi, in the Negev (24:62). But Abraham lived in Beersheba (22:19). The contrast between Abraham and Job in terms of their relationship with their children could not be more stark.

Names Occurring in Genesis 22 and Job

One final set of minor, though intriguing, intertextual links between Abraham and Job is that three of the names of Abraham's nephews (Uz, Buz, and Chesed) from the genealogy immediately following the Aqedah (Gen. 22:20–24) show up in the book of Job. Uz (Gen. 22:21) becomes a place name, the land where Job is located (Job 1:1). Buz (Gen. 22:21) becomes a gentilic (Buzite) in Job 32:2. And Chesed (Gen. 22:22) is pluralized to become a people group—the Chaldeans, who kill Job's servants and steal his camels (Job 1:17); and, of course, Abraham is from Ur of the Chaldeans (Gen. 11:31). This rather strange phenomenon of names linked to both Abraham and Job might be a further clue left by the author of Job to indicate that we should read the stories of these two patriarchs together.

Job's Response to the Aqedah

These intertextual connections have led me to wonder, for some time now, whether the book of Job could be thought of as a commentary on Abraham, intentionally juxtaposing Abraham's ominous silence in Genesis 22 with Job's vigorous speech toward God (which receives divine approval at the end of the book). Could the book of Job be thought of as, in some sense, an answer to Abraham?

58. Genesis 25:6 technically says that Abraham sent away the sons of his concubines, but makes no mention of sending away the sons of Keturah, his wife, who would have had a greater claim to his inheritance. Possibly to resolve this tension, Rashi interpreted "concubines" in Gen. 25 as singular, as a reference to Keturah. He may have been influenced by 1 Chron. 1:32, which says that Keturah was Abraham's concubine (not his wife). Some have resolved the contradiction between Gen. 25 and 1 Chron. 1 by suggesting that Keturah was a concubine before the death of Sarah and became Abraham's wife after; it has also been suggested that Keturah is an alternative name for Hagar. However, this doesn't solve the problem of the plural "concubines" in Gen. 25.

My hunch was corroborated when I read Judy Klitsner's *Subversive Sequels in the Bible*. In her brief section on Abraham and Job in the introduction to the book, which she uses to illustrate the idea of a "subversive sequel," Klitsner points to most (though not all) of the same intertextual connections between Abraham and Job that I have noted.[59]

Having had Klitsner's book recommended to me multiple times as I explained my research project comparing Abraham and Job, I finally picked up a copy and was both delighted (that I was not the only one who saw a connection between the Aqedah and Job) and dismayed (that she had stolen my thunder).[60] But when I read Klitsner's analysis more carefully, I realized that I was going to explore both Job and the Aqedah at much greater length than Klitsner does. More importantly, my reading of Job (particularly YHWH's speeches from the whirlwind and Job's response) is significantly different from Klitsner's.[61] So my understanding of how Job might be a "subversive sequel" to the Aqedah does not replicate Klitsner's approach.

My fundamental intuition about the relationship between Job and the Aqedah is that Job's vocal complaint to God functions as an implicit critique of Abraham's lack of protest on behalf of Isaac in Genesis 22. The book of Job thus models an alternative to silent obedience in the face of terrible circumstances.[62]

When I began working on this book, I wondered if Job's implicit criticism of Abraham meant that the author of Job disagreed with God's approval of Abraham in Genesis 22, especially as articulated by the angel speeches. If so, this would mean that the perspectives of Job and the Aqedah were in conflict. But as I dug deeper into Genesis 22, especially reading this narrative in the

59. Klitsner, *Subversive Sequels in the Bible: How Biblical Stories Mine and Undermine Each Other* (London: Maggid Books, 2001), xvii–xxxiii. It was Klitsner who first made me aware of the recurrence of people and place names in Gen. 22 and Job.

60. My thanks to Elie Kaunfer of the Hadar Institute, who on more than one occasion suggested that I read Klitsner, after patiently listening to my analysis of links I had discerned between the Aqedah and Job.

61. The difference is particularly evident in Klitsner's expansion of a brief section from her book on the Aqedah and Job into a more recent (2015) online article, in which she addresses in more detail how the book of Job interacts with the Aqedah. See Klitsner, "The Book of Job and Its Paradoxical Relationship with the *Akedah*," TheTorah.com, http://thetorah.com/the -book-of-job-and-its-paradoxical-relationship-with-the-akedah/.

62. At one point in his discussion of Job and Abraham, Walter Moberly notes, "It would be surprising if Abraham's paradigmatic fear of God should be seen as less pure than Job's in a story which is designed to display what fear of God really is" (Moberly, "Abraham and God in Genesis 22," 92). To which, I might respond, "The Bible is full of surprises!"

context of the larger Abraham story, it began to dawn on me that I might have been misconstruing the point of the Aqedah (including the angel's supposed validation of Abraham).

In the next chapter I will explore the possibility that the book of Job and Genesis 22 are in fundamental agreement about the validity of protest to God. Rather than exalting Abraham's silence as exemplary, even the Aqedah may be read as affirming God's desire for a vigorous dialogue partner.

7

Did Abraham Pass the Test?

Many modern interpreters who articulate their uneasiness with the Aqedah believe that they are reading against the grain of the text, exercising a hermeneutic of suspicion, in protesting what they assume the biblical text clearly teaches—namely, Abraham as a positive model of faithfulness to God. In this chapter, however, I will account for my skepticism about Abraham's response in Genesis 22 primarily on internal, inner-biblical grounds. In other words, I intend to do exegesis, not ideological criticism. Or to use Jewish terminology, I intend to propose a peshat reading of the text, in contrast to a midrashic reading.

I take seriously the warnings of both Jon Levenson and Walter Moberly (from Jewish and Christian perspectives, respectively) against suspicious readings of the Aqedah.[1] I am particularly aware of their claims that such readings tend to be arbitrary and extrinsic critiques, based on modern assumptions or predilections of the interpreter, which are simply juxtaposed with the ancient text. In response to these important warnings, I will attempt to show how Scripture itself may be understood to generate criticism of Abraham.

To accomplish this goal, I will explore the function of the Aqedah in the context of the Abraham story that precedes it; this will suggest a different reason for the test than is usually assumed. A contextual reading of the Aqedah leads me to conclude that Abraham's response was not optimal. As

1. See the discussion of Levenson's and Moberly's warnings in chap. 5.

a follow-up, I will address the fallout of the Moriah episode on Abraham's family, especially Isaac; this raises the question of whether it could have been possible for Abraham to have been faithful to God while keeping his family intact.

I will then turn to the significance of the two angel speeches, since these are usually taken as validating Abraham's response to God, implying that he passed the test with flying colors; I will propose an alternative interpretation of these speeches. The chapter will conclude by reflecting on the role of tradition in guiding a reading of Scripture and when and how a fresh reading might legitimately challenge tradition.

The Narrative Arc of the Promised Son

We need to start by considering the place and function of the Aqedah in the context of the larger Abraham story.

One common way of reading the Abraham story is to follow the narrative arc of *promise, delay, and fulfillment*—especially the promise concerning Abraham's descendents, through whom his line would continue and by whom the nations would bless themselves or each other.

This narrative arc moves from various articulations of the promise (Gen. 12:2; 13:16; 15:5; 17:4–6), to Sarai's barrenness (first noted in 11:30), the attempt to produce an heir through Hagar (in chap. 16), God's specification that the heir will come through Sarai/Sarah (17:15–16), a prediction that this would happen shortly (18:9–10, 14), and finally the birth of Isaac (21:1–7).

This narrative arc of the Abraham story reaches its culmination in Genesis 21, *prior* to the Aqedah. As J. Gerald Janzen notes, about chapter 21, "The narrative that began in 11:30 and 12:1–3 now comes to complex closure."[2] This raises the question of why we need the story of 22:1–19. What exactly is the function of the Aqedah in the larger Abraham story?[3]

The traditional interpretation is that Abraham is being tested for his willingness to give up the child of promise, the very one though whom future

---

2. Janzen, *Abraham and All the Families of the Earth: A Commentary on the Book of Genesis 12–50* (Grand Rapids: Eerdmans, 1993), 71. Jean Louis Ska is even more emphatic: "Every unprejudiced reader is convinced that the narrative cycle has reached its conclusion in Genesis 21. . . . Nothing prepares the audience for this dramatic turn of events in Genesis 22." Ska, "Genesis 22: What Questions Should We Ask the Text?," *Bib* 94, no. 2 (2013): 266 (entire article 257–67).

3. Fretheim asks, "Couldn't Abraham now just pass out of the picture, as he now does for all practical purposes?" Fretheim, "God, Abraham, and the Abuse of Isaac," *WW* 15, no. 1 (1995): 51 (entire article 49–57).

blessing would come. This is a test, in other words, of Abraham's whole-hearted commitment to God, placing this commitment above every earthly value (even God's promise of an heir).

And here we may compare the two parallel leave takings to which Abraham is called, linked by the repetition of *lek ləkā* (12:1 and 22:2), possibly rendered as "go yourself."[4] In 12:1 Abraham is called by God to leave his home and family, while in 22:2 he is called to sacrifice his son. In one case he is called to make a break with his past, and in the second case he is called to relinquish his future.[5]

This reading certainly has prima facie plausibility. When Israel was tested in the wilderness, as recorded in Exodus and Numbers, this was to prove their trust in God. *Prove* here has the sense of bringing out and realizing a potential—prove in practice. The potential must have been there, but it might be latent. And the stringent situation of testing can force the one being tested to rise to the occasion and show their mettle, so to speak.

4. Whereas the first word in the phrase *lek ləkā* is the imperative ("go"), the second word is what is traditionally known as the ethical dative (a term derived from Latin grammar). Consisting of the preposition *lə* (often meaning "for") affixed to a pronominal suffix (in this case "you") and following the verb, the meaning and function of this grammatical form is widely debated. For a discussion, see Jacobus A. Naudé, "Dative: Biblical Hebrew," in *Encyclopedia of Hebrew Language and Linguistics*, vol. 1, A–F, ed. Geoffrey Khan (Leiden: Brill, 2013), 655–58 (656–58 on the ethical dative). Although this grammatical form is often left untranslated, Naudé's analysis suggests that *lek ləkā* might be translated "Go yourself." The ethical dative is found in other places in the Aqedah, as when Abraham instructs the servants in Gen. 22:5 to "stay" (*šəbû-lākem*) with the donkey (this might be translated "Stay yourselves"). And in Gen. 22:8, Abraham tells Isaac that God will himself (*lô*) see to the sheep for the burnt offering (though the verb here is not an imperative).

5. This point is often made in the literature; see, for example, Gerhard von Rad, *Genesis: A Commentary*, rev. ed., trans. John H. Marks (Philadelphia: Westminster, 1972), 239; Fretheim, "God, Abraham, and the Abuse of Isaac," 51; Phyllis Trible, "Genesis 22: The Sacrifice of Sarah," in *"Not in Heaven": Coherence and Complexity in Biblical Narrative*, ed. Jason P. Rosenblatt and Joseph C. Sitterson Jr., ISBL (Bloomington: Indiana University Press, 1991), 173 (entire chapter 170–91). This linkage of Gen. 12:1 and 22:2 can be traced back to the rabbinic tradition, which viewed 12:1–3 and 22:1–19 as two of Abraham's ten trials or tests. The tradition of ten tests/trials is found in the Talmud (specifically the Mishnah) in Pirqe Avot 5:3 (although the text does not specify what they were). Prior to the Talmud, Jub. 17:17 and 19:3 mentioned Abraham's ten trials (but did not list them all). Later tradition, therefore, fills in the details, and various lists are found that typically combine episodes from Genesis (though not always the same ones) with extra-biblical stories. See, for example, Pirqe de-Rabbi Eliezer 26–31; Avot de-Rabbi Nathan 33a and 36b; Midrash Tehillim on Ps. 18:31; and the commentary of Maimonides (Rambam) on the Mishnah (Avot 5:3). Maimonides is the rare interpreter who derives all ten from Genesis (the command to leave his land is the first test and the binding of Isaac is the last). For these references, see Albert van der Heide, *"Now I Know": Five Centuries of Aqedah Exegesis*, ASJP 17 (Cham, Switzerland: Springer, 2017), 459–62 ("Appendix I: Abraham's Ten Trials").

So, is Abraham being tested to see if he would be willing to give up his son (and his future) out of commitment to God?

Problems with the Traditional Reading

The first problem with this interpretation is ethical. The commitment to God that Abraham has to demonstrate here involves *being willing to kill his very own son*. But how can this be a model for commitment to God? It works as a model only if we *abstract* from the very particularity of the text to some general axiom about the need for wholehearted obedience to God (an axiom that is obvious from elsewhere in Scripture and that doesn't need to be grounded in Gen. 22).

Likewise, the Christian typological interpretation of the Aqedah (where the death of Jesus as God's "only Son" is analogous to Isaac on the altar) falters on the dis-analogy between God offering his Son for our salvation (which in orthodox trinitarian theology is equivalent to God's *self*-giving) and Abraham being willing to sacrifice Isaac, a person over whom he does not (on any ethical account) have legitimate absolute power.[6] I could see Abraham being asked to make a *personal sacrifice* for God, but not sacrificing someone *else*—these are two very different things.[7]

But there is a second problem with the traditional reading of the Aqedah—namely, that it is unclear why this test is needed at all. The Abraham story gives absolutely no evidence of Abraham's special attachment to Isaac, such that giving him up would prove his commitment to God.

Abraham would seem, rather, to be attached to *Ishmael*, something that is very clear from chapters 17 and 21. When God tells Abraham that Isaac, not Ishmael, is the one through whom the covenant will be passed, this leads Abraham to plead for God not to forget Ishmael. He exclaims, "O that Ishmael

---

6. I am not contesting that certain New Testament texts (for example, John 3:16) may appeal to this analogy. My point is that we cannot reason from this midrashic New Testament take on the Aqedah back to its original meaning (especially since there is a further dis-analogy in that Isaac was not actually sacrificed, as Jesus was).

7. Moberly sidesteps this dis-analogy in his comment about "Abraham's self-sacrifice," in "Abraham and God in Genesis 22," in *The Bible, Theology, and Faith: A Study of Abraham and Jesus* (Cambridge: Cambridge University Press, 2000), 118. For Levenson's similar note about Abraham's "act of *self*-sacrifice," see "The Test," in *Inheriting Abraham: The Legacy of the Patriarch in Judaism, Christianity, and Islam*, LJI (Princeton: Princeton University Press, 2012), 69 (emphasis original). But Abraham is not (literally) sacrificing *himself*. Levenson is at pains to claim that in the ancient world of the text, Isaac would not have been regarded as an independent person with intrinsic value; rather, he was an extension of his father's line (and his father would have had the legitimate power of life and death over him).

might live in your sight!" (17:18). And when Sarah wants him to send Hagar and Ishmael away, we are told, "The matter was very distressing to Abraham on account of his son" (21:11).[8] In both cases, we find a significant difference from Abraham's response when God tells him to sacrifice Isaac.[9]

In fact, the account of what happens in Genesis 20 suggests that Abraham is so attached to Ishmael that he simply doesn't care about the replacement son that is promised.

We should remember that Abraham had passed Sarah off as his sister in Egypt back in chapter 12, with the result that Pharaoh took her into his harem. Abraham does this again in chapter 20, this time in Gerar, so the king of Gerar takes her into his harem. But note that chapter 20 comes *after* God announced that the covenant heir would be born to Sarah (17:16) and *after* God predicted that this would happen *shortly*—presumably within the next year (17:21; 18:10, 14). And yet, knowing this, Abraham goes ahead and passes Sarah off as his sister a *second time*, not caring that he might lose her (and the promised heir with her); indeed, she might even have been pregnant at the time.

Given that it isn't clear at all that Abraham is attached to Isaac, could it be that Abraham is being given a chance in chapter 22 to *prove his love* for his remaining son? After all, God's instructions to Abraham in 22:2 contain the following description of Isaac: "your son, your only one, *whom you love*—Isaac." So maybe Abraham's *love* for Isaac was being tested. As noted in the last chapter, it is possible that the phrase "whom you love" has the rhetorical effect not of a declarative statement of fact but rather of *suggesting* to

8. If anything, it is Sarah who is attached to Isaac (see esp. Gen. 21:10). Trible makes this point forcibly in "Genesis 22," 187–89. This "decisive parental difference between Sarah and Abraham" (187) leads to Trible's claim that the Aqedah would make more sense as a test of Sarah than of Abraham (if, as many interpreters assume, the test was about the relative strength of Abraham's love for Isaac versus his love for God).

9. There is also a significant difference between Hagar's response to the imminent death of Ishmael and Abraham's response to the imminent death of Isaac. While Hagar could not countenance the death of her son and so "lifted up her voice and wept" (21:16), Abraham is stoically silent. This difference stands out against the background of numerous similarities between the story of the banishment of Hagar and Ishmael and the Aqedah. To start with, instructions for the banishment and the sacrifice are both given by God to Abraham (21:12–13; 22:1–2). In both stories, Abraham "rose early in the morning" (21:14; 22:3). The deaths of Ishmael and Isaac are both prevented by the intervention of an angel (21:17; 22:11–12). This is followed by the announcement of future blessing (21:18; 22:16–17). In both cases, the reprieve for the son is linked to the parent seeing something they hadn't before; Hagar sees a well, Abraham a ram (21:19; 22:13). So the question arises as to why Abraham could not have cried out in grief, as Hagar did. The angel responds by asking, "What troubles you, Hagar?" (21:17) and Ishmael's life is spared. However, the angel has to *prevent* Abraham from going through with the sacrifice (22:11–12).

Abraham that he loves Isaac or of attempting to *evoke* his love for Isaac—with the sense of "You love him, don't you?"

But what would be evidence of this love? I suggest that Abraham could prove his love for Isaac by speaking out and protesting God's command to sacrifice him. Indeed, speaking out on behalf of Isaac might well *extend* and *deepen* Abraham's incipient love for his son (testing often brings to the surface and makes actual what is only potential).

Here it is significant that when the phrase "your son, your only one" is repeated later in the story, in Genesis 22:12 and 16 (spoken by the angel of YHWH), we do *not* find a repetition of "whom you love." These verses affirm Abraham's fear of God (22:12) and obedience to the divine word (22:16) in that "you have not withheld your son, your only one." But given that Abraham has just attempted to sacrifice Isaac, it makes sense that this God-fearing obedience would *not* qualify as love for him. And so that phrase is omitted.[10]

We may, therefore, need to rethink what YHWH means when he says through the angel, "Now I know that you are a God-fearer, since you have not withheld your son, your only one, from me" (22:12).[11] This statement describes what was *discovered* through the testing; but it is a logical fallacy

10. Jon Levenson proposes that the phrase "whom you love" is missing from the angel's proclamation because "the only point" that "the entire trial aims to prove is that Abraham's obedience is absolute and uncompromising"; and this obedience "has altogether overwhelmed his love of Isaac" (Levenson, *The Death and Resurrection of the Beloved Son: The Transformation of Child Sacrifice in Judaism and Christianity* [New Haven: Yale University Press, 1993], 137). I might agree that Abraham's obedience has overwhelmed his love for Isaac, though I see no evidence that he had ever loved Isaac. And I am just a bit suspicious of any religious commitment that is "absolute and uncompromising."

11. The word "since" in my translation of Gen. 22:12 interprets Abraham's attempt to sacrifice his son as a sign of his fear of God. But this is not the only possible translation for the multiple-duty conjunction *wə*, which is the only grammatical link between the statements "Now I know that you are a God-fearer" and "You have not withheld your son, your only son, from me." Given that this conjunction has various translation possibilities (including "and," "but," "now," "then," "since"), Tikva Frymer-Kensky translates it as "but," implying a contrast between genuine fear of God and the attempt to sacrifice Isaac: "Indeed, I know that you fear God, but (now) you have not held back your son, your only one, from me"; she therefore takes the attempt to sacrifice Isaac as compromising Abraham's fear of God. Frymer-Kensky, "Akeda: A View from the Bible," in *Beginning Anew: A Woman's Companion to the High Holy Days*, ed. Gail Twersky Reimer and Judith A. Kates (New York: Touchstone, 1997), 112 (entire chapter 127–44; nn. 345–46). Frymer-Kensky's contrast between fearing God and Abraham's willingness to sacrifice his son is consonant with the stance of the midwives in the Exodus story. When the king of Egypt commanded the midwives to kill Hebrew boys as they were born, "the midwives *feared God*; they did not do as the king of Egypt commanded them, but they *let the boys live*" (Exod. 1:17). Abraham is here implicitly contrasted with the Hebrew midwives.

to infer that this was the *purpose* of the test—especially if we have reason to believe otherwise.[12]

A professor may say to a student after a test, "Now I know that you are a C student." But that doesn't mean that this was the purpose of the test. The professor was hoping the student would put in some effort and get an A.

Even if we think that the angel was giving approval of Abraham's God-fearing readiness to give up his son (there *might* be something valued there, in that obedience to God is preferable to outright disobedience), there is no specific approval of Abraham's *silence*—which, as I have argued throughout this book, is contraindicated by the normative pattern of prayer in Scripture.

With this in mind, I am going to suggest that Abraham was being tested *not* for his unquestioning obedience (that is not something God wants) but rather for his *discernment of God's character*. I agree that he was being tested for his *trust* in God. But genuine trust is not equivalent to blind faith to do anything a voice from heaven tells you. Rather, trust in God requires knowledge or discernment of what sort of God this is.[13]

The Narrative Arc of Abraham's Discernment of God's Character

Here we should note that besides the narrative arc of the promise of descendents (which culminates with the birth of Isaac in Gen. 21), another narrative arc is discernable in the Abraham story. This is the arc of Abraham's growing relationship with God.

This is an important narrative arc since the Abraham story is about the genesis of a new relationship (which becomes formalized as a covenant in Gen. 15 and 17)—between a God whom later Scripture will distinguish radically

12. At one point Moberly admits that the angel articulates the result of the test, but he then goes on to assume (without any argument) that it was the purpose of the test too: "a result which presumably constituted its purpose in the first place." Moberly, "A Specimen Text: Genesis 22," in *Genesis 12–50*, OTG (Sheffield: Sheffield Academic Press, 1995), 40 (entire chapter 39–56).

13. Abraham could have discerned God's character from the promises God made to him about descendants and a land. Indeed, he could have interceded for Isaac by appealing to these promises, thus holding God to his own commitments. This is exactly what Moses does in his intercession on behalf of Israel after the golden calf. He implores God, "Remember Abraham, Isaac, and Israel, your servants, how you swore to them by your own self, saying to them, 'I will multiply your descendants like the stars of heaven, and all this land that I have promised I will give to your descendants, and they shall inherit it forever'" (Exod. 32:13). The result is that "the Lord changed his mind about the disaster that he planned to bring on his people" (32:14). There is no reason, in principle, why Abraham couldn't have also appealed to these very promises (articulated first in Gen. 12:2–3, then in the context of a covenant oath in 15:5, 7).

from the deities of the nations and a man with no explicit prior knowledge of this God.[14]

Jewish tradition is replete with stories of Abraham becoming a monotheist prior to traveling to Canaan, including a story about his smashing the idols in his father's workshop and another about his opposition to Nimrod in Babylon over worship of the one true God.[15] These stories likely take Joshua 24:2 as their point of departure: "Long ago your ancestors—Terah and his sons Abraham and Nahor—lived beyond the Euphrates and served other gods." However, the narrative of Genesis itself does not assume that Abraham started out as a monotheist, much less that he had a full understanding of the character of YHWH. Like the Israelites, who were later deformed by their bondage in Egypt, Abraham would have needed to undergo a significant process of reshaping regarding his attitude and behavior (and even his character).

So let us attend to Abraham's developing relationship with God in Genesis. Taking as our cue the various divine speeches addressed to Abraham between Genesis 12 and 22 (God never speaks to Abraham after 22:18), we may note the ups and downs of Abraham's verbal responses on each occasion.[16] These responses exhibit a growing and then declining degree of intimacy (and confidence) in the divine-human relationship.

Although God speaks to Abraham on two occasions in Genesis 12 (vv. 1–3, 7) and once in Genesis 13 (vv. 14–17), the first time Abraham responds verbally is in Genesis 15.[17] In that chapter God speaks multiple times, initially about the promise of an heir (15:1, 4–5) and then about the promise of land (15:7, 13–16, 18–20). Abraham responds with questions in both cases, honestly expressing his doubts (15:2–3, 8), and in both cases God takes his questions seriously and responds appropriately in order to bolster Abraham's faith.

14. The term *covenant* is specifically mentioned in Gen. 15:18 and 17:2. It is traditional to view chaps. 15 and 17 as two versions of the same covenant, the first told by the Yahwist writer, the second by the Priestly writer. In terms of narrative development, they could be viewed as two stages of the covenant that God makes with Abraham.

15. See Genesis Rabbah 38:13.

16. The fact that the Aqedah is the last recorded dialogue between God and Abraham has often been interpreted to mean that God is fully satisfied with Abraham and so the story has reached its fulfillment. However, it is also possible that God never speaks to Abraham again because God can do no more with Abraham, given his less than adequate response to the test in chap. 22.

17. Genesis 13:4 notes that when Abram returned to the place where he had built his first altar, he "called on the name of YHWH," which could be taken as address to the deity, though his words are not recounted. And in 14:22–23, Abram informs the king of Sodom of the substance of an oath he had sworn to YHWH, but there is no narrative recounting of this oath.

God's desire to respond to Abraham's concerns is evident throughout chapter 15. Indeed, a telling narrative note indicating that God's speech resumption in the midst of 15:5 suggests that God was at one point waiting on Abraham's response, but none came: "He brought him outside and said, 'Look toward heaven and count the stars, if you are able to count them.' [No response.] Then he said to him, 'So shall your descendants be'" (15:5).

God speaks again in Genesis 17, extensively about the covenant and circumcision (17:1–2, 3b–14) and also about the birth of Isaac through Sarah (17:15–16, 19–21). In all this Abraham speaks only once, asking God not to forget about Ishmael (17:18), which God agrees not to do, while reiterating the promise about Isaac (17:19–21). As in 15:5, it is possible that after speaking in 17:9–14, God waits on Abraham's response, which doesn't come, and so he resumes speaking in 17:15 ("And God said to Abraham").

The beginning of Genesis 18, when the three "men" visit Abraham and Sarah, records some speech from YHWH (distinguished as one among the three) concerning Sarah's giving birth (18:10, 13–14, and 15b). No speech of Abraham to God is reported, but Sarah speaks once in reply, to deny that she laughed (18:15a), to which God responds, "Oh yes, you did laugh" (18:15b).

Then comes the extended dialogue between God and Abraham in Genesis 18. God reveals his intentions about Sodom to Abraham (18:20–21), which generates Abraham's bold upbraiding of God about doing what is right (18:23–25), followed by God's agreement to spare the city for the sake of fifty righteous people (18:26). Then Abraham speaks five more times, as he brings the number down (18:27–28a, 29a, 30a, 31a, 32a), and each time God agrees (18:28b, 29b, 30b, 31b, 32b).[18]

Finally, in Genesis 22 God speaks twice at the beginning of the narrative (22:1a, 2) and twice more through an angel from heaven (22:11–12, 15–18). In all this Abraham says only one word, *Hinnēnî*, on two occasions (22:1b, 11b).[19]

18. Between Gen. 18 and 22, there are a few other places we might classify as Abraham's speech to God, although no actual words are quoted. In 20:17 we are told that Abraham prays for Abimelech, while in 21:11 he is distressed about Ishmael being sent away. That God replies to Abraham in 21:12–13 might imply that Abraham addressed his concerns to God, though it could be that God simply responds to Abraham's inner turmoil and not to actual speech (since none is recorded).

19. Similar to my own analysis, Paul Borgman organizes his exposition of the Abraham story around seven visits of God to Abraham (all of which he takes as tests of some sort). See Borgman, *Genesis: The Story We Haven't Heard* (Downers Grove, IL: InterVarsity, 2001), chaps. 3–6. While Borgman insightfully addresses Abraham's growing boldness in dialogue with God (especially

What is the nature of this God whom Abraham is coming to know? In all of the reported dialogues between YHWH and Abraham, YHWH is shown as a God who listens to his servant and tries to address his articulated needs (and in the case of God's rescue of Lot, even his unarticulated needs; Gen. 19).

So one way to think of this "relational" narrative arc is that it has to do with Abraham coming to understand the nature and character of the God who called him out of Haran.[20] And a *sign* of Abraham's growing (or diminishing) discernment of God's character is his willingness to speak up in the manner of the later psalmists and prophets, articulating his own needs and interceding on behalf of others.[21]

Genesis 18: A Teaching Moment for Abraham

This makes sense of the intentional opportunity God gives Abraham in Genesis 18 to learn more about divine mercy through the process of intercession, in order that Abraham might teach his children and household the way of YHWH. Here it is worth pausing to understand what is going on in Genesis 18 and how this episode sets us up for Genesis 22.[22]

In Genesis 18, three "men" have visited Abraham's camp and predicted that Sarah will have a son. Two of the "men" (angels, it turns out) depart for Sodom, while the third, which turns out to be YHWH himself, remains, for he has something he wants to tell Abraham.

---

in Gen. 15 and 18), his traditional reading of the seventh visit (Gen. 22) diverges significantly from mine.

20. Ellen Davis has a poignant reflection on the Aqedah in "'Take Your Son': The Binding of Isaac," in *Getting Involved with God: Rediscovering the Old Testament* (Cambridge: Cowley, 2001), 50–64. Central to her reflection is the question of what sort of God we (and Abraham) are dealing with in the text. "We need to know what kind of God we must reckon with" (52). "We have to ask, what does this story tell us about God?" (58). Indeed, this story tells us "something fundamental about the God of Israel" (61). Davis concludes that the Aqedah discloses to us "a God who is vulnerable" (repeated twice on 62), by which she means, initially, God's need to be sure of Abraham's faithfulness (62) and, ultimately, God's "excruciating vulnerability" in the death of Christ (63). Although it is a beautifully written piece, Davis's chapter does not challenge the traditional reading of the Aqedah. My own understanding of what we (and Abraham) should learn from the Aqedah moves in a different direction.

21. Leonard Sweet suggests that God desires relationship (even contentious relationship) rather than obedience. He applies this argument to the Aqedah, in Sweet, *Out of the Question . . . into the Mystery: Getting Lost in the Godlife Relationship* (Colorado Springs: Waterbrook, 2004), 37–48 (notes 217–20), 49–61 (notes 220–23).

22. Here we should note that these two episodes are united in the Parashah or lectionary reading in the Jewish Torah cycle, titled Vayera (18:1–22:24); this title is the first word of 18:1 ("And he appeared").

YHWH muses to himself: "Shall I hide from Abraham what I am about to do?" (18:17)—that is, concerning the cry of Sodom that has come to him. YHWH decides to inform Abraham of this cry in order that "he may charge his children and his household after him to keep the way of the LORD by doing righteousness and justice [ṣədāqâ ûmišhpāṭ]" (18:19).

When God tells Abraham that he is going down to see if the cry he has heard from Sodom demands judgment ("if not, I will know"; 18:20–21), he waits on Abraham's response (18:22).[23] But Abraham overinterprets God's statement that he is going to examine the situation in Sodom to mean that God has already decided to destroy the city (where his nephew Lot is living).[24] No doubt this is partly due to the reputation of Sodom (already alluded to in 13:10 and 14:21–24); but it is probably due also to Abraham's assumptions about the character of God and about what constitutes God's righteousness and justice.

But note, this is precisely what God wants to teach Abraham by revealing his intentions about Sodom. God wants Abraham to be able to instruct his children and his household in "the way of the LORD" so they will do "righteousness and justice." This means that Abraham must first *himself* be instructed in God's righteous ways.[25]

23. Many commentators suggest that the reading in the MT of 18:22 ("So the men turned from there, and went toward Sodom, while Abraham remained standing before the LORD") is an example of one of the eighteen *tiqqune sopherim* (scribal emendations) mentioned by the rabbis. If this is the case, perhaps the text originally said that YHWH remained standing before Abraham. The "original" reading is often taken by commentators to signify a stance of humility on YHWH's part, putting himself at Abraham's disposal, a point that it is assumed the rabbinic tradition could not countenance, which resulted in the change. However, Tim Hegg has shown that there is absolutely no textual evidence of any such original reading in any Hebrew manuscript or ancient version. Based on the fact that the rabbinic claim that 18:22 is one of the eighteen *tiqqune sopherim* is not found earlier than the late fifth to seventh centuries CE, Hegg argues that there was a theological and not a textual basis for the idea of a *tiqqune sopherim* at this point, arising from polemics with Christianity (having to do with whether the Shekinah was incarnate). For details, see Hegg, "Genesis 18:22 & the Tiqqune Sopherim: Textual, Midrashic, and for What Purpose?," paper given in the Masoretic Studies program unit of the Society of Biblical Literature, San Antonio, November 20, 2016, https://tr-pdf.s3-us-west-2.amazonaws.com/articles/gen18-22 %E2%80%93tiqqune-soferim.pdf.

24. For a lucid analysis of Abraham's misread of the situation, see Nathan MacDonald, "Listening to Abraham—Listening to Yhwh: Divine Justice and Mercy in Genesis 18:16–33," *CBQ* 66 (2004): 25–43.

25. The "way of the LORD" that God wants Abraham to learn, so that he may teach his children and household, may be read in light of Exod. 32:8, where YHWH tells Moses that in constructing the calf the people "turn aside from *the way* I commanded them" (referring to

What Is Revealed by God's Responses to Abraham?

Abraham does, indeed, intercede vigorously on Sodom's behalf, upbraiding God for unjustly planning to destroy the righteous/innocent with the wicked (18:23–25); he challenges God despite being, as he puts it, merely "dust and ashes" (18:27). In a series of requests that God save the city—initially for the sake of fifty righteous, which he eventually ratchets down to ten (as his last offer)—Abraham tests the extent of God's mercy; and God accedes to each request (18:23–33).

Contrary to a traditional reading of the text, there is no bargaining (or bartering or haggling) going on here, since bargaining involves two people starting at opposite ends and meeting in the middle. The dialogue in Genesis 18 is different. Abraham makes an opening offer of fifty; God says sure. Then Abraham says, how about forty-five; God says fine. Abraham proposes forty; God agrees. Then Abraham drops the "price" by ten instead of five, and offers thirty; God says, let's do it. Abraham then offers twenty; God agrees. Then Abraham says, I have one final offer—how about ten? God says, ten it is.

Now, the question is, What is God trying to teach Abraham about the "way of the LORD" from this exchange? If this were a used car sale, I would think the seller wants to give the car away. What sort of righteousness and justice is God displaying here? Certainly, one infused with mercy. As Jon Levenson puts it, "We should conclude that Abraham is to instruct the chosen nation in the ways of grace and mercy that characterize his God."[26] It is as if YHWH is looking for an excuse to save Sodom (and Lot).[27]

YHWH's instructions to Jeremiah might be relevant here. In 5:1 God tells the prophet,

> Run to and fro through the streets of Jerusalem,
>   look around and take note!

---

the moral path they should have taken); it may also be read in light of Moses's request to God in 33:13 to "show me *your ways*" (which, in context, are ways of mercy).

26. Levenson, *Inheriting Abraham*, 62. Although my interpretation of YHWH's "way" as characterized by mercy is based on a contextual reading of Gen. 18, Levenson grounds his conclusion in Moshe Weinfeld's study of the word pair "righteousness and justice" (*ṣədāqâ ûmišpāṭ*) in the Hebrew Bible and Mesopotamian literature, which suggests that it refers to "acts of kindness and mercy" (Levenson, *Inheriting Abraham*, 62, 219n33). Nathan MacDonald also cites Weinfeld's study ("Listening to Abraham—Listening to Yhwh," 37) and suggests that YHWH's "way" is that of "forgiving mercy" (40).

27. MacDonald, "Listening to Abraham—Listening to Yhwh," is particularly good on this point.

> Search its squares and see
> if you can find one person
> who acts justly
> and seeks truth—
> so that I may pardon Jerusalem.

This suggests that God might forestall destruction of a wicked city for just *one* righteous person. That Abraham stops at ten, however, suggests that he hasn't fully plumbed the depths of divine mercy.[28] He has not yet learned what God wanted to teach him. Nevertheless, God rescues Lot and his family through angelic agency (Gen. 19), even though Abraham hadn't thought to ask for that outright.

At one point during the rescue operation, when Lot was lingering in Sodom, the angels "seized him and his wife and his two daughters by the hand, *the LORD being merciful to him*, and they brought him out and left him outside the city" (Gen. 19:16). When the angels instruct Lot to flee to the hills, he tells them that he can't make it that far, and so (appealing to their favor or mercy [*ḥesed*]), he requests refuge in an outlying town, asking simply that the angels spare the town for his sake (19:18–20). And they agree, without discussion (19:21). Lot asks, on a smaller scale, for what Abraham couldn't. And it is immediately granted.[29]

What Did Abraham Learn?

So the question arises as to why Abraham did not simply ask God to spare Sodom for the sake of Lot and his family. We can only speculate; but it may be that he was somewhat intimidated, feeling guilty for asking for so much. We see evidence of his intimidation in the qualifying comments he makes in his second, fourth, and sixth requests, noting that he is just "dust and

28. Contra the speculations of commentators in the literature about why he couldn't go lower than ten (sometimes related to the Jewish tradition that a minimum of ten adults is required for a *minyan*).

29. The prominence of God's mercy is evident in the later reuse of the Sodom story in 2 Pet. 3. Ryan Juza has convincingly shown, by attending to a plethora of intertextual allusions, that 2 Pet. 3 draws on the Sodom story, in tandem with the flood story (filtered through the Jewish apocalyptic tradition), to address both judgment and mercy in the eschaton. See Juza, "Echoes of Sodom and Gomorrah on the Day of the Lord: Intertextuality and Tradition in 2 Peter 3:7–13," *BBR* 24 (2014): 227–45. While Peter's comment about "scoffers" who will come in the last days (3:3) alludes to Lot's future sons-in-law who thought he was joking about the coming fiery destruction (Gen. 19:14), the notion that God is patient, "not wanting any to perish" (2 Pet. 3:9), alludes to the rescue of Lot and his family (and 2 Pet. 2:6–9 explicitly refers to the rescue of Lot).

ashes," pleading that God not be angry with him, even though there is no
indication of any anger on God's part. He may have found it difficult to ask
for something so personal as the salvation of his nephew's family (which is
why this is unvoiced in the conversation). Perhaps he did not think that God
was *that* merciful.

So, at the end of his dialogue with God in Genesis 18, Abraham has *not*
quite learned what God wanted to teach him—even though Lot and his family have been saved.

It is not even clear that Abraham knows that they have been saved; the
narrative does not inform us of this. All we are told is that Abraham watched
from afar the smoke rising from the plain after Sodom's destruction (Gen.
19:27–28), perhaps with a sinking feeling in his stomach.

What Is Being Tested in Genesis 22?

So we may frame the question that wends its way throughout the Abraham
story as follows: How will Abraham be able to distinguish this God he is
coming to know from the gods of the nations? This sort of discernment will
be necessary so that Abraham will be equipped to "charge his children and
his household after him to keep the way of the LORD by doing righteousness
and justice" (18:19).

One indication that Abraham is confused about the character of the God
who called him back in chapter 12, who has been appearing to him over the
course of twenty-five years, is found in his explanation to Abimelech, the king
of Gerar, about why he passed Sarah off as his sister. Abraham says, "When
God caused me to wander from my father's house, I said to her, 'This is the
kindness you must do me: at every place to which we come, say of me, He is
my brother'" (20:13).

As many Bible readers know, the word for "God" in Hebrew (*'ĕlōhîm*) is
plural in form. Whether we should take it as "God" or "gods" depends on the
context and the grammar of the sentence. One of the grammatical indicators
is the form of the verb that goes with *'ĕlōhîm*, whether it is singular or plural.[30]

In 1 Samuel 4:7–8 the Philistines are portrayed as so confused about the
character of Israel's God that they first use *'ĕlōhîm* with a singular verb in

---

30. On this see Wilhelm Gesenius, *Gesenius' Hebrew Grammar*, ed. Emil Kautzsch, trans.
Arthur Ernest Cowley, 2nd ed. (Oxford: Clarendon, 1910), §145 (section on "Agreement between
the Members of a Sentence, especially between Subject and Predicate, in Respect of Gender
and Number").

verse 7 ("*'ĕlōhîm* has come into the camp") and then with a plural verb (and plural pronouns) in verse 8 ("Who can deliver us from the power of these mighty *'ĕlōhîm*? These are the *'ĕlōhîm* who struck the Egyptians with every sort of plague in the wilderness").[31]

Like the confused Philistines in 1 Samuel 4, Abraham uses the plural form of the verb "caused to wander" with *'ĕlōhîm* in his conversation with Abimelech (Gen. 20:13). Does this episode, coming just before the Aqedah, suggest that Abraham is unclear about whether the *'ĕlōhîm* he serves is one God or many?

It is possible that Abraham was merely accommodating his speech to the presumed polytheism of the pagan king (which was unnecessary, since God had already revealed himself to Abimelech in 20:3–7).[32] But even if Abraham was not confused about the unity of the divine nature, it is reasonable to think Abraham needs further guidance in distinguishing YHWH from the gods of the nations.

In light of the command that Abraham receives in 22:2 to sacrifice his son, we may put the question of Abraham's discernment of God's character more pointedly. Is the God of Abraham simply one of the pagan deities of Mesopotamia or Canaan who requires child sacrifice as a symbol of allegiance?[33] Or is he different, a God of mercy and love for his children, who was even willing to forgo judgment on Sodom for the sake of the righteous?[34] That was something

31. Many translations of Gen. 20:13 and 1 Sam. 4:7–8 render the verbs as singular or plural not in accordance with the Hebrew but in accordance with the expectations of the translator (Abraham is a monotheist, while the Philistines are polytheists). Thus almost all English translations have Abraham speak of God in the singular in Gen. 20:13, while the translations can't agree on whether the Philistines' statement in 1 Sam. 4:7 should be rendered as singular ("God" or "a god") or plural ("gods").

32. Whatever the motivation, Abraham's fudging on the nature of the true God is problematic for the one who is the father of the chosen people. Why couldn't he have been more forthright about the God he served? In other biblical texts, Israelites often communicate the nature of YHWH to those of other nations by proclaiming him to be "the God of heaven," an expression of God's universality and cosmic rule. Abraham uses this phrase later, when he commissions his servant to find a wife for Isaac (Gen. 24:3, 7). For the use of this designation, which occurs primarily in late biblical texts, whether in Hebrew or Aramaic, see 2 Chron. 36:23; Ezra 1:2; 5:11, 12; 6:9, 10; 7:12, 21, 23; Neh. 1:4, 5; 2:4, 20; Ps. 136:26; Dan. 2:18, 19, 37, 44; Jon. 1:9.

33. My question here evinces a certain overlap with Jon Levenson's claim about a possible correlation between the Aqedah and a shift in Israel's thinking from human to animal sacrifice; although Levenson thinks the text might reflect this shift, he does not think that it intends to *teach* this shift (*Death and Resurrection of the Beloved Son*, 113–14). My question, however, does not arise from (or depend on) a reconstructed history behind the text but relates to the text's own narrative world.

34. Even prior to the Abraham story, God is shown to be merciful (or at least restrained in judgment) in his response to human sin. Thus God makes garments of skin for the first couple (Gen. 3:21), gives Cain a sign of protection (4:15), and merely scatters the residents of Babel and confuses their language (11:1–9). Given the location of Babel in Mesopotamia (10:10–12) and the tradition

Abraham *should* have learned in chapter 18, so he could pass it on to his own children. But he didn't. The lesson was cut short—by Abraham himself.

And so in a final, climactic episode in the Abraham story, God gives Abraham another opportunity to learn and grow in the relationship. But God ups the ante this time; God raises the stakes. It's not his nephew Lot who will be destroyed (along with Sodom, his home). It is *Abraham's own son*. And it's not God who will do it; *Abraham* must do it *by his own hand*. If anything would force Abraham to speak out, to appeal to the mercy of God, this would be it. Abraham has the opportunity, in this test, to protest the command and intercede for his son's life, which would articulate his view of the character and ways of God—both in *what* he says to God and by *the fact* that he says it. And it would, further, show his love for Isaac (which would be a good thing, not an impediment to his commitment to God).

But Abraham doesn't speak out; he is silent.

Whereas Abraham *became* silent at the end of his intercession in Genesis 18 (he stopped the conversation earlier than he needed to and so never fully grasped the wideness in God's mercy), here, in Genesis 22, he never gets the conversation off the ground. He is simply silent. And this silence speaks volumes. It articulates a view of God as clearly as if he had used words. I would suggest that Abraham's silence speaks of God as a harsh taskmaster who is not to be challenged.[35] If that is what Abraham learned about God, we may wonder what he passed on to Isaac.

What Did Isaac Learn?

In the previous chapter, I noted that Isaac is not reported as returning with Abraham down the mountain. Indeed, in the remainder of the Abraham story there is no evidence that Abraham and Isaac ever see or speak to each other again after Genesis 22. Jon Levenson, however, objects to this line of thinking; he notes that just because the narrative does not mention any conversation or meeting between Abraham and Isaac after chapter 22, this does not mean that there was none, since they are not portrayed as speaking to each other before chapter 22.[36]

---

that Abraham's family is from the same region (11:27–32), we might wonder if (within the narrative world of Genesis) Abraham should have known of God's mercy or restraint in responding to sin.

35. Abraham's mindset may have been similar to that of the psalmist in Ps. 39, whose silence (39:1–2 [39:2–3 MT]) was grounded in his assumption that he was not allowed to dissent from, or protest, God's will (39:9 [39:10 MT]). See the discussion of this psalm in chap. 1.

36. Levenson, "The Test," 85–86.

Granted; but my point is different—not simply that they do not speak to each other but that they are clearly living apart after the Aqedah. So when Abraham sends his servant to find a bride for Isaac, Abraham himself is not able to personally connect with his son. When the servant brings Rebekah to Isaac, the text tells us that Isaac was living in Beer-lahai-roi, in the Negev, down at the southernmost extremity of the land (Gen. 24:62; also 25:11). But Abraham lives in Beersheba (22:19).[37] This gives more force to the idea that they had nothing more to do with each other after the Aqedah. And who can blame Isaac for this? What son would go home with a father who tried to sacrifice him to his God?

But Levenson has another objection to the idea that Isaac did not return from the mountain with Abraham. He suggests that there is no mention of Isaac at the end of the story because this is a test of Abraham; so the story appropriately starts with Abraham and ends with Abraham. Isaac "is not the focus, and his return requires no special mention."[38] But this explanation is complicated by the repetition of verbs from the start of the story at the end—with one significant change. When Abraham set out on the journey, we are told that after saddling the donkey, taking his servants and Isaac, and cutting the wood, he "arose and went" to the place God had told him (22:3). Although Abraham did not travel alone (he was accompanied by Isaac and the servants), the verbs for *arise* and *go* (*qûm* and *hālak*) are in the singular. So far, this supports Levenson's claim. But after Abraham returns from the mountain to his servants (with no mention of Isaac), we are told that "*they* arose and went" to Beersheba (22:19)—clearly including the servants but not Isaac.[39]

It looks like the text is intentionally making the point that Isaac did not return with his father. The next time father and son *meet*, if we may even call it that, is at Abraham's funeral (25:9); but by then it's too late for reconciliation.[40]

37. Beersheba is in the northern part of the Negev. We do not know the exact location of Beer-lahai-roi, but it is different from Beersheba.

38. Levenson, "The Test," 87.

39. This glaring absence of Isaac at the end of the Aqedah is noticed in Genesis Rabbah 56:11, which suggests a reason for his absence. "And Avraham returned to his young men (Gen. 22:19). And where was Itzchak? Rabbi Berechiah said in the name of the Rabbis from there [i.e., Babylon, in the Babylonian Talmud]: he sent him to Shem [Noah's son] to study Torah." Trans. from Sefaria.org (with my insertions in brackets), https://www.sefaria.org/Bereishit_Rabbah .56.11?lang=bi&with=all&lang2=en.

40. Another interpretation of Isaac's absence is found in Yalkut Reubeni (among other texts)—namely, that Isaac was taken to the garden of Eden (Paradise) for three years "to be healed from the wound inflicted on him by Abraham," though whether the wound was psychological trauma or an incision made by the knife is unclear (three years is thought to span from the Moriah incident until the finding of a wife for Isaac). Quoted in Shalom Spiegel, *The Last*

A Scattered, Broken Family

And what about Sarah? She is missing at the start of Genesis 22.[41] But she is also missing from Abraham's life for the rest of the Genesis account after chapter 22. The next time Sarah is mentioned we are told of her death, in Hebron, where she had been living (23:2).[42] Abraham travels (presumably from Beersheba) to Hebron to bury her; it does not seem that they have been living together, at least if we attend to the geographical references in Genesis.[43] Did Abraham's attempt to sacrifice Isaac result also in Sarah's alienation?

Or were they separated even prior to chapter 22? Could that be why Sarah is not mentioned at the start of the story? After all, when Abraham moves from Gerar (where he tries to pass Sarah off as his sister to the Philistine king), the next place he goes is Beersheba (though it is only named Beersheba after Abraham goes there; 21:31). This is where Hagar was living after she was sent away with Ishmael (21:14). Is Hagar the reason why Abraham went there? Were they living together? Did Sarah accompany him from Gerar to Beersheba, or did she go back to Hebron at that point, where they had previously been living?[44]

We don't have clear answers to these questions. But we clearly have a broken family. Not only is Isaac living in Beer-lahai-roi and Sarah in Hebron (at least after Gen. 22), but Ishmael has been living in the wilderness of Paran (21:20–21), and Hagar and Abraham are living in Beersheba (together or apart is unclear).[45]

Trial: On the Legends and Lore of the Command to Abraham to Offer Isaac as a Sacrifice; The Akedah (Woodstock, VT: Jewish Lights, 1993 [Heb. orig. 1950; Eng. orig. 1967]), 6.

41. Trible interprets Sarah's absence in the story as a function of a patriarchal bias in the text that marginalizes her. Trible, "Genesis 22," 182–92.

42. Given that the death of Sarah (Gen. 23) is the next narrative after the Aqedah (Gen. 22), various midrashim suggest that Sarah died when she heard that Abraham had taken her son to be sacrificed on the mountain. See, for example, Genesis Rabbah 58:5. For a translation, see Levenson, *Death and Resurrection of the Beloved Son*, 133.

43. The NJPS Tanakh and the NAB (rev. ed.) of Gen. 23:2 obscure the fact that Abraham traveled from Beersheba to Hebron to bury Sarah by translating the verb for "came" or "went" (*bô'*) as "proceeded," which is grammatically possible but which contextually ignores the geographical references.

44. In the context of an intriguing discussion of the significance of Beersheba in Gen. 21 and 22, Mark Brett comments, "This geographical irony is simply too great to dismiss." Brett, *Genesis: Procreation and the Politics of Identity*, OTR (London: Routledge, 2000), 76.

45. After Sarah's death, Abraham's family life takes a different turn. We are told that he took another wife, Keturah, through whom he had six sons (25:1–2), and he also had concubines, with sons by them (25:6).

These are not matters that are often discussed by interpreters of Genesis 22.[46] But they are important for a nuanced reading of the text. Abraham's family life is in tatters, to say the least; and by the end of the Moriah episode the dysfunctional family members are all scattered. But is this what God wants? Is this what faithfulness to God leads to?

So if God wants Abraham to instruct his children and household in God's way of righteousness and justice, we do well to ask, What did Isaac learn from the episode on the mountain in Genesis 22?

On the Mountain with the Boy

The fact that Abraham comes down the mountain alone, and is never reported as seeing Isaac again, prods me to ask if Abraham's attempt to sacrifice his son, without even attempting to stand up for the boy and plead with God for his life (as he pled on behalf of Sodom), did not have the effect of traumatizing Isaac and alienating him from his father.[47]

Picture Isaac traveling with his father for three days, mostly in silence; then the poignant but inconclusive conversation as they go up the mountain together. When they get there, Abraham builds an altar (something he did in other places, like Shechem, Bethel, and Hebron). But here things are different. He spreads out the wood on top of the altar and binds (*'āqad*) Isaac; this is the singularity (both a unique moment and a hapax legomenon) from which we derive the Jewish name for this story—the *Aqedah*, the binding of Isaac.

What is it like for Isaac, as his father trusses him up like a sheep for the slaughter (22:9), then picks up the knife?[48] The Hebrew word for "knife" here is *ma'ăkelet*; no ordinary knife, this is a butcher's cleaver (at least in later

---

46. Mark Brett is an exception. See Brett, *Genesis*, 72–76, where his focus is to understand the Genesis narrative as containing an implicit (subversive) critique of Israel's Persian-era identity politics.

47. Fretheim also wonders about this ("God, Abraham, and the Abuse of Isaac," 53) and concludes, "There is no escaping the trauma Isaac certainly endured" (57).

48. There is no instruction in Leviticus about binding the sacrificial animal for a burnt offering (Lev. 1:3–17; 6:8–13 [6:1–6 MT]). It is possible that Abraham bound Isaac so he would not resist (or flee); otherwise, Abraham might not have been able to complete the sacrifice. Genesis Rabbah 56:8 suggests that Isaac asked to be bound in case he were to struggle or flinch, which would result in a blemished sacrifice. "Father, I am a young man and I am concerned lest my body shake from fear of the knife and I will trouble you, and lest the slaughtering will be invalid and it will not be considered a sacrifice for you. Rather, tie me very well." Trans. from Sefaria.org, https://www.sefaria.org/Bereishit_Rabbah.56 .8?lang=bi&with=all&lang2=en.

Hebrew). And the boy lies there, watching while "Abraham stretched out his hand and took the knife to slaughter his son" (22:10).[49]

Only to be stopped by an insistent voice from heaven: "Abraham! Abraham!" (22:11). His name is repeated, as if the angel is desperate to stop him. And Isaac's life is spared. Not, as far as he knows, because of his father (*he* had tried to kill him) but by an angel, who forbade Abraham to stretch out his hand against the boy, then went on to say, "Do not . . . do anything to him." (22:12).[50]

I think I can safely say that if Isaac learned anything of the mercy of God, it was through the angel's intervention to stay his father's hand. Yet if he learned that it was *God* who had commanded his father to sacrifice him in the first place, this sense of mercy would not be pure and unvarnished. I think, minimally, that Isaac would be confused about the character of God.

And if Abraham's response to God's command in Genesis 22 did affect Isaac negatively, how could we view this response as exemplary? Wouldn't there be some alternative way to be faithful to God without traumatizing and alienating his son?

Father-Son Blessing after Genesis 22

Later, we are told by Abraham's servant (24:36) and by the narrator in a genealogy (25:5) that Abraham gave all he had to Isaac (possibly as compensation for what he went through on the mountain). But it is significant that Abraham never *blesses* Isaac. It was literally impossible to do, given that they never met again after chapter 22. Instead, we are told that after Abraham's death *God* blessed Isaac (25:11).[51] God made up for Abraham's failing. But was it ever fully made up? What would be the effect on Isaac of the estrangement and the resulting lack of direct blessing from his father?

49. The identical phrase "he took the knife" is found in one other place in the Old Testament (Judg. 19:29), as the Levite is about to dismember his concubine.

50. Indeed, the angel is so intent on stopping Abraham that there is a grammatical lapse in his words. The angel omits the direct object marker that would normally have preceded the Hebrew of "your hand" in the command, "Do not stretch out *your hand* to the young man" (22:12). Although this marker is often absent in Hebrew poetry, it is normally present in prose. Genesis 22:12 is the only place where this expected grammatical marker is missing in the Aqedah narrative.

51. That God, not Abraham, blessed Isaac is noted in Numbers Rabbah 11:2. However, the explanation given is that "in his pure and simple faith Abraham left this to God himself." Trans. Samuel Rapaport, in *The Sacred Books and Early Literature of the East*, vol. 4, *Medieval Hebrew, the Midrash, the Kabbalah* (New York: Parke, Austin, and Lipscomb, 1917), 115.

This makes me wonder if the lack of father-son blessing led to Isaac's later hyperfocus on his need to bless Esau, his firstborn, before he dies (27:4; see also 27:7, 10). He desperately wants to get the blessing right in the case of his own son, but he fails. Jacob, as we know, through deception, receives the blessing instead of Esau (27:19, 23, 29); and both Esau and Isaac are distraught that there is no blessing left for the firstborn (27:33–38).

Dysfunctional Family Life after Genesis 22

Perhaps it's too obvious, but then I wonder if the evident dysfunction in Isaac's own family can be traced back to the trauma of what happened on the mountain. Isaac and Rebekah play favorites (25:28); Jacob (with his mother's guidance) deceives his father to take his brother's blessing (27:5–29); Esau wants to kill Jacob, so he flees for his life (27:41–45).[52] Then Jacob's children (by two wives and two concubines) are wildly dysfunctional, the young Joseph boasting of his dreams of dominance in front of his older brothers (37:5–8), who plot to kill him (37:18–20), then sell him into slavery (37:23–28), and then deceive their father into thinking he is dead (37:31–35). And, of course, God worked it out for good (or so Joseph says [50:20], and that may be so); but that doesn't excuse the subethical, destructive behavior of Joseph's brothers or the prideful, boastful young Joseph. This is so far from Abraham's offspring learning the way of the YHWH (18:19) that it is clear something has broken down in the family system. As the modern Hebrew poet Haim Guri puts it, Isaac's heirs "are born / With a knife in their hearts."[53]

Isaac as a Diminished Character in the Book of Genesis

But one of the most pronounced effects of the Mount Moriah episode is the structure of the book of Genesis itself. Bible readers are familiar with the promises given to the three ancestors of Israel—Abraham, Isaac, and Jacob.

---

52. As Bruce Waltke puts it, "The family conflict now becomes full-blown in pursuit of the patriarch's [Isaac's] blessing. The future of the promises may be squandered by a family wrecked by jealousy, deception, and power struggles." Waltke with Cathi J. Fredricks, *Genesis: A Commentary* (Grand Rapids: Zondervan, 2001), 373.

53. Guri writes, "Isaac, as the story goes, was not sacrificed. / He lived for many years, / Saw all that was good until his eyes grew dim. / But he bequeathed that hour to his heirs. / They are born / With a knife in their hearts." Guri, "Yerushah" ["Heritage"], in *Shoshanat Ruḥot* (Bnei Brak, Israel: Hakibbutz Hameuchad, 1960), 83. Quoted in Glenda Abramson, "The Reinterpretation of the Akedah in Modern Hebrew Poetry," *Journal of Jewish Studies* 41, no. 1 (1990): 108 (entire article 101–14).

That triad is found over and over again in Scripture.[54] But the book of Genesis, after the Primeval History (Gen. 1–11), consists of the *Abraham* story (chaps. 12–25), the *Jacob* story (chaps. 25–35), and the *Joseph* story (chaps. 37–50), each introduced by reference to the father of the main character. But there is no comparable Isaac story.

The introductions to the stories of Abraham, Jacob, and Joseph all use the word *tôlədôt*, traditionally "generations," derived from the verb *yālad* (to give birth), with the sense of that which was generated or birthed by (or which developed from) the one named (in these three cases, it is their father). Thus Abraham's story begins, "These are the *tôlədôt* of Terah" (11:27). Jacob's story begins, "These are the *tôlədôt* of Isaac" (25:19). And Joseph's story begins, "These are the *tôlədôt* of Jacob" (37:2).

But there is no heading "These are the *tôlədôt* of Abraham."

Isaac has only one chapter that could be considered his own story (Gen. 26), where God blesses his every effort to dig wells wherever he travels, so that he has water, wealth, and peaceful relations with the Philistines. It is as if God is comforting Isaac with overabundant grace for what he went through on the mountain.

But apart from that chapter, Isaac appears only as a bit player in either Abraham's story or Jacob's story. He has no story of his own. Even in the Jacob story, Isaac does not appear in the narrative between the account of his blessing of Jacob (27:1–28:9) and the notice of his death (35:27–29); although his name is mentioned by others between these episodes, Isaac as a character simply disappears from view. He has no significant actions that advance the narrative of the promise. Indeed, Isaac is a much diminished, shadowy, and insubstantial character in Genesis.[55] Perhaps that is to be expected, given what he went through.

What Jacob Learned about the God of Isaac

One of the most intriguing bits of information we are given that bears on the question of what Isaac learned from the events of Genesis 22 is found in

54. A sampling of references to this triad of names includes Gen. 50:24; Exod. 2:24; 3:6, 15; 4:5; 6:3, 8; 32:13; 33:1; Lev. 26:42; Num. 32:11; Deut. 1:8; 6:10; 9:5; 29:13; 30:20; 34:4; 2 Kings 13:23; Jer. 33:26; Matt. 22:32; Acts 3:13; 7:32.

55. Elizabeth Boase recognizes the diminution of Isaac in "Life in the Shadows: The Role and Function of Isaac in Genesis—Synchronic and Diachronic Readings," *VT* 51, no. 3 (2001): 312–35. She describes Isaac as "shadowy, ill-defined and subordinate" (312) and also as "passive" (315, 322).

Genesis 31. In Jacob's conversation with his uncle Laban, which leads to a covenant between them, Jacob first affirms that despite Laban's underhandedness, the God of his fathers has protected him. And who is this God? He is, in Jacob's words, "the God of Abraham and the *Fear* [*pāḥad*] of Isaac" (31:42). Then when he and Laban swear the covenant oath, we are told, "Jacob swore by the *Fear* [*pāḥad*] of his father Isaac" (31:53).[56]

This is what Isaac passed down to Jacob, by intent or otherwise, about the character of his God—he is *The Fear*.[57] And my contextual reading of the Aqedah suggests that this use of the term "fear" does not have a positive connotation.[58] That God is to be feared was Abraham's legacy to his son.

Do the Angel Speeches Validate Abraham's Response to God?

I have tried to show that a careful reading of the Aqedah in the context of the earlier Abraham story, along with the later fallout of the test, leads to a reinterpretation of what was being tested and also of whether Abraham's response was optimal. This reinterpretation, however, seems to fly in the face of the two angel speeches, which are traditionally read as positively valuing Abraham's response. Doesn't the angel of YHWH (speaking on behalf of God) validate Abraham's unquestioning obedience?[59]

56. The Hebrew word for "fear" that Jacob uses is not *yir'â* but *pāḥad*. There is a scholarly opinion, first proposed by William Albright, that this word is derived from Semitic cognates meaning "thigh, hip, loins" and should be translated as "kinsman," so the phrase would be "the Kinsman of Isaac" (Albright, *From the Stone Age to Christianity: Monotheism and the Historical Process*, 2nd ed. [Garden City, NY: Doubleday, 1957], 348n71). Although there have been some supporters of this suggestion, not only is the evidence for this meaning scant, but *pāḥad* is one of the two standard Hebrew words for "fear" throughout the Hebrew Bible and fits the context of Gen. 31 very well. For an argument against Albright's suggestion, see Delbert R. Hillers, "Paḥad Yiṣḥāq," *JBL* 91 (1972): 90–92.

57. See Frederick Buechner's powerful novel *The Son of Laughter* (San Francisco: Harper-Collins, 1993) on the story of Isaac, told from the perspective of Jacob. Throughout the book Jacob pervasively refers to his father's God as "the Fear."

58. Both *yir'â* and *pāḥad* are used in equivalent ways for the fear of God/YHWH, although in many cases *pāḥad* clearly means "terror" or "dread" in a negative sense. David J. A. Clines argues that the sense or *denotation* of both *yir'â* and *pāḥad* is the emotion of being afraid (often, implicitly, of death). When this fear is *of God*, this emotion might lead to awe or reverence or to certain ethical or cultic actions, but these are *connotations* that the term "fear" may take on in certain contexts. Both *yir'â* and *pāḥad* simply mean being afraid (even of God). See Clines, "'The Fear of the Lord Is Wisdom' (Job 28:28): A Semantic and Contextual Study," in *Job 28: Cognition in Context*, ed. Ellen van Wolde, BibInt 64 (Leiden: Brill, 2003), 57–92. It is doubtful that there is much positive connotation to be had in the context of Gen. 31.

59. The New Testament also seems to validate Abraham's attempt to sacrifice Isaac. In Heb. 11:17–19, Abraham is praised for his faith in the resurrection (he believed God could raise Isaac), which is the reason why he went ahead with the sacrifice of his son. Beyond noting that

Although a surface reading may, indeed, suggest this, once we acknowledge the legitimacy of questioning Abraham, it becomes possible to read the two angel speeches differently, in light of our critical stance.

I already began to do this with respect to the first angel speech (Gen. 22:11–12). I previously noted that the statement "now I know that you are a God-fearer, since you have not withheld your son, your only one, from me" (22:12) signifies what was *discovered* from the test but does not necessarily reveal its *purpose* (what was being tested). Likewise, the omission of "whom you love" in the description of Abraham's relationship to his son could be read as containing an implicit negative judgment on Abraham's response, suggesting that it was not optimal. Couldn't Abraham have been faithful to God and also have exhibited love for his son?

Since the phrase "whom you love" is omitted from the description of Isaac also in the second angel speech (22:16), perhaps we might read other aspects of that speech (22:15–18) as less than fully approving.

God's Oath to Uphold the Prior Promises of Blessing Because of Abraham's Actions

For example, we might reconsider the significance of YHWH swearing by himself (22:16a) to fulfill the promises (stated in 22:17–18a) that he had previously made to Abraham.

> By myself I have sworn, declares YHWH: *Because you have done this thing, and have not withheld your son, your only one,* I will certainly bless you, and I will greatly multiply your offspring like the stars of the heaven and like the sand that is on the seashore, and your offspring shall possess the gate of their enemies. And by your offspring shall all the nations of the earth bless themselves, *because you have listened to my voice.* (22:16–18)

This oath (which is unusual in the book of Genesis) seems to be predicated on Abraham's actions, a point stated in 22:16b and 18b (italicized in the above quote). The specific reason given for YHWH's oath is that Abraham did not withhold his son, which explains the point of the opening general statement,

---

the explicit doctrine of resurrection did not arise until after the exile, I would point to Heb. 11:32, which lists none other than *Jephthah* as a hero of faith (in contrast to his portrayal as an unsavory character in Judg. 11). This is clearly based on extra-biblical tradition and not on the biblical text itself.

"because you have done this thing" (22:16b). I will shortly come to the angel's concluding general statement, "because you have listened to my voice" (22:18b).

Walter Moberly highlights the fact that when God initially promised to bless Abraham and increase his descendants, such that all the families of the earth would bless each other by him (12:1–3), none of this was explicitly tied to Abraham's actions. The promises of blessing were originally given unconditionally.[60] Likewise, Jon Levenson notes that prior to Genesis 22, God's promises to Abraham were "a matter of grace alone."[61]

But in the second angel speech of the Aqedah narrative, when God swears an oath to uphold his prior promises of blessing, Moberly takes this to mean that these promises are now tied to Abraham's actions: "Only here is God's blessing in some way dependent on Abraham's obedience." This leads him to ask, "How then should the angel of YHWH's words be related to the already-existing promise of blessing?"[62]

Moberly affirms that Abraham does not qualify to be a recipient of the blessing by his obedience, since the blessing was promised prior to his obedience; nevertheless, "There is a sense in which the basis for the blessing has changed."[63] He explains this somewhat paradoxical claim as follows: "Abraham's obedience has been incorporated into the divine promise."[64] I must admit that I find it difficult to know exactly how to understand this claim. What does "incorporated into" mean? Incorporated in what sense?

In an earlier article on the Aqedah, Moberly made a similar paradoxical point: "A promise which previously was grounded solely in the will and purpose of Yahweh is transformed so that it is now grounded *both* in the will of Yahweh *and* in the obedience of Abraham."[65]

Levenson is bolder in his formulation. Following a venerable tradition of Jewish interpretation (which wants to avoid the idea that God's gracious choice of Abraham was merely arbitrary), Levenson affirms that because of his obedience in Genesis 22, Abraham "to some degree merits the extraordinary promises that rest on his only/favored son." The result is that "the Aqedah

---

60. Moberly, "Abraham and God in Genesis 22," 119.
61. Levenson, "The Test," 84.
62. Moberly, "Abraham and God in Genesis 22," 119.
63. Moberly, "Abraham and God in Genesis 22," 119.
64. Moberly, "Abraham and God in Genesis 22," 120.
65. R. W. L. Moberly, "The Earliest Commentary on the Akedah," *VT* 38, no. 3 (1988): 320 (entire article 302–23).

has now become the basis for the Abrahamic covenant," or, put differently, "the Abrahamic covenant has now become a consequence of the Aqedah."[66]

Despite the differences in formulation, it is clear that both Moberly and Levenson agree on two points. First, they take Abraham's obedience as positive, such that linking the blessing to his actions (making blessing a consequence of his actions) represents divine approval of Abraham. But second, they also understand the linkage of blessing to Abraham's actions as something new and unprecedented in the narrative of Genesis.

However, both points can be challenged.

To start with the second point, the conditional element in the promises did not begin in Genesis 22. A conditional element was already articulated in Genesis 18, where YHWH desired Abraham to teach his children and household YHWH's way of righteousness and justice *in order to bring about* the fulfillment of the promises. YHWH says,

> I have chosen him, that he may charge his children and his household after him to keep the way of the LORD by doing righteousness and justice; *so that the LORD may bring about for Abraham what he has promised him.* (18:19)

The prior verse specified these promises—namely, that "Abraham shall become a great and mighty nation, and all the nations of the earth shall be blessed in him" (18:18).

This means that even before the Aqedah, Abraham had a responsibility to embody and communicate YHWH's normative standards of righteousness and justice—the "way of the LORD." It means, further, that prior to the Aqedah, God had intended that Abraham's embodiment and communication of this "way" would affect the reality of the blessing that God intended for the nations.[67]

---

66. Levenson, "The Test," 84.

67. Even prior to Gen. 18, at the very outset of the Abraham story, God issued an imperative to Abraham (then called Abram): "Be a blessing!" (12:2b). Although most modern translations render this imperative as a purpose statement ("that you might be a blessing," which is grammatically possible), Martin Buber (followed by Everett Fox and others) may be right to translate this "unprecedented imperative" more literally (Buber, *On the Bible: Eighteen Studies*, ed. Nahum N. Glazier [New York: Schocken Books, 1982; repr., Syracuse University Press, 2000], 86–87 [from the chapter titled "The Election of Israel: A Biblical Inquiry," 80–92]; see also Everett Fox, *The Five Books of Moses*, The Schocken Bible [New York: Schocken Books, 1995]). If, following Buber and Fox, we render 12:2b as an imperative, the promises of 12:3 ("I will bless those who bless you, and the one who curses you I will curse; and in you all the families of the earth shall

Indeed, it was precisely so that Abraham might learn about YHWH's "way" (and then model and communicate it) that God revealed his plans about Sodom to Abraham. It was a teaching moment. However, Abraham did not learn what God intended in Genesis 18.

But neither did he learn what God intended in Genesis 22—at least, not until God called off the sacrifice. This leads me to wonder if it would make more sense to think that YHWH needs to uphold the promises *by his own oath* precisely because they *cannot* be sustained by Abraham's less-than-fully-faithful response, evident in the Aqedah. The oath, in other words, is not a sign of approval of Abraham's actions, but is meant to compensate for the deficiency of his actions.[68]

So, while I agree with Moberly and Levenson that there is a change in the relationship between God's promises and Abraham's actions in Genesis 22:16–18, I think that the change is in precisely the opposite direction—namely, from conditional promises (chap. 18) to unconditional ones (chap. 22).

This change between Genesis 18 and 22 is parallel to the shift we saw in the aftermath of the golden calf episode (discussed in chap. 2). Whereas initially God's steadfast love (*ḥesed*) was for "those who love [God] and keep [God's] commandments" (Exod. 20:6), later God reveals to Moses that his love will continue despite Israel's idolatry and that this love is explicitly linked to forgiveness (34:7).[69] The difference between the golden calf episode and the Abraham story is that here God's compensation for the deficiency in the covenant partner is not the result of anyone standing in the breach (as Moses did). Rather, God steps into the breach himself. This is analogous to Isaiah 59:16, where YHWH "saw that there was no one, / and was appalled that there was no one to intervene; / so his own arm brought him victory, / and his righteousness upheld him."

---

be blessed") become grammatically the purpose statement of the imperative, and so designate the intended outcome of Abraham's obedience.

68. Note that in Deut. 9:5, which references "the promise that the Lord made on oath to your ancestors" (presumably in Gen. 22), the fulfillment of the promise (in Israel's possession of the land) is *disassociated* from their faithfulness: "It is not because of your righteousness or the uprightness of your heart that you are going in to occupy their land."

69. We see this shift in other places also, such as the book of Deuteronomy, where in 10:16 God commands Israel to circumcise their hearts, but when it turns out they are unable to do this and go into exile as a result, God promises to bring them back from exile and to circumcise their hearts himself, to enable them to keep the Torah (30:5–6). This circumcision of the heart after the disobedience that led to the exile has parallels to the heart of flesh promised in Ezek. 36:26–27 and the promise of a new covenant, with the Torah written on Israel's heart, in Jer. 31:31–33.

My suggestion, therefore, is that the oath in Genesis 22:16 signifies God's pledge or commitment that the divine purposes won't be thwarted by Abraham's lack; it is, furthermore, a sign of God's grace toward Abraham, reassuring him personally that the promises will, indeed, come to fruition—because God is faithful, even when we are not.[70]

The Blessing of the Nations and Abraham's Obedience

So far, I have been unpacking the possible meaning of the basis for YHWH's oath, stated in Genesis 22:16 (both generally, "because you have done this thing," and specifically, "and have not withheld your son, your only one"). But the angel's speech concludes with another general statement: "because you have listened to my voice" (22:18b). It might be thought, initially, that this concluding statement is equivalent to "because you have done this thing" (and applies to the entire oath). But it is more likely that it should be taken separately, applied specifically to the final statement about the blessing of the nations.[71]

This likelihood is not simply because it directly follows this promise of the blessing of the nations. It is also suggested by the change from the way the promise was expressed before Genesis 22 and its restatement here. Prior to the Aqedah, the promise was stated in terms of the nations blessing one another *by Abraham* (12:3; 18:18). But here for the first time the blessing is connected to Abraham's descendants: "*By your offspring* shall all the nations of the earth bless themselves" (22:18a).

This means that for the promise to be fulfilled, Abraham would need to have offspring. He would need to have obeyed the angel's command to stop the sacrifice and spare Isaac. This is why the angel links the promise to the sparing of Isaac: "By your offspring shall all the nations of the earth bless themselves, *because you have listened to my voice.*" Simply put, if Abraham had not desisted from the sacrifice when the angel called from heaven, there would be no offspring by which the nations could bless themselves.

70. Abraham's faithfulness in modeling YHWH's "way" (bringing blessing to the nations or to his own family) is quite mixed; and it is questionable whether he passes on to his children what God intends. For a discussion of the actions of the ancestors in Genesis in terms of whether they further God's intentions for blessing, see Middleton, "The Call of Abraham and the *Missio Dei*: Reframing the Purpose of Israel's Election in Genesis 12:1–3," in *Orthodoxy and Orthopraxis: Essays in Tribute to Paul Livermore*, ed. Douglas R. Cullum and J. Richard Middleton (Eugene, OR: Pickwick, 2020), 60–62 (entire chapter 44–64).

71. This was the position of Ibn Kaspi, *Gevia' Kesef* 14.35 (discussed in chap. 5). See van der Heide, *"Now I Know,"* 240.

Did Abraham Believe That God Would Provide a Substitute?

But there is one other consideration that bears on the question of whether or not Abraham's response to God in Genesis 22 was exemplary. In the previous chapter, I noted the possible meanings suggested by Levenson of Abraham's comment to his servants that he and the boy would return to them (22:5) and also his response to Isaac's question about the missing sacrificial animal (22:8). In both cases, I suggested that it was unclear what Abraham's intentions were, whether or not he planned to go through with the sacrifice of his son.

In the first case, one possible meaning of "We will worship, and we will return to you" (22:5) was that Abraham planned to intercede ("worship" could include prayer) on behalf of his son, asking God to call off the sacrifice. But (as even Levenson conceded), there is no evidence that Abraham did this.[72]

In the second case, the significant question is what Abraham meant when he told Isaac, "God himself will see to/provide the sheep for a burnt offering, my son" (22:8). Did he really believe his own words?[73] One sign of such belief would have been his search, when he got to the mountain, for a substitute animal. However, there is no reference to Abraham even checking to see if such an animal had been provided. Instead, having built an altar and placed the wood on it, he immediately proceeds to bind Isaac and place him on the altar (22:9).[74]

Abraham is so intent on the sacrifice that the angel calls his name twice ("Abraham, Abraham!" [22:11]); the repetition is most likely to ensure that he gets Abraham's attention. It is only *after* the angel instructs him not to go through with the sacrifice ("Do not stretch out your hand to the young man or do anything to him" [22:12]) that Abraham "lifted his eyes and saw" the ram that God had, indeed, provided (22:13)—as if only then did it dawn on him that there might, indeed, be a substitute sacrifice.

The details that the narrator provides about the location and circumstances of the ram are significant. When Abraham finally looks, he sees "a

72. Levenson, "The Test," 73.

73. I am here putting aside the semantic ambiguity of "my son" functioning as equivalent to "the sheep for the burnt offering" (discussed in the last chapter). Let us assume he meant what he said in a straightforward way.

74. The next verse ("Then Abraham stretched out his hand and took the knife to slaughter his son") functions literarily to slow down the action and keep the reader on the edge of their seat. It might also be an indication that Abraham himself was going slowly at this point, delaying the inevitable as long as possible.

ram behind, caught in a thicket by its horns" (22:13). A well-known textual issue here may bear on the interpretation of the situation. The word "behind" in my translation renders the Hebrew '*aḥar* (found in most manuscripts of the MT), but an alternative textual tradition has the word '*eḥad* instead (possibly due to scribal confusion of the final consonants, which are visually similar); so instead of "a ram behind," we would have "one ram."[75] But as Moberly points out, this use of "one" is redundant.[76] I think it is more likely that a scribe mistakenly changed '*aḥar* to '*eḥad*, rather than the other way around.[77] So, I think it means that Abraham couldn't see the ram in the direction he was facing; it was behind him, and he would have had to turn around to see it.[78]

In either case, whether we go with '*aḥar* or '*eḥad*, the text tells us that the ram had been caught by its horns in a thicket. The question is, How long had the ram been there?

Let us understand what is going on.[79] A ram is a male goat or sheep, and for its curled horns (from which a shofar is made) to be long enough to be caught in a thicket, it would have needed to be a fully grown specimen. A large, adult ram, full of testosterone, would have made a huge racket trying to extricate

75. This reading is found in manuscripts of the MT and the Samaritan Pentateuch, and also in Greek and Syriac translations (LXX and Peshitta). It is followed by the NIV, CEB, CEV, HCSB, NAB, NLT, NJB, and NJPS. By contrast, "behind" is found in the KJV, RSV, ASV, ESV, NET, and NASB. The REB hedges its bets with the translation, "Abraham looked round and there in a thicket he saw a ram caught by its horns."

76. Moberly, "Abraham and God in Genesis 22," 108n55.

77. To complicate matters, even if the text is taken to read '*aḥar*, there are a number of different translation possibilities. The word may be taken as a preposition or adverb of place ("behind") or of time ("after"/"afterward"). It can even be read in conjunction with the next word in the sentence, "caught" (*ne'ĕḥaz*); here, "after caught" means that Abraham saw the ram "after it had been caught." By far the most common rabbinic reading through the ages has been to take '*aḥar* as a reference to time ("afterward"), with the implication that *after* Abraham saw the ram, it became caught in the thicket (it was thus a perfectly timed miracle). For a discussion of these options, see van der Heide, "*Now I Know*," 474 ("Appendix V: After Caught").

78. In favor of reading '*aḥar* as a reference to place or position, not time, is the fact that the entire sentence in verse 13 has to do with what Abraham saw, pairing an object of sight with spatial-locator terms: "Abraham lifted his eyes and saw—there—a ram behind, caught in a thicket by its horns." This repeats some of the language from verse 4, which also pairs an object of sight with spatial locator terms: "On the third day Abraham lifted his eyes and saw the place from afar." In both cases, the reference is to his visual field. This point is made by Arlyn Sunshine Drew, "A Hermeneutic for the Aqedah Test: A Way beyond Jon Levenson's and Terence Fretheim's Models" (PhD diss., Andrews University, 2020), 130n231.

79. My interpretation here is indebted to Arlyn Drew's suggestion in "Hermeneutic for the Aqedah Test," 130n233.

its horns from the thicket that it was caught in. The fact that Abraham didn't hear the ram (and thus didn't look around for the source of the noise) when he first arrived suggests that the ram had already stopped struggling. In other words, it had been caught in the bushes (provided by God as a substitute) long before Abraham arrived and had exhausted itself. Such prior provision of a substitute would have flowed from the mercy of Abraham's God toward him (and also toward Isaac).[80] But if the ram had, indeed, been there (provided or "seen to" by God, as Abraham claimed God would do), Abraham clearly missed it. Did he even look to see if there was a substitute?

The unexpected character of Abraham's sighting of the ram is conveyed by the repetition of phrasing from earlier in the narrative, with a significant shift. In Genesis 22:4, Abraham has been scanning the horizon to catch a glimpse of his destination: "On the third day Abraham lifted his eyes and saw the place from afar." Although 22:13 repeats verbatim the statement, "Abraham lifted his eyes and saw," it adds the Hebrew *hinnēh* ("behold!" or "there!"), which calls attention to Abraham's surprise at what he sees—"a ram behind, caught in a thicket by its horns."[81] The contrast between what he expected to see in 22:4 and what he did not expect in 22:13 is stark.[82]

And if we think that the ram was still struggling to get free (having only recently become entangled), this means that Abraham was so hyperfocused on sacrificing his son that he shut out the noise of the struggle. In either case, Abraham did not even bother to investigate whether God had provided

80. This interpretation of God's prior provision of the ram is bolstered by the Jewish tradition (cited in chap. 5) of visual representations of the ram tied to a tree by a rope, which pictures the ram as even more securely tethered than if it had been accidentally caught by its horns in a bush. Also as discussed in chap. 5, these pictorial representations may be connected to the idea that the ram was created at twilight on the sixth day of creation (just before the first Sabbath)—that is, it was prepared long before Abraham arrived at Moriah.

81. Adele Berlin notes that the Hebrew *hinnēh* often follows a verb of perception (like "to see") and indicates "the perception of a character as distinct from that of the narrator." Berlin, *Poetics and Interpretation of Biblical Narrative*, BLS 9 (Winona Lake, IN: Eisenbrauns, 1994), 62.

82. This repetition of a phrase from earlier in the Aqedah, accompanied by a significant difference or shift, occurs in three other places in the narrative. As we have seen, in 22:12 and 16 there is the repetition of "your son, your only one" (from 22:2) but with "whom you love" omitted, which suggests that Abraham's attempt to sacrifice Isaac shows that he does not love him. We have also seen that 22:19 repeats "arose and went" from 22:3, though in plural form (with Abraham and the servants as subjects), thus suggesting that Isaac was missing. Although not noted before in our exposition, the final example of this repetition with difference is found in the twofold use of the verb for "he placed" in 22:6 and 22:9. In a tragic, ironic shift, instead of *placing* the wood (for the burnt offering) on Isaac, Abraham *places* Isaac on the wood (he is the burnt offering).

a substitute. This leads me to think that he did not believe his own words to Isaac ("God himself will see to/provide the sheep for a burnt offering" [22:8]). I am finding it more and more difficult to think well of Abraham in this story.

A Qualified Criticism of Abraham?

Despite my critical reading of Abraham's response to God in the Aqedah, I propose that we do not judge the patriarch too harshly. While I do not believe that he passed the test of discerning God's character with flying colors, he at least did not just turn away from God in disobedience.[83] Abraham genuinely, in the end, tried to obey the God he understood (inadequate as that understanding might have been).

If I were to construct a hierarchy of possible responses that Abraham might have made to God's request to sacrifice his son, I would put protest and intercession on behalf of Isaac at the top of the list, as the optimal response. Through such protest/intercession, Abraham would have demonstrated his profound discernment of God's character, that YHWH was merciful and compassionate. Or his intuition that God was merciful would have led him to prayer; and this intuition would have been confirmed and expanded by such prayer, resulting (I believe) in God rescinding the request. Such protest and intercession would have also demonstrated his love for Isaac, perhaps strengthening the tenuous bond between them.

But Abraham didn't speak out on behalf of his son.

Somewhat below this optimal response would be Abraham's genuine belief that God would provide a substitute—that is, he might have remained silent (against the general tenor of Scripture, which encourages bold prayer), yet trusted that somewhere along the journey or on the mountain itself, he might find an animal to sacrifice instead of his son. Yet when he arrived at the spot for the sacrifice, Abraham did not give even a cursory glance around the vicinity to see if God had provided a substitute; he simply bound his son and placed him on the altar. He did not look around until *after* the angel called off the sacrifice.

Yet the fact that he did eventually look around could be taken as a point in his favor. Perhaps Abraham is to be commended not simply for looking around but especially for offering up the ram "as a burnt offering instead of his son"

---

83. Fretheim explores what the consequences might have been if Abraham had disobeyed and "said no to God." Fretheim, "God, Abraham, and the Abuse of Isaac," 52, 56.

(22:13) *on his own initiative*. This was not something actually commanded by God.[84] In one sense, it was too little, too late. In another, it was better than nothing, in that it signified that Abraham finally understood that God did not want him to sacrifice his son. Evidence of his coming to this understanding is that Abraham names the site "YHWH sees/provides" (22:14).[85]

I am inclined to think that Abraham did not pass the test in Genesis 22. His silent obedience indicated that he did not discern God's merciful character (until the angel called off the sacrifice); and he did not show love for his son by interceding on his behalf.

Yet Abraham finally *did* come to understand that God didn't want him to sacrifice his son. If we consider his sacrificing the ram as analogous with a make-up test given by a generous professor, might we say that in this sense Abraham *just barely* passed the test of the discernment of God's character? Or is that conceding too much?

I certainly have no illusions that Walter Moberly or Jon Levenson would be satisfied with my interpretation of the Aqedah. However, I am not denigrating Abraham for being a monstrous child abuser or God for being an arbitrary and unethical deity in giving Abraham this test; nor am I claiming that the Aqedah tends to justify child abuse either today or in earlier times (these were some of their concerns).

Neither am I intending to disparage the long history of interpretation that exalts Abraham for his response in the Aqedah. Indeed, I respect that tradition. So when I titled part 3 of this book "Unbinding the Aqedah from the Straitjacket of Tradition," this was not intended as an insult. In biblical interpretation, no one comes to any text traditionless. Every reader is shaped by a whole series of prior readings and assumptions—and I am certainly no different. It would be impossible for me to offer an alternative reading of the Aqedah without standing on the shoulders of multitudinous others, who have already grappled with its meaning, and whose grappling I respect.

---

84. This point is made by Nahum M. Sarna: "Substitution of the ram for Isaac is a spontaneous gesture on the part of Abraham, performed at his own initiative and not divinely ordained." Sarna, *Genesis: The Traditional Hebrew Text with New JPS Translation*, JPS Torah Commentary (Philadelphia: Jewish Publication Society, 1989), 392.

85. Further evidence that Abraham may have come (finally) to understand God's mercy might be inferred from the words of the servant whom he sent to find a wife for Isaac. After meeting Rebekah, the servant says, "Blessed be the LORD, the God of my master Abraham, who has not forsaken his steadfast love and his faithfulness toward my master" (24:27). Even if Abraham was not able to teach his son Isaac the way of YHWH, he may have passed on to the remaining members of his household an understanding of God's mercy in preventing his sacrifice of his son.

Yet the question must be asked whether the tradition of prior interpretations of the Aqedah (each dependent on their particular historical context and
the assumptions and interests of the interpreters) should act as a straitjacket,
preventing new and fresh readings of the text. I believe they should not. Hence
I have attempted to "unbind" the Aqedah from the limitations of traditional
readings.

However, I agree entirely with Walter Moberly that new readings of the
Aqedah (especially any that are critical of Abraham) need to be grounded
in careful, contextual exegesis and not simply in the predilections of the interpreter.[86] Not only am I fully on board with Moberly here, this is precisely
what I have attempted to do in this book. Here I am also following the classic
advice concerning Scripture given in the Mishnah by the Hebrew sage with
the endearing name of Ben Bag Bag: "Turn it over, and [again] turn it over,
for all is therein. And look into it. And become gray and old therein. And do
not move away from it, for you have no better portion than it."[87]

My motivation is that a fresh encounter with this ancient text, from a new
angle, raising new considerations, might not only illuminate its meaning but
renew our experience of the God whom Jews and Christians believe may be
encountered precisely through this text.[88]

Imagining a New Ending to the Abraham Story

It is my claim that Abraham could have chosen the more excellent way of
protest (concerning God's command) and intercession (for his son). This

86. This is a point emphasized by Moberly in many of his writings, but especially in "Genesis
22 and the Hermeneutics of Suspicion," in *The Bible, Theology, and Faith: A Study of Abraham
and Jesus* (Cambridge: Cambridge University Press, 2000), 162–83. Thus he states, "Nothing
less than a rigorous, detailed, and persuasive exegesis could legitimately begin to make an alternative case" (174); the boldness to present an alternative interpretation "needs an exegetical
quality of corresponding rigour and persuasiveness" (175); it requires "convincing exegesis"
and "an exegetical basis" (176); and it "must be able to withstand the argued criticism that it
is a misreading of the text" (174).

87. Rabbi Ben Bag Bag, Pirqe Avot 5:22. Trans. from Sefaria.org, https://www.sefaria.org
/Pirkei_Avot.5.22?lang=bi&with=all&lang2=en. The word in brackets was added by the trasla-
tor for clarity.

88. Ellen Davis emphasizes the importance of biblical exegesis for Christians and Jews. Such
exegesis "is necessary for the ongoing life of the church and synagogue, whose identities—and even
existence as communities with a common story and language—depend on the recurrent experience
of hearing these texts as speaking of and to contemporary lives. And while that experience is not
predictable, it is contingent on the regular practice of exegesis by members of the communities
of faith, generation to generation." Davis, *Opening Israel's Scriptures* (Oxford: Oxford University
Press, 2019), 1.

would have had the salutary result of Abraham exhibiting (and growing in) his discernment of God's merciful character, and it would have demonstrated (and perhaps deepened) his love for his only remaining son.[89]

How might Isaac have turned out if he had witnessed his father's pleading on his behalf, with God's positive response to Abraham's intercession? Would he have returned from the mountain with Abraham? Would he have bequeathed to Jacob a different notion of God than "the Fear"?

And would there be a unit of narrative material, perhaps coming between Ishmael's genealogy (25:12–18) and the Jacob story (beginning in 25:19), focused on Isaac's life, beginning with: "Now these are the *tôlĕdôt* of Abraham"?

Given the way things turned out, we can only imagine.

---

89. I am aware that many readers may resist my alternative reading despite my exegesis. Therefore, let me state that one could take my critical interpretation of the Aqedah not as a simple replacement for a traditional pious interpretation but as a viable alternative reading. My exploration of the Aqedah would thus suggest that the meaning of this paradigmatic text is to some degree open-ended, capable of moving in different directions. Along with the traditional interpretation of Abraham's response as exemplary (a judgment derived, perhaps inaccurately, from the two angel speeches in Gen. 22:11–12 and 22:15–18, but especially from the history of interpretation), the text itself, especially when taken in context of the larger Abraham story and the biblical background of vigorous prayer, generates an alternative reading that allows us to question the legitimacy of Abraham's response.

Conclusion

The Gritty Spirituality of Lament

I began this book by asking whether Abraham's silence in Genesis 22 matters. This is more than a question about the interpretation of the Aqedah. It is fundamentally a theological question, which impacts our spirituality and ethics.

It is all too common in many churches around the world for believers to have absorbed the view that they must accept all calamities as the will of God, and many think that they must suffer in silence or even affirm God's role in the calamities. But this stance of absolute submission to the divine, exemplified by Abraham in Genesis 22, is not typical of biblical faith.

In contrast to the posture of unquestioning submission to God that informs spirituality in many faith traditions, the Hebrew Bible / Old Testament (and even the New Testament) assumes a stance of honesty toward God in prayer as normative; and such honesty often borders on vigorous protest.

Through my own experience of lament prayer, I have learned the importance of *not* being silent, precisely as a way of keeping faith with God in times of difficulty. Lament is thus a vocal analogue to Jacob's wrestling with God all night at the Jabbok, even becoming injured in the process, but refusing to give up until a blessing is received.[1] To put it differently, I have tried to follow

---

1. The narrative of Gen. 32:24–31 says that Jacob wrestled with a man all night, whereas Hosea says it was God (12:3) and an angel (12:4). Afterward, Jacob names the place Peniel ("face of God"), saying that he saw God face to face (32:30). Often, it is not until *after* the wrestling of lament prayer that we are able to affirm (or even believe) that we met *God* in the wrestling.

the advice of Cal Seerveld, one of my former professors, who titled a book of biblical meditations *Take Hold of God and Pull*.[2] Seerveld himself appealed to Jacob at the Jabbok in the preface to his book.[3]

A Surge of Interest in Lament

But the question of Abraham's silence in Genesis 22, along with the value of lament prayer, matters well beyond my personal experience. There has been a significant surge of interest in lament in recent times, evident in scholarly publications on the subject and in numerous popular works concerned for the life of faith in the context of a broken world. Seerveld's book of meditations could be viewed as an early example of the latter, arising as it did out of the complexities of the Vietnam War, the civil rights movement, and the assassinations of John F. Kennedy and Malcolm X, among other events.[4] While lament was implicit in *Take Hold of God and Pull*, Seerveld has gone on to address the value of lament much more explicitly, both in translating lament psalms and in setting them to music for congregational singing.[5]

Recent books on lament (and here I'm just looking at my own bookshelf) include titles like *Saying No to God* (2019), *Rejoicing in Lament* (2015), *Prophetic Lament* (2015), *The Psalms as Christian Lament* (2014), *Arguing with God* (2013), *Hurting with God* (2012), *Lyrics of Lament* (2010), *Evoking Lament* (2009), *Risking Truth: Reshaping the World through Prayers of Lament* (2008), *Rachel's Cry: Prayer of Lament and Rebirth of Hope* (2007), and *Lament: Reclaiming Practices in Pulpit, Pew, and Public Square* (2005).[6]

---

2. Calvin Seerveld, *Take Hold of God and Pull* (Palos Heights, IL: Trinity Pennyasheet Press, 1966; repr., Carlisle, UK: Paternoster, 1999).

3. Seerveld, *Take Hold of God and Pull*, xiii.

4. Seerveld explains the context that gave rise to the book. Seerveld, *Take Hold of God and Pull*, xi.

5. Calvin Seerveld, *Voicing God's Psalms*, Calvin Institute of Christian Worship Liturgical Studies (Grand Rapids: Eerdmans, 2005). Includes CD. Among the lament psalms included in the book are Pss. 3; 5; 13; 22; 25; 39; 42–43; 86; 139.

6. Matthew J. Korpman, *Saying No to God: A Radical Approach to Reading the Bible Faithfully* (Orange, CA: Quoir, 2019); J. Todd Billings, *Rejoicing in Lament: Wrestling with Incurable Cancer and Life in Christ* (Grand Rapids: Brazos, 2015); Soon-Chan Rah, *Prophetic Lament: A Call for Justice in Troubled Times* (Downers Grove, IL: InterVarsity, 2015); Bruce K. Waltke, James M. Houston, and Erika Moore, *The Psalms as Christian Lament: A Historical Commentary* (Grand Rapids: Eerdmans, 2014); Bernd Janowski, *Arguing with God: A Theological Anthropology of the Psalms*, trans. Armin Siedlecki (Louisville: Westminster John Knox, 2013); Glen Pemberton, *Hurting with God: Learning to Lament with the Psalms* (Abilene, TX: Abilene Christian University Press, 2012); Nancy C. Lee, *Lyrics of Lament: From Tragedy to Transformation* (Minneapolis: Fortress, 2010); Eva Harasta and Brian Brock, eds., *Evoking*

This list of titles just scratches the surface; there are many more books on lament than what I've cited. And this doesn't include the torrent of articles and blog posts on the subject, which shows no sign of stopping any time soon. There is even an episode of *The Simpsons* that explores lament, titled "Todd, Todd, Why Hast Thou Forsaken Me?"[7]

The Costly Loss of Lament

What has generated this intense interest in lament? I suggest two primary causes—one general and one specific. The first (general) cause is the loss of lament in the church (and in Western culture) and the gaping need this has generated. The fact is that over the centuries the Christian tradition has ignored (even suppressed) lament, to its own detriment; but the realities of the world, with its suffering and brokenness, are intruding into our lives in ways that cannot be ignored, and these realities cry out for some way to be addressed with honesty.[8]

Kathleen Billman and Daniel Migliore, in their book *Rachel's Cry*, have helpfully illustrated the complicated relationship of the Christian theological tradition to lament prayer, by examining the attitudes to lament in the writing of theologians such as Augustine, Luther, Calvin, and Barth.[9] Although the Jewish tradition has tended to be much more open to lament, I noted in chapter 5 the contradictory tendencies that developed during the rabbinic

---

*Lament: A Theological Discus*sion (New York: T&T Clark, 2009); Scott A. Ellington, *Risking Truth: Reshaping the World through Prayers of Lament* (Eugene, OR: Pickwick, 2008); Kathleen D. Billman and Daniel L. Migliore, *Rachel's Cry: Prayer of Lament and Rebirth of Hope* (Cleveland, OH: Pilgrim Press, 1999; repr., Eugene, OR: Wipf & Stock, 2007); Sally A. Brown and Patrick K. Miller, eds., *Lament: Reclaiming Practices in Pulpit, Pew, and Public Square* (Louisville: Westminster John Knox, 2005).

7. *The Simpsons*, season 31, episode 9, "Todd, Todd, Why Hast Thou Forsaken Me?," directed by Chris Clements, written by Tim Long and Miranda Thompson, aired December 1, 2019, on Fox, https://www.fox.com/the-simpsons. Todd is the name of the Simpson's Christian neighbor. Thanks to Nate Stenberg for this reference.

8. Note that two books addressing the COVID-19 pandemic propose lament (complaint and petition) as the appropriate response: N. T. Wright, *God and the Pandemic: A Christian Reflection on the Coronavirus and Its Aftermath* (Grand Rapids: Zondervan, 2020); Walter Brueggemann, *Virus as a Summons to Faith: Biblical Reflections in a Time of Loss, Grief, and Uncertainty* (Eugene, OR: Cascade, 2020). For a perspective on lament and the coronovirus from the majority world, see Federico G. Villanueva, "Lament during a Pandemic," *Langham Publishing* (blog), May 29, 2020, https://langhamliterature.org/blog/lament-during-pandemic?

9. Billman and Migliore, *Rachel's Cry*, 46–74. The chapter ends by addressing the more positive turn to lament in the theology of Jürgen Moltmann and liberation theologies. The complicated relationship of Augustine and Barth to lament is also addressed in Harasta and Brock, *Evoking Lament*, chaps. 4 and 5 on Barth (60–98) and chap. 11 on Augustine (183–203).

period, one strand affirming protest to God as valid, the other attempting to shut it down as sinful.

But long before the Christian or Jewish traditions in the Common Era, lament began to be a problem for ancient Israel. In his book *Protest against God: The Eclipse of a Biblical Tradition*, William S. Morrow has traced the decline of lament prayer after the exile, during the Second Temple period.[10] Morrow suggests that this eclipse was connected to a shift in the understanding of God and God's relationship to the world that was crystallized in the fifth century BCE and continued into the Common Era.[11] Not only was the God of Israel understood more and more to be universally powerful and transcendent, far above ordinary human concerns, which suggested that lament was inappropriate, but God's absolute righteousness implied that Israel's suffering constituted judgment, and so was justified.[12] This perhaps explains the rise of penitential prayer in the postexilic period, where rather than protest, the supplicant admits guilt and pleads for forgiveness (as in Neh. 9).[13]

10. Morrow, *Protest against God: The Eclipse of a Biblical Tradition*, Hebrew Bible Monographs 4 (Sheffield: Sheffield Phoenix, 2006); see also Morrow, "Violence and Transcendence in the Development of Biblical Religion," *Bulletin of the Canadian Society of Biblical Studies* 66 (2006/2007): 1–21. This was Morrow's presidential address given at the Canadian Society of Biblical Studies, May 28, 2006, York University, Toronto, ON (available online at https://www.academia.edu/7682452/Violence_and_Transcendence_in_the_Development_of_Biblical_Religion). This argument about the eclipse of lament is not unique to Morrow. It was earlier advanced by Claus Westermann, *Praise and Lament in the Psalms*, trans. Keith R. Crim and Richard N. Soulen from the 1965 German ed. (Atlanta: John Knox, 1981), 201–13, and is followed by many biblical scholars.

11. Morrow suggests that this eclipse of lament also characterizes the New Testament (*Protest against God*, 211). While I admit that lament seems less explicit in the New Testament than in the Old, the lament tradition underlies the narratives of the Passion Week, as well as many New Testament texts on petition and supplication (something I touched on in chap. 1). But this topic perhaps requires a separate essay, as does the question of whether the death of Jesus is modeled on the Aqedah.

12. Morrow explores the trend in chap. 5, "Exilic Critique of the Protest against God" (*Protest against God*, 106–28), linking it to Lamentations, Isaiah 40–55, and the Deuteronomic History (Joshua–Kings). For a summary of this point, see *Protest against God*, 136–38.

13. On the shift to penitential prayer, see Morrow, *Protest against God*, 161–67. Morrow also discusses the forms of lament (which tend to mix individual and communal elements) that endured after the exile, found in extra-biblical texts in the Apocrypha, Pseudepigrapha, and the Dead Sea Scrolls. Unlike the biblical lament psalms, these extra-biblical laments lack complaints about physical suffering or death (their focus is on enemies and sometimes the need for forgiveness) and tend to be in narrative contexts rather than collections for liturgical use. And the motif of protest to God falls by the wayside. On extra-biblical literature, see "Prayers for Indidivuals in Extra-Biblical Second Temple Literature," in *Protest against God*, 178–200. Also Morrow, "Violence and Transcendence," 9.

Morrow speculates on the causes underlying this theological shift, pointing to certain scriptural themes such as the Deuteronomic theology of reward and punishment and the prophetic writings, which typically viewed exile as judgment for Israel's sin.[14] He also cites the geopolitical situation of Israel under Persian rule, where the imperial reach of Persia outstripped even that of Assyria and Babylon, abetted by the Persian conception of a universal and transcendent deity found in the Zoroastrian religion. This new political and religious situation, in tandem with certain theological tendencies in Israel's Scriptures, led to a view of God as more distant and in full control of history, which challenged the felt intimacy with God found in lament psalms (and other biblical texts).[15]

The Impact of Walter Brueggemann

The second (specific) cause for the resurgent interest in lament in our time is the work of biblical scholar Walter Brueggemann. Through his many writings on the Old Testament, addressing its theological and ethical claims on contemporary faith communities, Brueggemann has almost single-handedly generated a serious return to the study and preaching of the Old Testament among pastors and theological students in many sectors of the North

14. It might be argued that it wasn't the Deuteronomic act-consequence schema per se that contributed to the decline of lament, but a rigid interpretation of this schema, where every example of suffering needed to be traced back to disobedience to God. And while the prophetic perspective certainly construed the exile as judgment for Israel's covenantal disobedience, there are laments embedded in various prophetic texts (as we have seen in chap. 2), something even Morrow admits.

15. Morrow (*Protest against God*, 134) suggests that the book of Job itself derives from a Persian-era context, in the Second Temple period, something I fully agree with. His analysis of the various points of view in the book leads him to take Job's friends, the wisdom interlude (chap. 28), and Elihu as all reflecting the theological shift of the period, which prohibits protest to God. His view of YHWH's speeches is more ambiguous, suggesting that these speeches undermine some aspects of both Job's view and those of his opponents, thus leaving the validity of Job's lament an open question. For Morrow's discussion of Job, see *Protest against God*, chap. 6, "Protest against God in the Axial Age" (129–46). While I agree with much of Morrow's analysis, my own exposition of YHWH's speeches (and Job's responses) leads me to think that the book of Job functions as a *critique* of the postexilic theological shift, reasserting the value and importance of the lament tradition in a time when it was being eclipsed. This late dating (in the Persian period) goes against the popular notion that Job is one of the oldest books in the Bible (if not the oldest), an opinion I have heard from many of my students, which they learned in church or from the internet (my impression is that a proposed early date is based on the story being set in a cultural context that seems to be Abrahamic). However, such an early date is simply unsustainable, given the multiple lines of evidence for the book's late date. Since I did not explicitly address the issue of dating in my two chapters on Job, I may need (at some point) to write a follow-up article on this subject.

American church, in quite diverse theological traditions. A significant part of Brueggemann's impact has been his call to reclaim lament as essential for the health of the church.

As early as the 1970s, Brueggemann began addressing the importance of lament as a crucial aspect of biblical faith in a number of writings on the Psalms and the prophetic books. An early exploration was the essay "From Hurt to Joy, from Death to Life" (1974), in which he claimed that "the lament witnesses to a robust form of faith" that both expressed and shaped Israel's honesty about pain and their dialogical relationship to God.[16] Other essays followed, such as "The Formfulness of Grief" (1977), in which he explored the relationship between the typical elements of a lament psalm and Elizabeth Kübler-Ross's analysis of the main elements of the grief process, all with a view to helping the church recover the importance of lament for life and liturgy.[17]

Then came *The Prophetic Imagination* (1978), in which Brueggemann proposed that a crucial aspect of the prophetic task was challenging the status quo by unmasking injustice and bringing pain to consciousness (which he called the "embrace of pathos"), along with the renewal (the "emergence of amazement") that may be generated from facing such pain with honesty.[18] In an article published a year later, Brueggemann spoke of two trajectories throughout the Old Testament that had important social implications, one of which was the "embrace of pain," associated with the Mosaic-prophetic traditions (equivalent to the "embrace of pathos" in *The Prophetic Imagination*).[19]

16. Brueggemann, "From Hurt to Joy, from Death to Life," *Int* 28 (1974): 3–19. Reprinted as Brueggemann, "From Hurt to Joy, from Death to Life," in *The Psalms and the Life of Faith*, ed. Patrick D. Miller (Minneapolis: Augsburg Fortress, 1995), 67–83. The quote is from *Psalms and the Life of Faith*, 68.

17. Brueggemann, "The Formfulness of Grief," *Int* 31 (1977): 263–75. Reprinted as Brueggemann, "The Formfulness of Grief," in Miller, *Psalms and the Life of Faith*, 84–97.

18. Brueggemann, *The Prophetic Imagination* (Philadelphia: Fortress, 1978), chap. 3: "Prophetic Criticism and the Embrace of Pathos" and chap. 4: "Prophetic Energizing and the Emergence of Amazement." There have been two more recent editions (2001, 2018) of this seminal book.

19. Brueggemann, "Trajectories in Old Testament Literature and the Sociology of Ancient Israel," *JBL* 98 (1979): 161–85. Brueggemann later expanded this analysis into a two-part article, "A Shape for Old Testament Theology, I: Structure Legitimation," *CBQ* 47 (1985): 28–46, and "A Shape for Old Testament Theology, II: Embrace of Pain," *CBQ* 47 (1985): 395–415. This two-part article is reprinted under the same titles as chaps. 1 and 2 in Brueggemann, *Old Testament Theology: Essays on Structure, Theme, and Text*, ed. Patrick D. Miller (Minneapolis: Fortress, 1992).

Not long after, Brueggemann addressed the importance of lament in an essay titled "Psalms and the Life of Faith: A Suggested Typology of Function" (1980) and followed this up with *The Message of the Psalms: A Theological Commentary* (1984), the first of many books he wrote on the Psalms.[20] In both the article and the book, Brueggemann treated lament psalms as a prime example of "disorientation," which was the ground of a "new orientation," possible only because Israel could bring their pain to God in honest appeal. Here we find a convergence of categories in Brueggemann's work on the Psalms and the prophets.[21]

But it was especially Brueggemann's 1986 essay, "The Costly Loss of Lament," that grabbed the attention of readers concerning the eclipse of lament in our time.[22] Here Brueggemann argued for the negative psychological and sociological consequences of the loss of lament prayer vis-à-vis matters of human identity and societal justice. His argument was that a recovery of lament prayer could contribute to healthy ego development, which itself is necessary for resistance to injustice and a commitment to human flourishing in the wider community.

Since that essay, Brueggemann has continued to write on lament. Among his many essays is a lengthy programmatic piece, called "Necessary Conditions of a Good Loud Lament," published in 2003.[23] Brueggemann began the essay by tracing the turn to lament in biblical studies, pastoral care, and the church at large, ending with a warning that our entrenchment in totalizing ideologies means that it will be very difficult for lament to really take hold in contemporary society. The bulk of the essay then worked through a list of ten "theological preconditions" for the serious practice of lament in our time.

20. Brueggemann, *The Message of the Psalms: A Theological Commentary*, Augsburg Old Testament Studies (Minneapolis: Augsburg, 1984), esp. "Psalms of Disorientation," 51–121; Brueggemann, "Psalms and the Life of Faith: A Suggested Typology of Function," *JSOT* 17 (1980): 3–32 (reprinted under the same title as chap. 1 in *Psalms and the Life of Faith*, 3–32). This article generated a response from John Goldingay, "The Dynamic Cycle of Praise and Prayer in the Psalms," *JSOT* 20 (1981): 85–90; this was followed by Brueggemann, "Response to John Goldingay's 'The Dynamic Cycle of Praise and Prayer,'" *JSOT* 22 (1982): 141–42.

21. In "Psalms and the Life of Faith: A Suggested Typology of Function," Brueggemann uses the category of "reorientation," which became "new orientation" in *Message of the Psalms*.

22. Brueggemann, "The Costly Loss of Lament," *JSOT* 36 (1986): 57–71 (reprinted under the same title as chap. 5 in *Psalms and the Life of Faith*, 98–111). This article generated a response about the corresponding loss of genuine praise: Rolf Jacobson, "The Costly Loss of Praise," *ThTo* 57, no. 3 (2000): 375–85.

23. Brueggemann, "Necessary Conditions of a Good Loud Lament," *HBT* 25 (2003): 19–49.

It is not my intent to rehearse all of Brueggemann's arguments about the importance of lament. Rather, I will highlight what I have found to be most valuable in lament, which is relevant not only for my own life but for the renewal of faith today.

A Dialectic of Resistance and Submission

Lament prayer, whether in the Psalter or elsewhere in the Bible, contains an implicit theological claim—namely, that God welcomes honesty in the divine-human relationship. To put it another way, the God of the Bible desires a dialogue partner with *chutzpah*.[24]

This honesty or *chutzpah* is, however, not in contrast to trust or submission. Take, for example, the two-pronged prayers of Jeremiah and Habakkuk. In Jeremiah's case, he first affirms what is supposed to be true of God: "You will be in the right, O LORD, / when I lay charges against you." Then he supplements this affirmation with a complaint: "But let me put my case to you. / Why does the way of the guilty prosper? / Why do all who are treacherous thrive?" (12:1). Similarly, Habakkuk first confesses to God, "Your eyes are too pure to behold evil, / and you cannot look on wrongdoing." But then he boldly goes on to ask, "Why do you look on the treacherous, / and are silent when the wicked swallow those more righteous than they?" (1:13).

Both of these prophets first acknowledge what is believed to be true of the God of Israel (equivalent to the confession of trust in lament psalms); they then follow this up with a complaint, in the form of questions (which is also typical of lament psalms). In neither case is the confession of trust in contrast to the complaint. Indeed, it is the *ground* of the complaint.[25]

But as Psalm 22 indicates, it is possible to begin immediately with complaint: "My God, my God, why have you forsaken me?" Likewise, Jeremiah's

24. Belden C. Lane explores a Christian appreciation of the Jewish tradition of "boldness towards heaven," in "*Hutzpa K'lapei Shamaya*: A Christian Response to the Jewish Tradition of Arguing with God," *JES* 23 (1986): 567–86. Lane speaks of "an audacious faith, almost bordering on insolence" that is "especially prevalent in the rarefied air above Mt. Sinai" (567). This fits very well my discussion in chap. 2 of Moses, who exemplifies the attitude of "boldness towards heaven" (the *Hutzpa K'lapei Shamaya* of Lane's title).

25. Brueggemann suggests that such prayers (along with those of Moses, Abraham in Gen. 18, and Job) evidence "mutuality between incommensurate partners," which is an alternative to both one-dimensional absolutism on God's part and unfettered human autonomy. Brueggemann, "Concluding Reflections," in *Shaking Heaven and Earth: Essays in Honor of Walter Brueggemann and Charles B. Cousar*, ed. Christine Roy Yoder et al. (Louisville: Westminster John Knox, 2005), 159 (entire chapter 157–62).

prayer in 20:7–18 opens with the accusation: "O LORD, you have enticed me, / and I was enticed; / you have overpowered me, / and you have prevailed." In both these prayers, the positive statements of trust in God come later—in Psalm 22:3–5, 9–10, and especially 22–31 (22:4–6, 10–11, 23–32 MT), and in Jeremiah 20:11–13.

By contrast, Psalm 88 exhibits an almost unrelenting focus on complaint, implicating God personally in the suffering: "You have put me in the depths of the Pit, / in the regions dark and deep" (88:6 [88:7 MT]). "I suffer your terrors; I am desperate. / Your wrath has swept over me; / your dread assaults destroy me" (88:15b–16 [16b–17 MT]). Yet, even in the absence of any clear affirmation of trust (beyond the phrase "God of my salvation" in 88:1 [88:2 MT]), the very fact that this abrasive psalm is addressed to God is testimony to the implicit trust that the one praying has in the God being addressed.[26]

This gritty spirituality of vigorous human agency vis-à-vis God is well illustrated by Jesus as he contemplates his own death (Luke 22:42). With no contradiction, he embodies the dialectic of resistance and submission, or boldness and trust, when he pleads, "Father, . . . remove this cup from me" (resistance/boldness), yet affirms "not my will but yours be done" (submission/ trust).

Lament and Healthy Ego Development

The value of lament, with its boldness (and even resistance) toward God, not as an alternative to submission but in addition to submission, is illustrated by the theory of personality development known as Object-Relations Theory, propounded by D. W. Winnicott and others. This theory suggests that the healthy ego-development of a child occurs when that child is first bonded in physical intimacy with its mother, which is the prime example of submission or surrender to a genuine Other outside of the self—hence the name Object-Relations Theory. Without this bonding, a child never learns to trust; and trust is essential both to healthy relationships in general and to the religious life in particular.

---

26. A particularly poignant example of post-biblical lament is found in the liturgical poetry or *piyyutim* of Isaac bar Shalom, who accuses God of remaining silent during the massacre of Jews during the Second Crusade in Germany (1147 CE). One poem begins: "There is none like You among the dumb, / Keeping silence and being still in the face of those who aggrieve us." For the poem and analysis, see Jakob J. Petuchowski, *Theology and Poetry: Studies in the Medieval Piyyut*, Littman Library of Jewish Civilization (London: Routledge & Kegan Paul, 1978), 71–83.

But Winnicott suggests that, along with surrender, healthy ego-development also needs the experience of the child's *initiative* vis-à-vis the mother, to which the mother is responsive. She uses the metaphor of the child's experience of "omnipotence," which may be an overstatement, but it gets the point across. "A true self," Winnicott notes, "begins to have life through the strength given to the infant's weak ego by the mother's implementation of the infant's omnipotent expressions."[27] If the mother always initiates, and the child is simply compliant, it develops not a strong ego but rather a "false self," which then exposes the child later in life to the manipulations of others, including ideologies and fundamentalisms of various sorts.

Walter Brueggemann applies Winnicott's insights to the life of faith, noting, "Where there is lament, the believer is able to take initiative with God and so develop over against God the ego-strength that is necessary for responsible faith. But where the capacity to initiate lament is absent, one is left only with praise and doxology. God then is omnipotent, always to be praised. The believer is nothing."[28] He goes on to add that "the absence of lament makes a religion of coercive obedience the only possibility."[29]

This raises the important issue of the implications of lament for ethics. Brueggemann's insight is that our participation in lament prayer may strengthen our sense of self-identity, so we are not so easily manipulated by others or fall prey to ideologies. And his linking of lament to prophetic criticism has implications for naming injustice and uncovering the forms of our contemporary bondage to ideologies that perpetuate violence—whether between or within societies.

Lament and the Discernment of God's Character

I would go further than Brueggemann, by suggesting that lament is connected to ethics not just because of a strengthened sense of identity but also through the discernment of God's compassion that typically accompanies lament. This is the *theological* importance of lament.

Indeed, it may be that part of the motivation for lament prayer (beyond the wellspring of pain that cannot be denied) comes from the divine-human relationship that lament assumes—an understanding of a God who positively

27. Winnicott, *The Maturational Processes and the Facilitating Environment: Studies in the Theory of Emotional Development* (Madison, WI: International Universities Press, 1965), 145.
28. Brueggemann, "Costly Loss of Lament," 103.
29. Brueggemann, "Costly Loss of Lament," 104.

invites such prayer. Whether or not such prayers (in the Psalter or elsewhere) explicitly include a confession of trust, they *depend implicitly* on such trust. The child of an abusive parent, cowering in the corner of a room, would not typically protest that parent's behavior or ask the parent to act differently. It takes a high degree of trust for a child honestly to voice criticism of a parent—whether that criticism is voiced in anger or only tremulously. The sine qua non of lament is thus a discernment of the character of God as one who desires and welcomes honesty, even abrasive and audacious honesty. This discernment may motivate one to pray with boldness.

In an essay on Psalm 22, feminist theologian Cynthia Rigby suggests that the possibility of being heard by a *Thou* who is the transcendent Creator of the universe may embolden the one praying.[30] This is what, she hypothesizes, engenders the shift in Psalm 22 from petition and complaint to praise (starting in 22:21b). Even though the psalmist has not actually been delivered from his troubles, he is confident that God has heard his cries.

In contrast to some feminist theologians, who claim that only a God of immanence (and not transcendence) can be helpful to oppressed women, Rigby cites examples of African American and Filipina women who are able to trust a transcendent and powerful God even when this God does not bring obvious liberation from oppressive situations, precisely because they understand that God is *able* to liberate. The transcendent God they believe in, who is outside the situation of oppression, may be appealed to—in petition and complaint. Indeed, this God welcomes independent subjects who grapple with God. Thus Rigby notes that those who "feel free to blame and to trust in the God in whom they believe seem to be able to muster the energy to survive," even in difficult situations.[31] That the Lord of the universe would host (even welcome) prayers that express pain and need, is what ultimately generates hope, and, with it, energy for creative living in the human community.

This suggests that beyond one's understanding of God providing the *basis* or *motivation* for lament, something may be *learned* from the experience of lament. This was true in my case. Lament led to a fresh discernment of the character of God. Beyond my initial experience of lament prayer in a time of personal darkness (noted in the introduction), years later I participated

---

30. Rigby, "Someone to Blame, Someone to Trust: Divine Power and the Self-Recovery of the Oppressed," in *Power, Powerlessness and the Divine: New Inquiries in Bible and Theology*, ed. Cynthia L. Rigby (Atlanta: Scholars Press, 1997), 79–102.
31. Rigby, "Someone to Blame, Someone to Trust," 86.

(on separate occasions) in a week of communal academic study shaped by Christian liturgy, where a lament psalm was integrated into both morning and evening prayers. Even though I was not at the time in a place of lament and could not identify with the specific complaints in these psalms, this regular hearing of words addressing God with the psalmist's troubles served to generate a deep sense of gratitude for God's attentiveness and mercy.[32]

Lament and Ethical Transformation

Abraham Heschel speaks of the possibility of a new revelation of God, shattering our prior complacency. This is his imaginative description: "A tremor seizes our limbs; our nerves are struck, quiver like strings; our whole being bursts into shudders. But then a cry, wrested from our very core, fills the world around us, as if a mountain were suddenly about to place itself in front of us. It is one word: GOD."[33]

My experience of God has been much more mundane—and tame—by comparison. Instead of a high-voltage flash of insight, I have come to know God's presence in the darkness of suffering. This discernment was gradual and came through my own (halting) prayers of lament. Nevertheless, when Heschel goes on to make the point that while "inspiration passes, having been inspired never passes," I find this verified in my experience.[34]

One of the lasting impacts of lament is an ethical sensibility. Not only can the practice of lament strengthen our sense of self (Brueggemann's point), it may open us up to empathy for others in their suffering. In Exodus 23:9, Israel is enjoined, "You shall not oppress a resident alien; you know the heart of an alien, for you were aliens in the land of Egypt." Leviticus 19:34 is similar: "You shall love the alien as yourself, for you were aliens in the land of Egypt." The logic is that shared experience of suffering has positive ethical consequences.[35]

---

32. My thanks to The Colossian Forum for these liturgical experiences in summer 2013 and 2014, which kicked off a multidisciplinary research project, eventually published as *Evolution and the Fall*, ed. William T. Cavanaugh and James K. A. Smith (Grand Rapids: Eerdmans, 2017).

33. Abraham Joshua Heschel, *Man Is Not Alone: A Philosophy of Religion* (New York: Farrar, Straus & Giroux, 1951), 78.

34. Heschel, *Man Is Not Alone*, 78. Of course, a single initial experience of God is no guarantee of an enduring relationship. Jesus's parable of the sower (or the soils) amply illustrates this (Matt. 13:1–23; Mark 4:1–20; Luke 8:4–15). Of the four types of soil that receive the seed, only one type produces good growth. An initial experience of grace needs to be nurtured and tended. Or as Paul puts it in Phil. 2:12, "Work out your own salvation with fear and trembling."

35. Deuteronomy 10:18–19 goes even further in grounding love for the alien or stranger (Hebrew *gēr*) also in the character and actions of YHWH, "who loves the strangers, providing

Yet these consequences are not necessary. While the experience of suffering can, indeed, result in our compassion for the suffering of others, suffering may also close us off from others. Sometimes the experience of suffering can deplete our energy and reduce our ability to give much of ourselves to others. In some cases, protectively walling ourselves off from others may result from privileging our suffering and valorizing our own identity as victims.[36] This is a particular problem in the world today, where identity is often defined in oppositional categories of us versus them. Although tribalism has been a pernicious feature of most cultures throughout human history, a sense of oppositional identity, with its accompanying demonizing of others, has become rampant in our time.

Our contemporary tribalism is exacerbated by our connectivity through social media, where algorithms embedded in the system lead us to link primarily with like-minded people—for good or ill. While it is possible to find those on a similar spiritual journey through the internet, it is also easy for white supremacists, jihadists, and others nursing a sense of victimization to band together.[37]

The fact is that suffering by itself does not inevitably result in an increase of empathy. Such empathy is generated, I submit, by the discernment of God's compassion, which both grounds and welcomes our lament and is revealed through our participation in lament.

Lament thus has the potential to prevent us from succumbing to one of two extremes—falling into ethical paralysis and despair in the face of suffering (either our own or that of the world) or transmuting our suffering into vitriolic anger and violence against others.[38] Lament can be the beginning of a journey of ethical transformation.

---

them food and clothing. You shall also love the stranger, for you were strangers in the land of Egypt."

36. Shai Held's insightful discussion of the Torah's exhortation to love the *gēr* includes the honest admission that while suffering ought to open us to empathy for others, it can also lead to a sense of entitlement and privilege. See Held's meditation on the parashah (Jewish lectionary reading) known as Mishpatim (Exod. 21:1–24:18), titled, "Turning Memory into Empathy: The Torah's Ethical Charge," in *The Heart of Torah* (Philadelphia: Jewish Publication Society, 2017), 1:176 (entire chapter 175–78).

37. For a fuller analysis of tribalism, including the experience that may give rise to it and the theology that undergirds it, see J. Richard Middleton, "The Challenge of the Kingdom," in *A New Heaven and a New Earth: Reclaiming Biblical Eschatology* (Grand Rapids: Baker Academic, 2014), 263–82; and Middleton, "Created in the Image of a Violent God?," in *The Liberating Image: The* Imago Dei *in Genesis 1* (Grand Rapids: Brazos, 2005), 235–69.

38. These very extremes are evident in God's warning to Cain. Prior to Cain's murder of his brother, God asked, "Why are you angry, and why has your countenance fallen?" (Gen.

Abraham's Missed Opportunity

This is why Abraham's silence is so tragic. The Aqedah testifies to the patriarch's missed opportunity for lament. In lieu of Abraham's lament, this book represents my own lament on Abraham's behalf, my grappling with God about Abraham's resounding silence.

But I continue to wonder: Suppose Abraham had not been silent. Suppose he had been so sure of the mercy of God that he could wrestle with God, arguing back, challenging God—interceding for his son. Or suppose Abraham *wasn't* sure of God's mercy but took the risk to lament anyway. He might have come to know the compassion of this God, who hosted (and affirmed) Job's complaint—which brought Job comfort in the end.

Yet despite Abraham's failure to lament, God was gracious and kept faith with Abraham, continuing to work through this fractured family—ultimately to bring redemption to the world.

And the God of Abraham continues to welcome lament even today.

4:6). Brian Walsh and I have explored similar extremes of paralysis and violence in the lyrics of Bruce Cockburn's songs, linking these extremes to different ways we may deal with anger. In the song "Gavin's Woodpile," Cockburn describes native peoples being poisoned by a contaminated river, while "a helpless rage seems to set my brain on fire"; and he admits, "I'm paralyzed in the face of it all." But in "Tropic Moon," Cockburn describes revolutionaries who want to demolish an unjust regime and explains, "In the rage of the hearts of these men / is the seed of a wind they call kingdom come." See Middleton and Walsh, "Theology at the Rim of a Broken Wheel: Bruce Cockburn and Christian Faith in a Postmodern World," *Grail* 9, no. 2 (June 1993): 15–39.

Scripture Index

Subject Index